# RELIGION, CULTURE, CURRICULUM, AND DIVERSITY IN 21ST CENTURY AMERICA

Edited by

**Mary Alice Trent
Trevor Grizzle
Margaret Sehorn
Andrew Lang
Elsa Rogers**

University Press of America,® Inc.
Lanham · Boulder · New York · Toronto · Plymouth, UK

**Copyright © 2007 by**
**University Press of America,® Inc.**
4501 Forbes Boulevard
Suite 200
Lanham, Maryland 20706
UPA Acquisitions Department (301) 459-3366

Estover Road
Plymouth PL6 7PY
United Kingdom

Library of Congress Control Number: 2006933309
ISBN-13: 978-0-7618-3558-5 (paperback : alk. paper)
ISBN-10: 0-7618-3558-X (paperback : alk. paper)

⊖™ The paper used in this publication meets the minimum
requirements of American National Standard for Information
Sciences—Permanence of Paper for Printed Library Materials,
ANSI Z39.48—1984

# Contents

## Part Two
## Religion, Diversity, and Culture

# Part One

## Diversity, Christianity, and Curriculum

# Diversity and Disability: Richness or Roadblock to Effective Learning

## DR. EVEN CULP
## PROF. EVIE LINDBERG

Educators live in a time of multiple directives for teaching students with learning disabilities. Educational mandates such as the Individuals with Disabilities Act (IDEA) and No Child Left Behind (NCLB) have prompted educational systems to assess how well teachers instruct students within the classroom. Educators are asked to teach utilizing scientifically based research practices, curriculum, brain research, and technology, hoping to reach as many children as possible in an effort to leave no child behind. The public schools now apply these effective teaching practices to demonstrate adequate yearly progress (AYP). Schools found wanting face the consequences of sanctions, including the implementation of student transfers, supplemental tutorial plans, and the possibility of state takeover. Colleges and universities, both public and private, are also faced with similar teacher accountability and institutional accreditation. Therefore, the question must be asked, college and university professors use effective teaching practices to reach their students who are struggling academically?

Professors often encounter students who have been on an individual educational program and have little or no knowledge of how to successfully navigate the university system. Professors may also encounter stu-

**Dr. Even Culp** is Professor and Director of MultiMedia Institute at Oral Roberts University in Tulsa, OK, and **Ms. Evie Lindberg** is Assistant Professor in the School of Education at Oral Roberts University.

dents with undiagnosed educational issues that arise as a result of the intensive college and university programs. Often these students are unaware of what educational support is available to them. Students with special needs arrive as freshmen at college or universities having been under the IDEA law throughout their public school experience. Through IDEA students have an individual education plan (IEP) with annual objectives, accommodations, and modifications (if necessary), supplemental services with a behavioral or transition plan written (if necessary) all of which is reviewed yearly by the child's IEP team. In high school, students often do not pay attention to the IEP. Mom, dad, or a guardian have often looked after these details. As the student enters college, no one may realize the accommodations or modifications needed for success. The student may not be able to confidently verbalize this information to an individual in authority when a parent/guardian is no longer able to legally make these decisions.

The Americans with Disabilities Act and Section 504 of the Rehabilitation Act espouse the same intent, which is "equal access and equal opportunity." The obligation of the institution (public or private) as a whole is to provide qualified individuals with disabilities equal access and equal opportunity to any programs, goods, or services it offers or contracts with to offer.

Students who did not qualify for service under IDEA were provided services under Section 504 of the Rehabilitation Act. Section 504, enacted in 1973 and amended in 1978, provides that no otherwise qualified individual with a disability in the United States, as defined in section 7(20), shall, solely by reason of her or his disability, be excluded from the participation in, be denied the benefits of , or be subjected to discrimination under any program or activity receiving Federal financial assistance or under any program or activity conducted by any Executive agency or by the United States Postal Service, (Section 504 of the Rehabilitation Act). The last law that college and university professors need to understand is the Americans with Disabilities Act.

The Americans with Disabilities Act (ADA; Public Law 101-336), was passed in 1990 and provides comprehensive civil rights protections to individuals with disabilities in the areas of employment, public accommodations, state and local government services, and telecommunications. The ADA expanded the scope of Section 504 beyond those entities receiving federal funding. An individual with a disability is a person who has a physical or mental impairment that substantially limits one or more major life activities, has a record of such an impairment, or is regarded as having such an impairment. This law requires public and private sectors as well as colleges and universities to provide accommodations for individuals with disabilities if the appropriate documentation has been supplied. When presented proper documentation, professors are bound by law to accommodate the student and to keep this information confidential at all times.

The Family Educational Rights and Privacy Act (FERPA) is a law that provides privacy to all students 18 years or older. The Family Educational Rights and Privacy Act (FERPA) (20 U.S.C. § 1232g; 34 CFR Part 99) is a federal law that protects the privacy of student education records. The law applies to all schools that receive funds under an applicable program of the U.S. Department of Education. Though FERPA gives parents certain rights with respect to their children's education records, these rights transfer to the student when he or she reaches the age of 18 or attends a school beyond the high school level. How then are professors to ascertain a student's situation such as LD, one of the other thirteen categories housed in IDEA, or other medical problems (i.e., bipolar) if a student's files cannot be accessed and/or a student's family cannot be contacted for verification of a suspected educational or medical problem?

Few students reach their freshman year possessing the skills to persevere through some of the natural challenges without assistance. Most LD students have even fewer skills, since they have been sheltered more than the average high school student. Typically, these students are ill prepared to be their own advocate and are more intimidated by the whole college/university experience. Some proactive LD students will go to the University's Student Services. After an assessment, these students take documentation to their teachers. This documentation articulates what type of accommodation the students need to facilitate their learning. All other LD students enter classes undisclosed and undocumented. Other students arrive on campus having done well in their high school or junior college experience. Some find they are unable to handle the academic load at the university. Many of these students have never had a problem and do not know how to handle this new situation. Often these students are unaware of what educational support is available to them. How can faculty teaching at Christian colleges and universities positively impact these students?

Colleges and universities are different from high school programs. College and university professors do not see students every day; some courses meet once a week, others two or three times a week, and few meet every day. So in the short time professors have with students in class, what support is necessary when professors are unaware that a problem may even exist?

Learning-disabled students disclose easier in classes where they know the teacher is interested in each student's success. One way Dr. Even Culp at Oral Roberts University handles this situation is to tell the class in his introductory remarks, "If anyone in this class has any learning challenges, needed accommodations, test anxiety, or problems that you feel I should know about, please seek me out. Let me know, so we can work together throughout the semester. This way we can avoid uncomfortable situations later on in the semester." Once a student discloses to him privately that they have concerns, Dr. Culp is able to find out if the student has been to the Disabilities Services Center. If they have not been diagnosed but they are concerned, then he can direct them to Disabilities Services. The student may be tested to identify the challenge.

Assistant Professor Evie Lindberg of Oral Roberts University addresses the situation in a different manner. In her initial classes she has the students complete several learning profiles, one on learning styles, multiple intelligence, study habits, and a little about their past educational challenges that they may have experienced. In addition, she has them write down things they like, places they have been, and anything interesting they want to share. She explains that, based on their learning styles and multiple intelligence, she will adjust her subject matter to their unique learning needs. By the student being part of this process and by having some background knowledge of the students themselves, Professor Lindberg is able to activate background knowledge by using students' names, drawing upon information about their cultural background or the personal experiences they have shared in an effort to make the subject matter relevant. Marzano (1992) explains it this way: "What an individual considers to be important is probably a function of the extent to which it meets one of two conditions: it is perceived as instrumental in satisfying a basic need, or it is perceived as instrumental in the attainment of a personal goal" (p.11).

For learning to take place, a learning community must be created, according to Lenz and Deshler (2004). "A learning community is an environment where learning is valued and accessible for all learners and where teachers and students work together to make sure everyone in the community is learning" (p.104). By creating an environment where the student is enriched and provided opportunities for active participation, the student feels safe and empowered and begins to take ownership of their learning. Lindberg believes that when students take ownership in the learning process, they will take a much bigger percentage of the knowledge of the course with them into the world.

Research has shown that teachers often do not even know that a student has a disability, is frustrated, or is having trouble learning until well into the semester when patterns of failure have long been established (Lenz & Trent, 1994).

Since LD students must self-disclose their learning challenges in college, what teacher attributes facilitate relationship and dialogue? "Abilities to carry on effective relationships with others, to speak clearly and concisely, to lead and interact in group environments, and to listen with understanding and empathy are most important for all teachers" (Rubin & Feezel, 1986). Meadows (1998) cited teacher warmth as a key facet of effective pedagogy.

These relationships help faculty obtain genuine feedback to assess how well students with varied learning styles and skills are mastering course objectives. By building rapport and trust, teachers not only connect with the students; they build positive interactions among students as they participate in activities and learn substantive content. As a result, students are more likely to attend classes, have more positive attitudes, and show higher achievement (Van Sickle & Spector, 1996). Teachers play a major role in creating, perpetuating, or extinguishing stereotypes about competence; building or tearing down self-perceptions; molding expectations for success or failure; or sending disheartening messages or encouraging students to develop their abilities (Eccles, 1995).

In practice teacher immediacy behavior positively impacts learning outcomes (Christensen & Menzel, 1998). Humor and self-disclosure both proved to be characteristics of effective teachers (Nussbaum, Comadena & Holladay, 1987). In contrast, "significant and somewhat discouraging, teacher behavior that students perceive as negative demotivated students more than positive teacher behaviors motivated students" (Gorham and Christophel, 1992). Obviously, a teacher's ability to create relationships and utilize effective interpersonal skills (both verbal and nonverbal) impacts learning.

Whether or not teachers are aware of students' learning challenges, they can accommodate these challenges through multiple instructional strategies and activities. Much of college education involves reading and listening, so college professors expect students to be auditory learners (Johnson, 1994). "Forty percent of us are visual learners, 40% are kinesthetic/tactile learners, 15% are auditory, and about 5% mostly use our olfactory/gustatory attributes" (Johnson). "When learning style preferences are taken into account, learner achievement and satisfaction have shown an increase" (Penland, 1984). There is also a relationship between teacher immediacy behaviors of eye contact and physical proximity and improved student learning (Gorham, 1988). Smiling, vocal expressiveness, and a relaxed body position were shown to enhance student learning as well (Richmond, Gorham, & McCroskey, 1987). As teachers utilize multiple teaching techniques that encompass various learning styles, all students benefit.

Learning disabilities are not the only distractions to the classroom. Technology, which may enhance classroom instruction, now provides all students with a new array of options and distractions. Cell phones, text messaging, and wireless laptop connectivity allow students to be physically present while engaged elsewhere. A solution to these student distractions is more activities designed to actively engage the student in the learning process. Well-designed lessons focus on higher levels of learning: application, interpretation, and problem-solving. These learning activities are best facilitated through discussion, group work, problem-based learning, simulation, and hands-on projects. Such learner-engaged activities will enhance student outcomes.

Engagement skills and classroom culture bear directly on classroom learning. Beyond the classroom, students and faculty live in a broader academic reality with different demands, expectations, and support systems.

What other campus resources impact student learning? It is important that struggling students avail themselves of university resources for success. Faculty need to be familiar with student support services. Most colleges offer supplemental support systems such as assessment of disabilities, peer tutoring, writing labs, remedial courses, and study skill courses. Since struggling students may not be aware or seek out these services, teachers are the critical link to these services. As faculty members identify student inadequacies, faculty can direct students to the appropriate service. Some students may resist, but hopefully, the student will respond to the faculty members' counsel.

The culture of many colleges still rewards tenure and rank based more on scholarly publications and research than effective teaching. As a result, few college teachers invest much time acquiring knowledge and skills in instructional design, human development, learning theory, or presentational skills. Most colleges offer faculty opportunities to enhance performance in these areas.

By law colleges admit students with learning disabilities. Faculty need to facilitate these students' success. As a Christian institution may we surpass the law and create a godly, caring environment. Ephesians 1: 3-8 sets the tone, telling each of us that we are chosen, accepted, favored, adopted and redeemed. May our students experience this care in our classrooms. Skilled and caring faculty can improve learning success rates by enhancing classroom culture and developing effective engagement techniques. As faculty connect LD students with institutional support beyond the classroom, the total learning environment will better serve all participants. Through these steps, Christian colleges and universities can make a positive difference for students with learning challenges.

The purpose of the following activities is to generate a dialogue among faculty about resources for students who are challenged academically. By the end of the activity, faculty will have identified teaching strategies to help a struggling student. Faculty will also have identified resources available to the student offered by their university.

## 1. Role play

Regardless of the number of participants, divide the attendees in groups of six to ten members. Make as many groups as needed. One person will play the role of student and present the problem to one faculty member. (See scenario for details on the problem.) The faculty member should respond as they typically would do to assist the student. The exchange should last four to six minutes. Each group will sit in a circle around the "student and teacher" and observe the role play. Assign the observers to one of three topic subgroups.

## 2. Observe

While observing one subgroup will make a list of all the strategies/methods they might use to help this student. The second subgroup will make a list of resources available to the student at the university. The third subgroup will identify university resources or programs that better equip faculty to respond to such students.

## 3. Brainstorm/Collaborate

After the role play, each subgroup will take five to ten minutes to generate their list of suggestions.

## 4. Report/Suggest

Next, have each subgroup briefly report their findings to all attendees. If you have multiple groups, have all subgroups dealing with teaching interventions share first, university resources share second, and faculty resources share last.

## 5. Reflect/Apply

Have a person record all responses. These will be emailed to attendees along with other web resources after the event. Finally, have a facilitator reflect on comments, and encourage faculty to apply the ideas shared, and then bring closure to the session.

**Note:**    Scenario one is for faculty in general.
Scenario two is for use with teachers focusing on special education issues.

# Ima Your Student
# Educational Evaluation
# Scenario 1 Fact Sheet

Use with Non-special Education Teachers—
this student is undiagnosed.

**Ima Your Student**
Date of Birth:  02/29/1984
Sex:           Female
Age:           20 years, 7 months
Sophomore in the college (Considered in 14.0 grade level)

## Background Information

She is an African American who is a sophomore at Oral Roberts University. Her major is Theology. She has struggled in school subject matter all her life and complains of having difficulty staying focused. She works part-time as a bank teller. She is currently taking sixteen hours. She has difficulty writing research papers and written responses on exams.

## Summary of specific test findings

Ima's academic skills as observed by different faculty are described within the low range. Her fluency with academic tasks and her ability to apply academic skills are both within the low average range. Her academic knowledge has been described as within the average range. Ima's performance is average in reading comprehension; low average in basic reading skills, basic writing skills, and written expression; and low in math calculation skills and math reasoning. However, Ima's strengths on her subtest are in reading comprehension and reading vocabulary.

## Learning Profile

Ima likes the latter part of the day to do her work. She may like a little food or a drink with her when she studies and prefers soft lamplight in a more relaxed atmosphere. When she studies, she prefers a warmer room with moderate noise. She is an auditory learner. Areas to strengthen are in the area of visual motor integration.

# Ima Your Student
# Educational Evaluation
# Scenario 2 Fact Sheet

Use this scenario for Special Education Teachers.

**Ima Your Student**
Date of Birth:   02/29/1984
Sex:             Female
Age:             20 years, 7 months
Sophomore in the college (Considered in 14.0 grade level)

## Background Information

She is a Caucasian student and a sophomore at Oral Roberts University in Tulsa, OK. Her major is Theology. She is currently taking sixteen hours. She has struggled in school subject matter all her life and was diagnosed in fourth grade as having a learning disability. She has difficulty writing research papers and written responses on exams. She complains of having difficulty staying focused. She works part-time at Wal-Mart.

At the age of thirteen, she was in a car accident, paralyzing her legs. Her mobility around campus doesn't appear to hamper her at this time.

## Summary of specific test findings

Ima's academic skills as observed by different faculty are described within the low range. Her fluency with academic tasks and her ability to apply academic skills are both within the low average range. Her academic knowledge has been described as within the average range. Ima's performance is average in reading comprehension; low average in basic reading skills, basic writing skills, and written expression; and low in math calculation skills and math reasoning. However, Ima's strengths on her subtest are in reading comprehension and reading vocabulary.

## Learning Profile

Ima likes the latter part of the day to do her work. She may like a little food or a drink with her when she studies and prefers soft lamplight in a more relaxed atmosphere. When she studies she prefers a warmer room with moderate noise. She is an auditory learner. Areas to strengthen are in the area of visual motor integration.

# Role-play

**Before this skit begins:**
Select someone to role-play the student and someone to play the faculty member. The audience should be separated into three groups as noted earlier in number one.

## Characters

**Professor Norton**: He has been at this university for seven years, has taught New Testament for a long time, and is well liked by the students and the university. He is also Ima's university advisor.

**Ima Your Student**: Ima is African American and has been in this New Testament class now for six weeks and has become frustrated. She studies hard, but still made a "D" on her exam and a "D" on her first research paper.

## Scene

This scene takes place at the end of a New Testament class in which Ima has just scored a "D" on her exam. Ima waits until all the students leave and approaches Professor Norton, at which time the following conversation ensues.

**Ima** (speaking timidly): "Professor Norton, can I speak to you for a minute?"

**Professor Norton** (Looking up from gathering his materials after class): "Sure, Ima, what can I help you with today?"

**Ima**: "I am a theology major and I want to do well, but I do not understand why I did so poorly on your exam. Two weeks ago I received a "D" on my first paper. In school I have always struggled in writing and have often had difficulty staying focused.

**Professor Norton**: "How many hours are you taking this semester?"

**Ima**: "I am currently taking sixteen hours, and I work part-time as a bank teller. I do not want to fail this course, what can I do?"

Continue dialogue for four to six minutes then stop role-play. Break into groups to discuss the topics in number two.

## Group A

- What strategies/methods/questions would you discuss with the student to better aid her?
- What can Ima do on her own to help herself develop better writing skills?

## Group B

- What resources within the college/university are available to students like Ima to help with their areas of apparent weaknesses?

## Group C

- What resources are available within your college/universities that are available to the professor to help him/her with a student like Ima?
- What legal issue must the professor be mindful of when making recommendations to the student?

# References

Berlo, D. K. (1960). *The process of communication.* New York: Hold, Rinehard, & Winston.

Christensen, L. J., & Menzel, K. E. (1998) The linear relationship between student reports of teacher immediacy behaviors and perceptions of state motivation, and of cognitive, affective, and behavioral learning, *Communication Education, 47,* 82-90.

Deshler, D. D., & Lenz, K. B. (2004). Evidence-based inclusive practices in middle and secondary schools. *Teaching Content to All.* Copyright © Pearson Education, Inc.

Eccles, J. S. (1995). *Issues related to gender equity.* Background paper prepared for Equity Blueprint Committee. Washington, D.C.: American Association for the Advancement of Science, Project 1061.

Gorham, J. (1988). The relationship between verbal teacher immediacy behaviors and student learning. *Communication Education, 37,* 40-53.

Gorham, J., & Christophel, D. M. (1992). Students' perceptions of teachers' behaviors as motivating and demotivating factors in college classes. *Communication Quarterly, 40,* 239-252.

Johnson, H. (1994). Confessions of an auditory learner. *Adult & Continuing Education Today*, *24*(3), 5.

Lenz, B. K., Adams, G., & Fisher, J. (1994). *The Learning Expressways Folder*. Lawrence, KS: Edge Enterprises.

Lenz, B. K., & Deshler, D. D. with Kissam, B. R. (2004). *Teaching content to all evidence-based inclusive practices in middle and secondary schools*. Boston, MA: Allyn & Bacon Publishers.

Marzano, R. J. (1992). *A different kind of classroom: Teaching with dimensions of learning*. Alexandria, VA: Association for Supervision and Curriculum Development.

Meadows, L. (1998, January). Effective teaching in an urban middle school. Paper presented at an annual meeting of the Association for the Education of Teachers in Science, Minneapolis, MN.

Nussbaum, J. F., Comadena, M. E., & Holladay, S. J. (1987). Classroom verbal behavior of highly effective teachers. *Journal of Thought*, *22*(4), 73-80.

Penland, P. R. (1984). What we know about adult learning styles. In C. H. Shulman (Ed.), *Adults and the Changing Workplace* (pp. 67-78). Arlington, VA: American Vocational Association.

Richmond, V. P., Gorham, J. S., & McCroskey, J. C. (1987). The relationship between selected immediacy behaviors and cognitive learning. In M. McLaughlin (Ed.), *Communication Yearbook 10* (pp. 574-590). Beverly Hills, CA: Sage.

Rubin, R. B., & Feezel, J. D. (1986). Elements of teacher communication competence. *Communication Education*, *35*, 254-268.

Tileston, D.W. (2005). *Ten best teaching practices* (2nd Ed.). Thousand Oaks, CA: Corwin Press.

Van Sickle, M., & Spector, B. (1996). Caring relationships in science classrooms: A symbolic interactions study. *Journal of Research in Science Teaching*, *33* (4), 433-454.

# Building a Community of Learners and Thinkers: An Examination of Black Literature Courses

TASHA L. GOODE, ED. D. CANDIDATE

African-American literature courses are a scarcity among non-historically African-American colleges and universities. In fact, the issue of race is rarely discussed in open and honest settings in which students feel comfortable sharing their views (Dr. Trent, personal communication, October 23, 2005). However, African-American literature is a vibrant aspect of American literature as the black experience in America is directly tied to the history of the building of this country (Young-Minor, 2002, 2003). Although some educators fail to see the inherent value of including African-American history as a part of American history, this neglectful act does not negate the fact that African-American literature is derived from this history (McCabe, 1996). For this reason, African-American literature should be included in the literature courses offered by the English departments of colleges and universities throughout the United States.

Upon researching Africa-American literature courses, one can conclude that there is a great need for more opportunities to examine race and culture. Educators relate that African-American students are just as likely to experience an emotional and spiritual disjointedness to Africa-American literature and its history, as their Caucasian counterparts. Unfortunately, many African-American students today are unaware of

**Tasha L. Goode**, a native of Queens, NY, is ED. D. candidate in the School of Education at Oral Roberts University in Tulsa, OK.

the rich history they share with the African-American authors they are studying. Research indicates that African-American students view African-Americans as a complaining group of disillusioned individuals who refuse to acknowledge the various strides this community has accomplished (Young-Minor, 2002, 2003).

Since all students bring their own assumptions when analyzing literature, critical thinking can occur when students are taught to question these assumptions to forge understanding which continues throughout one's life (Young, 2002). The literature available leans more towards the need to start the process of incorporating African-American literature in the early formative years. Often the incorporation of African-American literature into the program is viewed as being too risky, but this connotation stifles scholarly and personal liberty. Unfortunately, the designers of curriculum are more concerned with meeting state and national standards as opposed to developing critical thinking and discourse (Davis, 2002).

Despite the fact that African-American history and literature should be a considered a worthy topic at any time of the year (Taylor, 1997), this is not the case in non-historically African-American colleges and universities. The real issue lies in the fact that most authors of historical texts have long chosen to portray African Americans in a negative light. This inaccurate portrayal helped to perpetuate fixed stereotypes in American society, especially in the formative years (Barksdale-Ladd & Hefflin, 2001; McCabe, 1996). This continual process of the elimination of African Americans as constructive, valuable members of society does a disservice to all Americans, not just the African-American community. Educational institutions have a responsibility, as a supplement to the home, to promote mutual respect for persons of ethnically diverse backgrounds. Just as the human body needs vitamin supplements when the body does not attain adequate nutrition from food intake, the school must also act as a leveling agent to bridge gaps where there exists a deficiency of understanding. For these reasons schools must take care to acquire textbooks that promote healthy practices of thought (McCabe, 1996).

Research also indicates that when African-American children are taught about their rich heritage at an earlier age, they develop a sense of belonging. The counseling concept of bibliotherapy uses books to encourage self-esteem and an awareness of oneself in relation to society. Literature directed towards the specific ethnicity of the child assists the child in developing self-efficacy. The ancient Egyptians used literature as a means of nourishing the soul. Thus the use of literature in fostering healing is not a novel concept. However, many educators have not yet discovered the inherent benefit of using African-American literature to help students cope with personal issues (Ford, Harris, Howard, Tyson, 2000).

When African-American children are able to read literature that accurately represents their culture, they develop an affinity with the characters, which then allows them to relate these experiences to real world experiences. Because children bring their personal experiences and beliefs about culture into the classroom and these beliefs can be easily modified, literature can also influence their value systems (Ford, et. al., 2000). Literature needs to reflect the African-American experience with accurate depiction of African-Americans portrayed in pragmatic milieus (Barksdale-Ladd & Hefflin, 2001).

African-American literature classes seem to have a recurrent theme of critical reflection. The learning theories that appear to be most closely aligned with teaching African-American literature and literature in general are thematic instruction and transformational learning. Thematic instruction is the practice of choosing a specific theme and appropriate assistive learning materials that help the students accrue knowledge via learning environments that reflect the world in which they live. This in turn allows them to apply critical thinking skills as they consider how to best use the new information they acquired to solve a particular problem. Similar to thematic instruction, which is based on cognitive theories (Wisconsin Center for Education Research, 2005), transformational learning is also a cognitively based learning theory. This learning approach closely resembles the manner in which educators teach African-American literature classes in that this theory advocates critical reflection to encourage a paradigm shift in thought leading to lasting and continual change. Preconceived ideology is challenged and then replaced by a new perception, which leads to an increasingly developed and reflective manner of thought. Critical reflection is crucial to transformational learning as this is where true growth occurs (Merriam, 2004; Neese, 2003). Transformational learning does not occur unless cognitive development takes place (Mezirow, 2004). African-American literature courses indeed seek to develop cognitive development along with critical reflection, which can then result in a transformational experience that continues throughout one's life.

The first word that accurately describes the Seminar 451: African-American Literature course offered only every two years at Oral Roberts University (ORU) is community. The students all relate to the class as a community of learners in which the professor, Dr. Mary Alice Trent, a rhetorician and professor of African-American Literature with the English department at ORU, facilitates the discussions. The students feel safe to share, discuss, argue, cry, reflect, and encourage one another. The text—a mammoth tome of collected works by African-American writers, poets, educators, leaders, and activists—created interest and sparked, at times, heated but genuine oral communication among the students. This concept of community in education is one that, while often mentioned and hailed as a vital part of the educative process, is severely lacking in many colleges and universities. I took this class as an undergraduate student at ORU, and I never felt more comfortable to verbally express my ideas as when I was in this class. Before taking this course, I previously believed that the concept of community was a joke; an oversimplified, idealistic view that could never be achieved. I was wrong. However, there were students who were not cognizant of how important African-American literature is to American culture. Dr. Trent masterfully handled both the inquisitive and the skeptical with respect and ease in an inclusive manner that allowed honest discussion to take place and critical thinking to occur. Unfortunately, this style of teaching is not the norm.

For this paper, I searched long and diligently for information about how to develop and present a curriculum centered on African-American literature. I was rewarded with a few interesting articles on the topic of presenting African-American literature but became most interested in the apparent lack of regularity with which colleges and universities offer such a course. I have always believed that given the inherent history of African Americans in the United States, African-American history and literature should not be singled out as being separate from the American history and literature courses. As I further researched this topic and interviewed Dr. Trent, this view was enhanced and intensified. I became increasingly convinced that by offering more opportunities for students to learn about African-American culture (i.e., via history and literature courses) at the secondary, junior high, and elementary school levels, post secondary students would be better prepared for the encounters they will face when entering school at the college and university levels.

The seminar course centers on the literary works of African Americans from the year 1619 to the present. The program is decidedly focused on the significance of African-American literature and committed to helping students understand how African-American history relates to American history and that both are juxtaposed within one another. Inherent within the framework of the class is the idea that students from all racial and ethnic backgrounds could benefit from taking this course as members of American society. The backdrop of the class is tied directly to understanding the background history of African-Americans in America. The literary writings of African-American literature are derived from this rich, turbulent history. Dr. Trent reports that as an educator of African-American literature she is grappling with the onus of decreased interest on the part of both faculty and students in these classes even before she enters the classroom (Dr. Trent, personal communication, October 23, 2005). Unfortunately, this lack of interest is not limited to the Caucasian population but is readily apparent within the African-American student population as well (Young-Minor, 2002, 2003). The fact that the course is only offered every two years is a major factor. Increased commitment to diversity and cultural relations should include more ethnically diverse selections within the literature course repertoire. That is not to say that the classics should be disposed of, but rather that African-American literature possesses an equal weight in terms of its beneficial impact on student learning (Davis, 2002; MCcabe, 1996).

As Dr. Trent stated in the interview, "any time you seek to shift or sift the status quo in the literary cannon, then this comes with a shifting or sifting of the power structure of the literary establishment" (Dr. Trent, personal communication, October 23, 2005). The delicate issue of race is at the nexus of the program. Despite the fact that race is at the heart of many classical literary works, many times race is not verbally communicated, but this is not an indication of the absence of race but rather of its intricate taboo status. Although race can often be seen as "the albatross around the neck," (Dr. Trent, personal communication, October 23, 2005) in the African-American seminar, race is openly discussed. The writings and authors analyzed, such as Phyllis Wheatley, Ouledah Equiano, Countee Cullen, Langston Hughes, Zora Neale Hurston, and so forth, are highly conscious of the issues of their race and the struggle for equality by African Americans. Instead of shrinking from the subject matter of race, this program is built around helping the students to candidly converse on this issue and to get them to understand the different ways in which people view race and race relations in America. All Americans were both "affected and infected by [racial] oppression" (Dr. Trent, personal communication, October 23, 2005).

In order for a program of this nature to thrive, the professor must be wholly comfortable with himself / herself and not possess an issue with race. This focuses on assisting students in becoming comfortable with themselves and others from ethnically diverse backgrounds. For this reason, the professor must not have racial prejudices that will in any way hinder student learning (Dr. Trent, personal communication, October 23, 2005; Far North Parent-Professional Partnerships, 2005; West, 2000). This is where the concept of community within this African-American literature program truly takes place and actually assists the professor in establishing an environment whereby students are free to engage and converse. Dr. Trent (2005) acknowledges that:

> We are still fighting a civil war in our minds [. . . .] When you travel in a bubble, you associate with those of a like mind [. . . .] There are many layers [to wade through] and you have to be ready because you don't know what may come forth, and if you encourage [students to take] the layers off, you must be prepared for what you'll encounter (personal communication, October 23, 2005).

Additionally, the program focuses on the role of religion in the lives of the individuals discussed, as well as the issue of cultural literacy and cultural relevancy. Historically speaking, educational institutions were originally established to teach Christian values, alongside the traditional educational elements. The founding fathers of education were concerned that a lack of knowledge of the scriptures and application to life would result in an inadequate education. Education was never meant to become a separate entity from the teachings of God, as understanding of the scriptures fostered knowledge. Students were considered to be wise when they were able to excel at recitation and application of the scriptures as well as the traditional elements of education (Masrden, 1994). This concept is similar to transformational learning discussed earlier, which fosters this kind of process, forcing the individual to critically reflect on issues to create a new sense of understanding (Caffarella, & Merriam, 1999). African-American literary works often possess an underlying Christian element in which a transformation from one set ideology propels the character into an elevated realm of spiritual and personal enlightenment (Dr. Trent, personal communication, October 23, 2005).

Moreover, Dr. Trent maintains that culturally literate and relevant students are those who are vibrantly cognizant of past and present general knowledge (e.g. history, culture, arts, science, literature, music, technology, etc.) and their place within this spectrum. They are also characterized by their inherent ability to articulate this acquired knowledge throughout their academic and social discourse. The program recognizes that students may not be entering the course with a working knowledge of a broad expanse of topics; therefore the program seeks to rectify this neglect with insightful, thought provoking, profound, and at times prolific literary material (Dr. Trent, personal communication, October 23, 2005; McShay, 2005; Young-Minor, 2002, 2003). Cultural relevancy necessitates that the instructor values the unique qualities of each student while being careful not to inhibit learning, thus allowing time and opportunity for personal evolvement (Far North Parent-Professional Partnerships, 2005). Dr. Trent (2005) asserts that:

> In keeping with the Christian tradition in America, we know that many African-American writers have used their religious background to influence their literature. For example, one early African-American writer is Phyllis Wheatley, who spoke of God in her poetry. Others include Richard Allen, Sojourner Truth, James Baldwin, and Maya Angelou, just to name a few. The Negro spirituals, in fact, epitomized both an aesthetic elegance and a code of communication among the people. From jazz, the blues, and rap to folklore, fiction and poetry, African-American artists have influenced mainstream American culture, art, music, language and so forth. Making students aware of this rich legacy, educators must design a curriculum that explores the history, language, and literature of historically marginalized people in America (personal communication, October 23, 2005).

Dr. Trent uses the works of rhetoricians such as Linda Flowers, Ken McCurry, Lile Brannon, Theresa Enos, Kenneth Burke, and Peter Albow as her base for establishing a critical thinking foundation for the program. According to Dr. Trent, these rhetoricians all advocate critical thinking as a valuable outcome of the reading and writing learning experience. She also uses cultural, historical, contextual, biographical analyses, as well as deconstructionist theory, for reading workshops, and of course, she uses Christianity as the backdrop for the discussions (Dr. Trent, personal communication, October 23, 2005).

However, this course also follows the thematic instructional and transformational learning approaches, which organizes a curriculum around a major theme in conjunction with the standard institutional learning objectives and outcomes and seeks to cause a transformation in how the students view the subject and thus the world. The designing of the course consists of selection of the theme, creation of the integrated curriculum, development of the mode of instruction (e.g. the selection of the appropriate text), and a symposium that incorporates collaborative efforts of the part of the students. The research methods of instruction behind thematic instruction are the sociocognitive, cognitive flexibility, and authentic instruction and assessment theories. The sociocognitive theory avers that when prior knowledge is confronted and challenged through novel concepts and ideas in which cognitive disequilibrium occurs, one's original perceptional knowledge base is altered. This new acquired knowledge then assists the students in behaving responsibly in the current educational setting that parallels real world learning experiences (Wisconsin Center for Education Research, 2005). The acquisition of the textbook used for the class is imperative, as this tome must accurately represent the culture and nature of the theme (Barksdale-Ladd & Hefflin, 2001).

The cognitive flexibility theory states that students should be able to recognize differing aspects of knowledge, applying this knowledge as needed at a later date to assist in solving a problematic situation. The authentic instruction and assessment theory mentions that students must learn to develop meaning built upon previous knowledge in a manner that illustrates genuine application of the information into a real world setting. In this wise, students can then apply cross-disciplinary tactics to incorporate this new knowledge into other areas of academic and social life (Wisconsin Center for Education Research, 2005).

Under the transformational learning approach, the course seeks to cause a paradigm shift of sorts in the mind of the students. The program is designed to engage the students by utilizing the Socratic method of asking probing questions to elicit responses that would force the students to examine their beliefs. This challenge then leads to critical thinking or reflection as the students mull over the new information and checks this intrusive material against preconceived, long held ideology. Once the new material is found to be more beneficial to the life experiences of the students, a transformation occurs as the students receive the new information and begin to form a more developed outlook on their life and the environment surrounding them (Caffarella, & Merriam, 1999; Merriam, 2004; Mezirow, 2004; Neese, 2003; Young, 2003).

Knowledge is the key that unlocks the mysteries of the world. As an equalizer, knowledge dispels ignorance which conflicts with the values of America's foundation but leads to deterioration of the mores of society when knowledge is rejected. America is seen as a democratic society, but this connotation denotes the image of an enlightened citizenry in which individuals are viewed as knowledgeable and prudent. As knowledge is still commonly viewed as power, those who lack knowledge are at risk of disenfranchisement and lack of power. Although critical thinking skills are vital to the educative process, the future of education will depend on ethically-centered creative thinking (Cook, 1990).

The inclusion of African-American history and literature in a mainstream educational curriculum at all colleges and universities in North America is an excellent example of this new order of thinking and learning. In making this paradigm shift, educators must consider the needs of the students, explore possibilities, value the cultures of all students, and empower all students to acquire ownership of content matter and demonstrate intellectual capacity. The paradigm shift will occur when educators recognize the need for change and embrace flexibility with an open mind, compassionate heart, and iron will to hold fast to their moral center, infusing and reflecting the future into the present while respecting the past (Schwahn & Spady, 2002).

Teaching African-American history in mainstream education is a wise gesture necessary to properly equip students with all they need to succeed in retaining knowledge and understanding. Withholding valuable information vital to their understanding of how race relations operate throughout the world is detrimental to the future success of the students as professional. The time to teach students the correct history of America is now (Dr. Trent, personal communication, October 23, 2005). In 2 Timothy 4:3, Paul warns that there will come a time when humanity will be unreceptive to the truth and seek those teachers who will tell the people what they wish to hear, utterly rejecting the truth (King James Version). This phenomenon began with the earliest history books neglecting to candidly narrate an accurate account of the history of African-Americans in America and their veritable important contributions to the foundation of this country and the deception has continued until this present day (Dr. Trent, personal communication, October 23, 2005).

African-American literature has yet to be truly valued for its contributions to American thought. Studying diverse literary works can only serve to enhance the worldview of the students. If the faculty members of non-historically African-American colleges and universities want to have their campuses truly reflect a non-biased viewpoint of its student body, then they must now consider the need to include African-American literature as a vital part of the literary curriculum. African-American history is a major component of American history that can no longer be ignored. For many years, African-Americans have fought to be included in the great words of the Constitution as equals in a country rife with inequality and biased nefarious practices. For many years, African-Americans have watched as they were portrayed in an unfavorable light, their treatment in American society a dark cloud looming over this great country (Davis, 2002; Dr. Trent, personal communication, October 23, 2005; McCAbe, 1996).

This country is large enough to embrace the African-American tradition of literary works and its people resilient enough to withstand the pressure of honest discourse on racial issues. Race is a factor that this country has yet to acknowledge in a genuine manner. The inclusion of African-American literature will provide the stepping stone to build a foundation of change. African-American children must be taught at the elementary, junior high, and secondary levels to value the strength inherent within their ancestry and to reach out for the glorious futures that their ancestors fought and died for so long ago. They must be allowed to hear the true stories of slavery and see the road in which their ancestors traveled. They must be allowed to see honest reflections of themselves in literary works. The struggle is not over and in many ways has only just begun. Colleges and universities have long been considered as institutions of change. As pioneers, they should be the initiators of racial change in American society by advocating a curriculum at all levels of education that depicts African-Americans in a positive light. African-American literature stands ready as the tool by which to begin this process (Barsdale-Ladd & Hefflin, 2001; Dr. Trent, personal communication, October 23, 2005; Ford, et al., 2000; Taylor, 1997).

Despite the many strides African Americans have made in this country, in some ways society is more segregated now than this country was fifty years ago. More and more students are choosing to not associate with others outside of their ethnic backgrounds. Home schooling, while a necessary tool for some families, can become, in some instances, a breeding ground for a racist ideology as children only associate with those of a like mind. Churches have long been traditionally segregated entities, and even today there exist few predominately white churches in which people of color are truly accepted and vice versa (Dr. Trent, personal communication, October 23, 2005).

As far as we have come as a country, we have yet to truly embrace one another as individuals, uniquely different but equally valuable. No longer should we allow ourselves to consider ourselves as colorblind individuals. The inability to see, value, and accept the various hues of our peers is the inability to accept, value, and see those individuals as vital members of the American community. One should not have to pretend not to see another's ethnicity in order to accept him or her as one of his or her own. I challenge the notion of color blindness and tolerance. While most equate tolerance with compassion, this word also carries the negative connotation of enduring. This would suggest that a person of color is to be endured rather than embraced. African-Americans have endured many years of hardship and deserve to be included in "We the People" (Dr. Trent, personal communication, October 23, 2005).

# References

All Scripture taken from the New Living Translation of the Holy Bible.

Barksdale-Ladd, M. A. & Hefflin, B. R. (2001). African American children's literature that helps students find themselves: Selection guidelines for grades k-3. *The Reading Teacher, 54*(8), 810-19.

Caffarella, R. S. & Merriam, S. B. (999). *Learning in adulthood: A comprehensive guide.* Jossey-Bass: San Francisco, CA.

Cook, W. J. (1990). *Strategic planning for America's schools.* The Cambridge Group: Montgomery, AL.

Davis, D. M. (2002). Good morning, revolution: The unpopular works of Langston Hughes and the implications for curriculum developers. *JCT, 18*(2), 77-86.

Far North Parent-Professional Partnerships. Retrieved October 27, 2005 from World Wide Web: http://www.alaskachd.org/partnership/content/building7.html

Ford, D. Y., Harris III, J. J., Howard, T. C., & Tyson, C. A. (2000). Multicultural literature and gifted Black students: Promoting self-understanding, awareness, and pride. *Roeper Review, 22*(4), 235-40.

Marsden, G. M. (1994). *The soul of the American university: From Protestant establishment to established nonbelief.* Oxford University Press: New York.

McCabe, P. P. (1996). A case grammar analysis of the representation of African-Americans in current fifth grade social studies textbooks. *Reading Horizons, 36,* 380-401.

McShay, Y. M. (2005). Positive change affects educators and learners. *The Delta Kappa Gamma Bulletin, 71*(2), 57-8.

Merriam, S. B. (2004). The role of cognitive development in Mezirow's transformational learning theory. *Adult Education Quarterly, 55*(1), 60-8.

Mezirow, J. (2004). Forum comment on Sharan Merriam's "The role of cognitive development in Mezirow's transformational learning theory." *Adult Education Quarterly, 55*(1), 69-70.

Neese, R. (2003). A transformational journey from clinician to educator. *The Journal of Continuing Education in Nursing, 34*(6), 258-62.

Schwahn, C. J. & Spady, W. G. (2002). *Total leaders: Applying the best future-focused change strategies to education.* Scarecrow Education: Lanham, MD.

Taylor, G. S. (1997). Using historical fiction and biography to make African American history come alive. *The New England Reading Association Journal, 33*(1), 15-20.

Young, K. (2002). Poetic intervention in teaching and learning. *JCT, 18*(4), '59-78.

Young-Minor, E. (2003). Performance pedagogies for African American literature: Teaching Shange at Ole Miss. *Radical Teacher, 65,* 27-32.

West, G. (2000). "It takes time": The generative potential of transgressive teaching. *Radical Teacher, 58,* 21-5.

Wisconsin Center for Education Research. Creating and effective foreign language classroom. Retrieved October 19, 2005 from World Wide Web: http://www.wcer.wisc.edu/step/ep301/Fall2000/Tochonites/theme.html

# Cultural Competence Education: A User-Friendly Instrument to Assess Professional Development Needs

## DR. SHERRI DESSIREA TAPP

Culture is a set of learned beliefs and behaviors shaping how members view and experience the world. People bring to social encounters worldviews and behaviors that have been shaped by their culture of origin and that were learned as children. Individuals also bring their cultures of affiliation. Cultures of affiliation may include in part religious groups, ethnic groups, social classes, and voluntary and professional organizations, which they have come to embrace (Robbins, Fantone, Hermann, Alexander, & Zweifler, 1998, p. 811).

More than three decades have passed since Lewis (1969) wrote:

> We cannot hide the fact that racism is encountered in counseling in many forms. We cannot hide it, so we have got to face it . . . we must not allow the presence of racism to choke our efforts, to prevent progress in human relationships, to make us less human, to undermine our confidence and ability to do a job. (p. 54)

Minority group experiences are generally seen and analyzed from a white, middle-class perspective (Sue et al., 1982, p. 48). As a result, many human services professionals lack understanding and knowledge about

**Dr. Sherri Dessirea Tapp** is Assistant Professor in the Graduate School of Education at Oral Roberts University in Tulsa, OK

ethnic worldviews and values and their consequent interaction with an oppressive society.

Educators, Social Workers, Medical and other Helping professionals should be culturally sensitive with children and families who are Black, Puerto Rican, Native American, Asian, or any other marginalized ethnicity. Educators should also be culturally sensitive and competent in terms of socioeconomic status, gender and culture. While the intent to protect and advocate is an honorable one, many such professionals are loathe to admit much less be upfront about the inequality with which people are treated based upon race, gender, and social class (Cunningham, 1993, p.2). To be African American or Chicano or Native American or Asian American is to be often seen as different, though not in any positive sense, for we often conceptualize different as deficient despite the objective reality (p. 2). The browning of our country is evident everywhere (Rodriguez, 1998, p.1). Yet, in the course of human service provision, more children of color are removed from their homes than Caucasian children (Courtney, Barth, Berrick, Brooks & Devon, 1996, p. 100).

A recent assessment was conducted of five states with large numbers of children placed in some form of foster care that included Texas, Michigan, New York, Illinois, and California. This assessment revealed that children of color are represented three to ten times as much as Caucasian children in state custody. The same study found that the National Center on Child Abuse and Neglect has reported since 1988 that children of color are more likely to be over-represented in child maltreatment reports when we consider the number of children of color in the child population (Courtney et al, 1996, p. 101). After a referral is made, allegations of abuse regarding children of color are more likely to be confirmed by social services providers working as Child Welfare Specialists than referrals alleging the abuse or neglect of Caucasian children. The racism that has permeated child welfare services is demonstrated in three ways: (a) by the types of services made available, (b) by unfair treatment based on ethnicity within the system, and (c) by failing to follow through on plans to make changes within the system (Courtney et al, 1996, p. 105). While larger numbers of Black children have been served by public agencies, Caucasian parents have been given more support than other parents (Courtney et al, 1996, p. 106).

Once in the state custody system, over half of the families who had children in custody received no service recommendations (Courtney et al, 1996, p. 106). In other words, no efforts were made to facilitate services that would result in over half of the families being reunited. Native American children were the least likely to have services recommended.

> Situations such as these indicated a need for increasing the cultural competency of the social service providers in the system. Culturally competent social service professionals possess the skills that allow them to compare and contrast values, norms, customs, and institutions of groups of people who are from a variety of backgrounds. These professionals understand the effects of stereotyping, discrimination and oppression on the provision of social services to those families in need. (Poole, 1998, p. 12).

To assist in resolving this problem, cultural competence in specific areas is necessary, such as awareness, knowledge, and skills. The awareness category has to do with the social services providers' awareness of their own meaning schemes and how they may manifest during interactions with families in the form of culturally insensitive behaviors (Ponterotto et al., 1996, p. 248).

Knowledge refers to the social services providers' knowledge of their own worldview, as well as the worldview of the person or family being served and of other culture-specific information, including the impact of racism on clients, models of acculturation, and racial identity development (p. 248). Practitioners have to be familiar enough with the respective culture of the people they are serving to know differences within and among groups. For example, they need to realize that not all Hispanics and Latinas are alike in everything and that Black people in Tulsa, Oklahoma, are not automatically the same as Black people in Castro Valley, California. Likewise, they must be aware that one band of Blackfeet cannot be expected to automatically have the same values and beliefs as a clan of another Native American Tribal group, or as other groups of Blackfeet.

Another area of competence is skill—that is, being able to "make adjustments to work effectively in cross-cultural situations" (Poole, 1998). Skill has to do with the social workers' ability to translate awareness and knowledge into culturally competent social services practice (Ponterotto et al, 1996, p. 248). Defining cultural competence as just accepting and valuing the cultures of others is much too broad (Poole, 1998, p. 2). To exercise cultural competence, social service providers are encouraged to recognize there are good and bad components within every culture. Exercising cultural competence involves practicing tolerance but rejecting any cultural aspects that harm or oppress other people.

Marginalized populations are those groups of people who have historically had little if any voice in the society in which they live. Children of marginalized populations in the system had fewer visits with their families, fewer services in general, and less contact with their social worker than those in the non-marginalized population (Courtney, 1996). For example,

> A comprehensive 1994 federal study of child welfare cases in all 50 states compared children's natural families based on a number of different characteristics and found in every case that black children were more likely than white children to be removed from the home regardless of specific family problems. For example, even when there was no substance abuse problem in the home, black children were still removed 32 percent of the time while white children were removed only 21 percent of the time. Similarly, if a parent was employed, black children were removed in 36 percent of cases. Latino children in 34 percent of cases and white children in only 22 percent. This national study was commissioned by the federal Department of Health and Human Services and conducted by Westat, a private research firm. ( < http://www.nycfuture.org /3/index.htm > , parag. 39).

Although Black children comprised only 15% of the child population in the United States in 1995, they represented 49% of children in foster care that same year. Caucasian children represented 36% of the child population in out of home care for that year (Morton, 1999). Poverty plays a critical role in a child's removal from a home. A national survey of abuse and neglect cases in the mid-1980's found that children in families with incomes below $15,000 were 5 times more likely to be victimized by their parents than those with incomes above that level. Low-income parents are often under greater stress and are more poorly educated than those in higher income brackets, and Black and Latino families are far more likely to be poor than white families (http://www.nycfuture.org/ 3/index.htm parag. 51).

The education of and services to children can be enhanced when educators, social services workers, and other helping professionals become aware of the reality that white privilege and other factors prohibit cultural competence. Giving these professionals who have chosen to perform a very difficult job an opportunity to raise their own consciousness can result in children being better educated and fewer children being removed from their homes.

There is wide agreement among scholars that becoming culturally competent is a developmental process (Beamer, 1992, p. 288). Cultural competence involves both external and internal adjustments. It is not just external. Internal cultural competence must also be promoted, encouraged, and facilitated. Social workers cannot merely be cognizant of the fact that they are to provide services for families of different ethnicities. Child welfare and other social workers must also experience raised consciousness to discover their personal realities about dealing with families of color. "Critical consciousness facilitates analysis of problems within their context for the purpose of enabling people together to transform their reality rather than merely understanding it or adapting to it with less discomfort" (Cunningham, 1993, p. 7).

> The problem was that in order to deliver needed services, the service providers must be culturally competent. There was no way to identify this cultural competence. This lack of an identifying process thwarted the continuing education process that could lead to heightened awareness of cultural appreciation within organizations that serve the public.

The development of a user-friendly instrument to identify cultural appreciation was needed to promote cultural appreciation and enhance service provision. Such an instrument may set the stage for a transformative learning experience for social services professionals. "This may involve new ways of understanding and using knowledge or new ways of understanding oneself and acting in interpersonal relationships" (Merriam, 1995). The development of an instrument that identifies cultural competence may facilitate child welfare or other helping professionals becoming aware of how they perceive and interact with people of different ethnicities. At that point, they may apply this new knowledge to enhance the interpersonal relationships they have with children and families of color. By doing so, service provision may be improved.

A study was undertaken to develop and establish the validity and reliability of an instrument to identify cultural competence in human services workers. The instrument that was developed was patterned after Assessing The Learning Strategies of Adults (ATLAS) and therefore utilized a design similar to that for creating ATLAS (Conti& Kolody, 1999(a), 1999 (b)). This process involved analyses using various multivariate procedures with data collected from social services workers with the Multicultural Counseling Knowledge and Awareness Scale (MCKAS) and the Quick Discrimination Index (Ponterotto, et al., 1995, 1027). In order to develop a user-friendly instrument with a flow-chart design for identifying cultural competency in social workers, workers at the Oklahoma Department of Human Services completed two existing instruments that assess cultural competence. The participants were all currently employed by the Oklahoma State Department of Human Services (DHS). The DHS is comprised of a number of divisions providing a myriad of services to children, families, and individuals. Its mission is to assist individuals and families in need to help themselves lead healthier, more independent and productive lives (www.okdhs.org/statement/ dismissingstatement.htm).

According to the agency's Monthly Statistical Bulletin, social services personnel at the DHS in May of 2001 served 13,551 families receiving Temporary Assistance for Needy Families; 1,162 people needing Adult Protective Services; 144,197 people requiring Child Support Enforcement Services; and 9,728 children requiring Developmental Disability Services. Also during May, there were 730 elderly people who received adult day services; 109,441 families who received Food Stamp services; 439,787 individuals who were provided Medicaid services; and 49,106 people who received State Supplemental Disabled Services for the blind and the elderly. Additionally, there were 2,590 children who were assessed for abuse and neglect by Child Welfare Specialists, and 6,132 children were served in foster care placements (www.okdhs.org/ finances/bulletin/ bulletin 0105/t33.htm).

The Department of Human Services (DHS) has approximately 5,000 employees who directly provide social services to clients. They are classified with the following titles: Social Services Specialist, Social Services Supervisor, Child Welfare Specialist, Child Welfare Supervisor, and Youth Guidance Specialist. They are located in offices throughout the 77 counties in the state of Oklahoma. More than 1,200 social workers were sent an e-mail through the DHS system and invited to participate in the study. The e-mail message provided a link to a website that contained the form for participating in the study.

The responses of the participants were completely anonymous because there were no identifiers in the responses that were electronically recorded. In response to these e-mail requests, 768 responses were received in a one-week period from Department of Human Services employees. This is a response rate of 70% of those invited to participate and represents approximately 15% of the 5,000 of the employees providing direct services. Responses from the participants were compared to demographic variables to assure that the two instruments were appropriate for the group.

Factor analysis was conducted in order to examine the structure of the Multicultural Counseling Knowledge and Awareness Scale and the Quick Discrimination Index to determine if the structures were confirmed with the responses of the social workers at the Department of Human Services. The Multicultural Counseling Knowledge and Awareness Scale (MKCAS) is a 32-item counselor self-rating scale initially called the Multicultural Counseling Awareness Scale developed by Ponterotto, Sanchez, and Magids in 1991. The MKCAS uses a 7-point Likert-type format to measure multicultural knowledge/skills and awareness, with responses ranging from not at all true (1) to totally true (7). The MKCAS and accompanying demographic questionnaire require 15 to 25 minutes to complete. The MKCAS is conceptually grounded in the Division 17 competency report of the American Psychological Association (Sue et al., 1982), which states that multicultural competence consists of knowledge, awareness and skills.

The Quick Discrimination Index (QDI) was developed to fill a need for a reliable, valid, and moderate-length self-report measure of attitudes regarding racial diversity and women's equality (Ponterotto et al., 1995, p. 1017). There were three coordinated studies on the development and initial validation of the QDI. Study 1 focused on item development, content validity, internal consistency reliability, and criterion-related validity. Study 2 focused on the factor structure of the QDI while further examining criterion-related validity and internal consistency. This study also assessed the stability of responses to the QDI over time. Finally, Study 3 incorporated confirmatory factor analysis to test the factor structure found in Study 2 and examined measures of convergent and discriminant validity and social desirability contamination (p. 1017).

Items were generated from the literature on discrimination, prejudice, and "modern racism" and from the development team's applied work in the area. An attempt was made to tap both the cognitive and affective components of prejudicial attitudes. Roughly 40 statements were initially written. Each item statement was examined by the research team, and redundant, unclear, and confusing items were eliminated. Twenty-eight remaining items were placed on a 5-point Likert-type scale: 1 =

Strongly Disagree; 2 = Disagree; 3 = Not Sure; 4 = Agree; and 5 = Strongly Agree (Ponterotto et al., 1995, p. 1018).

To assess the content validity of the prototype Quick Discrimination Index, five individuals with expertise in the topical area and in psychological measurement who were not part of the development team rated each item on a 5-point Likert-type scale for domain appropriateness and clarity. Items receiving a mean of less than 4.0 a "5" rating indicated highly domain appropriate and very clear on either domain appropriateness or clarity were eliminated or rewritten. This procedure resulted in a final prototype pool of 25 items. The total score range is from 25 to 125 with higher scores indicating more positive attitudes toward multiculturalism and women's equality (Ponterotto et al., 1995, p. 1018).

The 25-item (QDI) was then the subject of a 2-hour focus group conducted by the senior author with seven graduate students in education. Focus group members completed the instrument and then discussed both their affective and cognitive reactions to the items. Focus group members completed the QDI in 6 to 13 minutes (Ponterotto et al., 1995, p. 1018). The principle components factoring method with varimax rotation was employed with both existing instruments. This process resulted in confirming the structure of both the Multicultural Counseling Knowledge and Awareness Scale and the Quick

Construct validity addresses the underlying theory of an instrument. Following the design for the development of Assessing The Learning Strategies of AdultS, the construct validity for the Cultural Appreciation in Lifelong Learning instrument rests with the validity of the 62 items in the Multicultural Counseling Knowledge and Awareness Scale and the Quick Discrimination Index. Both of these instruments have their validity reported in published documents. The demographic data for the social workers at the Department of Human Services (DHS) and the analyses examining the relationship of the demographic variables for this group and the instruments indicate that these instruments are appropriate for measuring cultural competency for social workers. Moreover, the factor analyses for both instruments confirm that they are measuring cultural competency in the same way for social workers as for other groups with whom the instruments have been tested, which include educators. Since the items from the two instruments have established construct validity and since the instruments are useful with the DHS group, the pool of items for the Cultural Appreciation in Lifelong Learning instrument have construct validity.

Construct validity was established by conducting a confirmatory factor analysis on each instrument to demonstrate that human services responses were similar to the published results for the instrument. In addition, cluster analysis was used to identify the groups that possessed different levels of cultural competency based on the concepts in the literature that are measured by the two instruments.

Content validity pertains to the sampling adequacy of the content of the instrument (Kerlinger, 1973, p. 458). In this study, content validity focused on developing items that accurately placed respondents in one of four groups identified in the cluster analysis. One way to statistically determine content validity is to use discriminate analysis. Discriminate analysis is a useful tool to identify the process that separates groups created by a cluster analysis (Conti, 1996, p. 71). Discriminant analysis is a statistical technique that allows the investigation of the differences between two or more groups in relationship to several variables simultaneously (Klecka, 1980, p. 7). In discriminate analysis as with other multivariate techniques, the emphasis is upon analyzing the variables together rather than individually; the purpose of multivariate procedures is to examine the interaction of the multiple variables (Conti, 1993). "Discriminate analysis requires the researcher to make meaningful decisions about the data and to impose sense upon it" (p. 90). Discriminant analysis can be used either to describe the way groups differ or to predict membership in a group. In this study, discriminate analysis was used to investigate what separated the four groups that emerged from the cluster analysis.

Discriminant analysis is a useful tool for identifying the *process* that separates the clusters and therefore for helping to describe the clusters. By using the various clusters as the groups and by using the variables from the cluster analysis as the set of discriminating variables, one can generate an analysis that produces a structure matrix which describes the process that separates the various clusters into distinct groups and which yields a discriminant function that is a formula that can be used for predicting placement in the various clusters.(Conti, 1996, p. 71)

Content validity was established by using discriminant analysis to create precise items for an instrument using a flow-chart design. Criterion-related validity was established by comparing participant responses on the new instrument to their responses on the items used to create the new instrument. Finally, reliability was established by the test-retest method.

Several traditional and innovative steps were taken to develop an instrument to identify cultural awareness of social workers. Innovative steps involved using existing instruments to provide the source for the pool of items, collecting data via the Internet, and using multivariate analyses to determine the structure and content of the new instrument. The result of the combination of these steps was the creation of a new instrument with a flow-chart design that can be completed in less than two minutes and which classifies respondents into one of four groups of cultural appreciation. This instrument was named Cultural Appreciation in Lifelong Learning (CALL) and may be referred to as CALL.

The 768 participants that provided the data for developing the Cultural Appreciation in Lifelong Learning instrument were all currently employed by the Oklahoma State Department of Human Services (DHS). As has been the tradition with social services in America, the overwhelming majority of respondents were female with four-fifths female and one-fifth male. The average age of the participants was 42.7 with a standard deviation of 10.4. Nearly three-fourths of the participants were over the age of 35 years of age.

The U.S. Census Bureau reported that for the State of Oklahoma the estimated ethnicity statewide for 1999 was distributed as follows: African American—7.5%, American Indian or Alaskan Native—7.5%, Asian or Pacific—1.0%, Caucasian—80%, and Hispanic—4.0% (http://www.odoc.state. ok.us). Although nearly three-fourths of the participants in this study were Caucasian, the sample was slightly more diverse than the state population. The two largest minority groups in the state are Native Americans and African Americans. Those identifying themselves as African American made up nearly 10% of the sample, and Native Americans comprised over 11% of respondents. Thus, this representative sample of Department of Human Services is somewhat more ethnically diverse than the general population of the state.

Respondents were asked to provide information as to the length of time they have been employed with the Department of Human Services (DHS) and whether or not they worked in a metro or non-metro county. Nearly one-fourth (23.5%) of the participants in this sample had less than 2 years of experience on the job while over a third (35.6%) had 8 to 10 years experience and approximately two-fifths (40.9%) have over 10 years of experience. Over 300 (42%) staff members have worked for the DHS less than 5 years. Thus, the Department of Human Services is nearly evenly divided into a very experienced group and a much less experienced group. While 60% had over 5 years of experience as DHS employees, 40% of the staff in the sample had 5 years or less experience working in the agency. Nearly one-fourth of the less-experienced group is comprised of new employees with less than 2 years of experience in the agency.

The mean for the number of years of experience for the 433 participants who perceived diversity issues as related to societal causes was 9.6 with a standard deviation of 8.37. The median was 7.00 years of experience. The mean for the number of years of experience for the 335 participants who perceived diversity issues as related to the individual perspective was 10.27 with a standard deviation of 7.96. The median was 9.00 years of experience.

The mean for the number of years of experience for the 158 people who acknowledged a lack of knowledge concerning cultural diversity was 10.29 with a standard deviation of 7.64. The median was 10.0 years of experience. The mean for the number of years of experience for the 177 people who have some knowledge of cultural issues, but have chosen not to support cultural diversity, was 10.25 with a standard deviation of 8.26. The median was 8.00 years of experience.

While experience is a tremendous resource for adult learning, fixed habits and patterns also develop over time (Knowles, 1970, p. 44). Therefore, those newer employees may be very open to training related to cultural awareness. Finally, there are large groups at the more-experienced level within DHS. These entered the agency during vastly different social eras. Those that had 6-10 years of experience began working with families in the Department of Human Services during the second administration of President Clinton. Those with 11-15 years of experience came to work for DHS during President Clinton's first administration. Employees of the Department of Human Services with 16-20 years of experience were hired during President Bush's administration, and those with 21-25 years of DHS experience came to work for the agency during the Reagan administration. Very few DHS employees remain with the agency for more than 25 years. Thus, the levels and training needs for cultural appreciation for this group may vary widely because of this diverse experience.

Nearly two-thirds (65.88%) of respondents worked in non-metro counties while the remainder work in or around the Tulsa, Oklahoma City, or McAlester areas which are all classified as metropolitan areas within DHS. Those working in metropolitan areas have a greater opportunity to serve people of diverse cultures and ethnicities because more people live in the metropolitan areas than in the non-metro areas. For example, there are approximately 792,000 people living within Tulsa County and approximately 1,000,000 people living in the Oklahoma County area. At the two-cluster solution 37.0% of the respondents in the group perceiving diversity issues as related to societal causes worked in a metro location while 62.6% did not. Of those who perceived diversity issues as related to the individual perspective 30.1% worked in a metro location and 69.6% did not. At the four-cluster solution 37.1% of those in the group of 197 who viewed traditional values as limiting multicultural groups worked in a metro location while 62.4% did not. Of those 236 participants who viewed traditional values as being somewhat useful to multicultural groups, 36.9% worked in a metro location and 62.7% did not. Of those 158 participants who acknowledged a lack of knowledge concerning cultural diversity, 32.3% worked in a metro location and 67.7% did not. Of those 177 participants who have some cultural knowledge but chose not to support cultural diversity, 28.2% worked in a metro location and 71.2% did not.

There are several positions within the Department of Human Services. Child Welfare and Social Services Specialists are those workers providing direct services to children and families on a daily basis. Child Welfare and Social Services supervisors also provide some direct services to families on a more limited basis. Nearly two-thirds (62.66%) of the respondents were specialists who provide direct services to clients. Just over one-fourth of respondents were Child Welfare Specialists. A little more than one-tenth of the respondents worked in supervisor capacities. Slightly more than one-fourth of participants were Youth Guidance Specialist staff, clerical staff, and administrative personnel. While the Youth Guidance Specialists have regular direct contact with clients, the clerical and administrative staff members generally do not.

Social Services Specialists comprised 38.1% of the group perceiving diversity issues as related to societal causes, Child Welfare Specialists were 27.7%, and Social Services and Child Welfare Supervisors made up 12.9% of respondents in this group. Of those who perceive diversity issues from an individual perspective, Social Services Specialists comprised 35.8% of the group, Child Welfare Specialists comprised 21.8%, and Social Services and Child Welfare Supervisors made up 8.7% of that group.

The Department of Human Services employees participating in the survey were asked to answer a total of 62 questions from the Multicultural Counseling Knowledge and Awareness Scale (MKCAS) and the Quick Discrimination Index (QDI). Scores for the 32 items on the MKCAS may range from 32 to 224. The distribution of scores for the MKCAS had a range from 76 to 208. The mean score on the MKCAS was 146.65 with a standard deviation of 22.98. The median score was 146. Thus, the responses were distributed across the scale with the indicators of central tendency for the group falling near but slightly above the midpoint of 128 for the scale. At the two-cluster solution those in the group perceiving diversity issues as related to societal causes had a mean score of 161.70 with a standard deviation of 9.10. The median score for this group was 161.00. Those in the group perceiving diversity issues from an individual perspective had a mean score of 127.20 with a standard deviation of 13.61. The median score for this group was 128.00.

The paper version of CALL has three pages that use a flow-chart design, two pages that describe the four groups identified by the instrument, and a page with directions. CALL is printed on colored cards that are half page sheets of a standard-sized, 8.5 "x 11" page. Six colored cards pages are bound at the top to form a small booklet. Like Assessing the Leaning Strategies of AdultS, "sentence stems, which are in the top box on the page, lead to options in other boxes which complete the stem. Connecting arrows direct the respondent to the options. Each option leads the respondent to another box which either instructs the respondent to proceed to another colored card or which provides information about the respondent's correct group placement" (Conti & Kolody, 1999, p. 16). These pages make up the entire packet for the CALL instrument. CALL can be completed by professionals in one to two minutes. In the model packet printed for the field testing of CALL, the pages that linked to choices on the first item were printed on orange and yellow paper. These pages can be any color as long as they are coordinated with the option boxes on the first item. Also, since some people have difficulty discerning various colors, either page numbers or some other coding system may be used. Cultural Appreciation in Lifelong Learning (CALL) is a valid and reliable instrument for identifying cultural appreciation. Additionally, four distinct groups exist related to cultural appreciation.

Cultural appreciation can be identified by exploring the concepts of knowledge and awareness. Awareness and knowledge are two components of cultural competence (Ponterotto et al., 1994, p. 17). Awareness is concerned with one's own cultural socialization and accompanying predispositions. Knowledge has to do with the learner's knowledge of the worldviews and value patterns of culturally diverse people. These two components interact to create four distinct groups in terms of the appreciation of cultural diversity.

For the Cultural Appreciation in Lifelong Learning instrument, each of the four groups was given a non-gender-specific name that would not reflect any type of bias toward the group. The four names selected for each group are (a) Group 1–Chris; (b) Group 2–Alex; (c) Group 3–Lee; and (d) Group 4–Lynn. The first initials of each group combine to form the word CALL. The following descriptors are given for each group in the Cultural Appreciation in Lifelong Learning booklet. Each description is based upon the items from the structure matrix that was used to form the groups.

## Chris

Those in this group enthusiastically embrace cultural diversity. They feel that societal forces are firmly established that are often repressive to culturally diverse groups. They are very familiar with the impact and operations of oppression and realize that racial discrimination is deeply rooted in society. They understand the role culture has played in the development of an identity and worldview of those in culturally diverse groups.

## Alex

Those in this group appreciate cultural diversity. They feel that societal forces have greatly impacted and have limited opportunities for culturally diverse groups. They understand the role culture has played in the development of an identity and worldview of those in culturally diverse groups but believe that culturally diverse groups can benefit from assuming some mainstream traditional values.

## Lee

Those in this group do not eagerly embrace cultural diversity. They believe that the individual, rather than societal forces, is the major factor influencing a person's social situation. They do not believe that forces such as oppression and racism are deeply rooted in society and are not aware of many institutional barriers that restrict minority groups. They accept mainstream traditional values. They acknowledge that they have very little knowledge of ways for various ethnic groups to adopt the cultural traits of other groups, but they are aware that being born a minority in this society brings with it far more challenges than faced by White people.

## Lynn

Those in this group are opposed to cultural diversity. They strongly believe that the individual, rather than societal forces, is the major factor influencing a person's social situation. They do not believe that forces such as oppression and racism are deeply rooted in society, and they feel that far too much attention has been directed toward multicultural or minority issues in society. They are somewhat aware that being born a minority in this society brings with it more challenges than faced by White people and have some knowledge of ways for various ethnic groups to adopt the cultural traits of other groups. Despite this awareness and knowledge, they reject concepts related to cultural diversity and firmly believe that people should marry within their own race. Within the four groups there is clear distinction as each group demonstrates varying degrees of knowledge and awareness regarding cultural appreciation.

Cultural Appreciation in Lifelong Learning (CALL) is used to facilitate correct placement in groups formed by the Multicultural Counseling Knowledge and Awareness Scale and the Quick Discrimination Index. The responses from practitioners in the Department of Human Services were used to conduct the cluster analysis to uncover the groups with varying levels of cultural appreciation. The use of discriminant analysis allowed for identifying the processes that separated these groups and provided the structure matrix of items for writing the precise item for identifying placement in the group. Field testing with practitioners provided clarity and feedback on these items. Finally, the items were organized into a booklet that could easily be administered, and a website was created for the instrument (http://members.cox.net/drtapp). Thus, the format and process for creating ATLAS was also very effective for creating CALL.

Cultural Appreciation in Lifelong Learning can be used by those conducting the training, as well as by those receiving training. In this way, it can be utilized to raise the educator's awareness regarding the personal degree of cultural appreciation. This could lead to an examination of personal worldviews, which in turn could lead to an opportunity for a perspective transformation. Cultural Appreciation in Lifelong Learning (CALL) can also be used to stimulate discussions around how those that are exemplary in a particular area became that way. It is through dialogue that adults attempt to understand and to learn what is valid in the assertions made by others and attempt to achieve consensual validation for our own assertions (Mezirow, 1990, p. 354).

CALL should be used to stimulate thinking and dialogue on the issue of cultural diversity in social services provision, the attitudes of the workers, managers, and administrators and how these attitudes impact the quality of the services being provided. Regardless of group placement, everyone has the potential to grow in cultural appreciation. Dialogue should be encouraged as to how that growth can be cultivated.

Cultural Appreciation in Lifelong Learning (CALL) is the result of a product-oriented study. It was developed with adult participants from the United States. CALL warrants further study to find out if it is applicable in international arenas. Research should be conducted to determine how social services workers are prepared to work with the general population outside of the United States and how ethnic diversity is addressed during that preparation. Cultural Appreciation in Lifelong Learning (CALL) was developed to promote consciousness raising among those charged with providing services to people and their families. Studies should be conducted to explore consciousness raising related to cultural appreciation and ultimately a transformed life. This sort of inquiry should also address whether people can or have the desire to change.

Inquiry is warranted as a result of this study to determine how adult educators might cultivate the desire to change within learners. There are various characteristics that make one learner more amenable to change than another. The attitude of the learner needs to be studied to determine its role in amenability to change. Additionally, the origin of people's attitudes toward various cultures and ethnicities is worthy of study. Research should examine and seek to determine not only where attitudes come from, but whether or not they are fixed.

Finally, further study is warranted to generate alternatives for how the Chris, Alex, Lee and Lynn groups may interact with each other to collectively enhance their cultural appreciation. This study should include discussion regarding what role the facilitator plays in stimulating such interaction. Such research should also explore the attitudinal posture of the facilitator and its impact on interaction between the groups.

# References

Beamer, L. (1992). Learning intercultural communication competence. *The Journal of Business Communication*, 29 (3) 285300.

Conti, G. J. (1993). *Using discriminant analysis in adult education. Proceedings of the 34th Adult Education Research Conference* (pp. 8489). Pennsylvania State University, University Park, PA.

Conti, G. J. (1996). *Using cluster analysis in adult education. Proceedings of the 37th Annual Adult Education Research Conference*, (pp. 6772). University of South Florida: Tampa.

Conti, G. J., & Kolody, R. C. (1999). *Guide for using ATLAS: Assessing The Learning Strategies of Adults.* Stillwater, OK: Oklahoma State University.

Courtney, M.E., Barth, R. P.,Berrick, J.D.,Brooks, D.,et al. (1996). Race and child welfare services: Past research and future directions. *Child Welfare* 75(2),99

Cunningham, P. (1993). Let's Get Real: A critical look at the practice of adult education. *Journal of Adult Education*, 22(1), 3-15.

Kerlinger, F. N. (1973). *Foundations of behavioral research.* New York:Holt, Rinehart and Winston.

Klecka, W. R. (1980). *Discriminant analysis.* Beverly Hills, CA: Sage.

Knowles, M. S. (1970). *The modern practice of adult education andragogy versus pedagogy.* New York: Association Press.

Lewis, S. O. (1969). Racism encountered in counseling part I. *Counselor Education and Supervision*, 9, p. 49-54.

Merriam, S.(1995). *Selected writings on philosophy and adult education* (2nd ed.). Malaber, FL: Krieger

Mezirow, J.(1990). *Fostering critical reflection in adulthood a guide to transformative and emancipatory learning.* San Francisco, CA: JosseyBass Inc.

Morton, L. L., et. al., *Determinants of withdrawal from the bilingual career track when entering high school. Guidance and Counselling* v. 14 no. 3 (Spring 1999) p. 14-20

Poole, D.L.(1998).Politically correct or culturally competent? *Health and Social Work*, 23, 14

Ponterotto, J. G., Reiger, B. P., Barrett, A. Sparks, R. (1994). Assessing multicultural counseling competence: A review of instrumentation. *Journal of Counseling and Development*, 72 (3), 316322.

Ponterotto, J. G., Burkard, A., Reiger, B. P., Grieger, I., D'Onofrio, A., Dubuisson, A., Heenehan, M., Millstein, B., Parisi, M., Rath, J. F., & Sax, G.(1995). Development and initial validation of the Quick Discrimination Index (QDI). *Educational and Psychological Measurement*, 55 (6) 10261031.

Ponterotto, J. G., & Alexander, C. M. (1996). *Handbook of multicultural assessment: Clinical, psychological, and educational applications*. San Francisco, CA: JosseyBass Publishers.

Robbins, L. S., Fantone, J. C., Hermann, J., Alexander, G. L., and Zweifler, A. J. (1998). Culture, communication, and the informal curriculum: Improving cultural awareness and sensitivity training in medical school. *Academic Medicine*, 73, 831-833.

Rodriguez, D. M., (1998). Diversity training brings staff closer [diversity workshop, Piscataway, N.J.]. *The Education Digest*, v 64, No. 1, 28-31

Sue, D. W., Bernier, J. E., Durran, A., Feinberg, L., Pedersen, P., Smith, E. J., & Vasquez-Nuttall, E. (1982). Position paper: Cross-cultural counseling competencies. *Counseling Psychologist*, 10 (2), 45-52.

# Encouraging Multicultural Diversity in the Curriculum

## DR. LINDA GRAY

What an educator means by the term "diversity" in the English class-room has changed in recent decades. In the late 1960s and early 70s, institutions of higher learning expected their relatively small numbers of minority students to adapt to the majority culture and the traditional curriculum. No one seemed to give much thought to what the students brought to the university or to the concept of adapting the curriculum to the students. Then later, in an attempt to recognize aspects of minority students and their cultures, textbooks began including token works of literature by minority authors—Black authors primarily—and some curricula incorporated a multicultural unit. Today the understanding of diversity in the classroom means understanding the complexity that diversity truly encompasses—issues of society, ethics, and application (Wathington, 2002).

In our rapidly changing classrooms in the U.S., teachers face new issues concerning diversity and the curriculum. In the past few decades, the literary canon has changed in the textbooks to include multicultural literature, histories of various ethnic groups, and a range of perspectives on some of life's milestones. Teachers may react to such textbook and classroom changes by embracing change, openly resisting change, or thinking they've adapted but inadvertently continuing to teach as they always have.

---

**Dr. Linda Gray** is Professor of English at Oral Roberts University.

A look at literature anthologies from a few decades ago reveals the significant change in which types of literary works are included in textbooks used in American literature courses. Older anthologies rarely included works from African-American, Native American, Hispanic, and Asian writers; however, most—if not all—current American literature anthologies include literary works from all of these groups. A comparison of *The Norton Introduction to Literature*, the 1977 edition and the current edition, reveals the extent of how different the selections are. Both books have nearly the same number of entries—418 in 1977 and 415 in the current edition. However, the earlier edition has only 13 works by minority writers—equaling 3.1% of the works in the book. By contrast, the current edition has 40 works by ethnic minorities, which comprises 9.6% of the works in the book.

The changing U.S. culture is reflected in the changing canon, as illustrated in the comparison of the two editions of the *Norton Anthology*. As any experienced teacher knows, adopting a new textbook for use in a course automatically creates extra work for the teacher as he or she must get acquainted with different material. Some teachers simply prefer to hold to their "tried and true" old standbys, and if forced to change to new textbooks, they may teach only those selections that were in the old book. Consequently, even though the canon has changed, not all teachers have embraced these changes. Other teachers welcome new course content, viewing the change as adding a new spark of life to their courses.

The same range of reactions can describe what happens when diversity issues and content are incorporated in the classroom. Is cultural diversity an important part of education in today's world? Do teachers have an obligation to deal with diversity issues in their courses?

Barbara Scott (1994), in her article "Integrating Race, Class, Gender, and Sexual Orientation into the college Curriculum," explains that faculty "have an academic responsibility and a moral obligation to provide students with an inclusive education that will enable them to deal with the contingencies of living in a diverse world." If teachers are to engage, educate, and prepare students for the modern world, which is characterized by international travel, culturally diverse countries, and frequent multicultural interactions, then we must incorporate diversity in our classrooms—or better still, "transform our curriculum multiculturally." Scott points out that there is a difference between incorporating diversity and transforming curriculum, as the latter reflects a holistic approach that truly revises the curriculum, not a cut-and-paste insertion of token snippets of multicultural content, more typical of curricula a couple of decades ago.

In *Teaching with a Multicultural Perspective*, the authors, Patricia and Leonard Davidman (1994), distinguish four ways diversity shows up in the curriculum:

1. The "contributions approach," which highlights cultural holidays and events without really affecting the traditional curriculum.
2. The "additive approach," which inserts cultural content and themes in isolation, such as including a cultural unit within the existing unit. Although more inclusive than the first approach, this one is still minimal because the dominant culture is still viewed as the norm.
3. The "transformative approach," which changes the underlying structure of the curriculum so that diversity is central (not marginal) to the course.
4. The "decision-making and social action approach," which involves application of the transformative approach. Students make careful decisions and develop ways to take action on their decisions and to show civic responsibility.

Both of the first two approaches, which simply insert somewhat fragmented multicultural information into an existing curriculum, are low on Bloom's Taxonomy (Huitt, 2004) by simply expecting recall or comprehension of multicultural facts. The latter two approaches rank higher on Bloom's Taxonomy by engaging synthesis and evaluation skills. Enabling students to reach these higher levels is what educators seek so that students learn to think critically about what they learn and consequently become thoughtful adults.

Methods for how to truly transform a curriculum must involve the larger picture and the major goals for the curriculum. The journal *Diversity Digest* (1997) offers several pointers for effectively transforming the curriculum of a school or university, including incorporating the intended diversity goals into the mission statement—being careful to recognize that diversity is complex and involves setting numerous goals, not just one simplified one. Placing the goals for diversity within the mission statement naturally ensures the transformation for all aspects of the school or university, and it encourages creating programs and activities among the departments and involves faculty dialog and development. Assessment of diversity courses and programs is also important, as is trying to tie diversity goals to student life programs, not just curricular programs.

Once the direction toward multicultural recognition and goals are established at the university level, academic departments and individual professors need to put their own courses in line with university goals. Specific guidelines for courses are offered by Leonard and Patricia Davidman (1994) to help the teacher deliberately consider how his or her own course materials and teaching practices reflect multicultural goals. These include evaluating if and how the course content and teaching methods promote educational equity, cultural pluralism, and a multicultural perspective. The teacher should also look at how both the campus and neighboring community can serve as a venue for teaching diversity. The Davidmans also advise the teacher to make sure students understand the rationale for a multicultural curriculum and caution the teacher to be alert for unintended consequences of requiring multicultural courses.

There are numerous benefits of truly transforming a curriculum multiculturally, according to Barbara Scott and to the findings from a task force on multicultural curriculum transformation at Northern Illinois University. Benefits include the following:

- More students are reached (Provost's Task Force, 2001). People tend to respond to stories, characters, and situations similar to their own, so if the textbooks (quite commonly anthologies) include selections and perspectives that readers can relate to, then the books and teachers can reach more students.
- Students are more actively involved in the learning process (Scott, 1994). Students are more likely to be actively involved in their own educations if they like what they are studying.
- The curriculum becomes more accurate and balanced (Provost's Task Force, 2001). America is a multicultural nation, and the curriculum should reflect the nation's population.
- Biases and stereotypes in curriculum are exposed and changed (Provost's Task Force, 2001). Transforming the curriculum to present various perspectives and include literature by mi-

norities helps eliminate misleading and inaccurate perceptions people have about each other.

- Students are better prepared to work in a global environment (Provost's Task Force, 2001). Culture shock and cross-cultural misunderstanding are less likely to occur on the job if people have already learned about different cultures and world perspectives.
- Student evaluations improve (Scott, 1994). Students who like their classes and feel the course material is relevant are more likely to rate the course high.
- Faculty are revitalized and improved their job satisfaction (Scott, 1994). A multiculturally diverse curriculum that invigorates students results in faculty enthusiasm.
- Both students and teachers increase their awareness and appreciation of cultural heritages, perspectives, and contributions (Provost's Task Force, 2001).

Despite these and other benefits of a multiculturally transformed curriculum, not all teachers welcome such curricular changes, and even some who do, do so only minimally. Patricia Helton, Vice President for Student Life at Eastern Mennonite University, points out that students often learn more than the stated course objectives and content; they also learn and internalize the less obvious attitudes, values, and viewpoints of the professors. In other words, students pick up a hidden curriculum—the professors' real feelings about diversity and multicultural inclusion in the class (Helton 2000).

Vice President Helton (2000) conducted research involving 200 teachers (teachers identified as leaders in diversity issues) to ascertain "the factors that influence faculty to transform their courses and to measure the perceived" results. She discovered that all of the teachers had intrinsic motivation—such as morality and identifying with marginalized student groups—for transforming their courses multiculturally. She also found that only 57% of the specialty courses involving gender and ethnicity and gay/lesbian studies were taught by the diversity experts. Only 34% of the diversity experts were involved in diversity training.

Research on the other end of the education component—the students—was carried out by Barbara Gold, Associate Dean of Faculty at Hamilton College in New York (2001). Her results indicated that students generally didn't want a diversity requirement as part of their degree programs because they felt diversity should be an integral part of other courses, not a separate course or not something that should be isolated or emphasized. The students understood the importance of transforming the entire course curriculum and the inadequacy of the "contributive" and "additive" approaches. The students also appreciated faculty who made it clear that they could discuss diversity issues in an open and tolerant atmosphere without fear of having to appear politically correct.

But even with faculty and students all agreeing on a multicultural curriculum, such a curriculum may be difficult to achieve because of other factors, such as the cost of the textbooks. When three of us English professors at Oral Roberts University worked on creating textbooks—a combination anthology/workbook—for the university's two general education English courses, we chose which works we wanted to include in the anthology (Epperson, 1999). Although purposely choosing to include works by ethnic minorities, we were dismayed to discover how much more expensive the copyrights cost for contemporary authors, especially authors presenting diverse backgrounds and worldviews, including writers like Amy Tan, Leslie Marmon Silko, and Maya Angelou. By contrast, many if not most of the old standards in the literary canon are relatively inexpensive or are public domain and thus free to use.

The fact that high copyright costs had such an effect on the decisions of which selections to include in the anthology was surprising to us editors. It was frustrating to have to eliminate some of our first choices because the copyright costs would make the textbooks too expensive for the students. It was also frustrating because we really wanted the students to read, enjoy, and benefit from these works as the teachers did. Having high copyright fees can limit the exposure these fine essays, short stories, and poems have. Ironically, the copyright holder (the author, estate, or publisher) may receive less in compensation if the fees are higher, simply because the costs limit the inclusion of expensive literary works in a broader spectrum of anthologies. Less expensive works are more affordable and thus more practical to include in a larger array of textbooks. Such a situation is a simple case of basic economics.

Consequently, as editors for the English anthology, we had to select very carefully in order to balance costs and still offer a broad representation of authors so that class discussions and assignments could incorporate an ethnic diverse content. Some costly first choices had to be abandoned entirely while other expensive selections were kept but were only affordable by eliminating two or three other less expensive works. In the end, the anthologies and workbook pages offer a solid basis for diversity education and a good range of writers; however, the process was challenging, and we were saddened that trying to transform the curriculum was made more difficult because of copyright fees.

What was learned from the process is that choosing texts and developing a curriculum that reflects cultural diversity don't just happen automatically. It takes intentional work on the part of the professor and requires continual reassessment. The Council on Interracial Books for Children (1976) created a set of criteria for assessing children's books for racial and sexual bias. Although now 30 years old, the list still serves as a seminal work in the analysis of such biases and doesn't need much updating. However, in an effort to incorporate new technology in recent years and to adapt the criteria for college-level texts and electronic media, the following criteria are modifications of the Council's original guidelines:

1. **Check the graphics** for visual stereotypes, tokenism, and biases.
2. **Check the content** for racist and sexist attitudes in less obvious ways, such as using white standards of success to measure the success of other cultures or showing women in only traditional female roles.
3. **Look at the lifestyles** to see if the lifestyles of American minorities or other cultures are shown favorably.
4. **Evaluate the relationships among people** to see if people of color and females of all races function in primary roles and not just supporting roles.
5. **Examine the heroes** to see if they reflect the heroes of typical white Americans or if they are based on the struggles for justice and equality as viewed by diverse populations.
6. **Consider the effects** the texts and electronic materials have on a person's self-image.
7. **Consider the author's or graphic artist's background** to see if the work deals with a multicultural theme and to determine what qualifies the author or artist to deal with the subject matter.
8. **Check out the author's perspective** to determine if the author writes out of a cultural as well as personal context.

9. **Look for loaded words,** which show bias and negative connotations.
10. **Look at the copyright date** because works before the Civil Rights Movement tend to portray racist and sexual biases.

Using guidelines such as these to help identify problematic books is an excellent step toward recognizing areas of bias and toward developing a more diverse course content, but faculty do need to go beyond textbooks in order to transform the curriculum fully. Setting multicultural perspectives as a part of the larger goals of the educational institution helps ensure a more integrated curriculum, one that is not isolated but rather involves all faculty and crosses the spectrum of courses and academic departments. Transforming the curriculum can be challenging as well as enlightening, but the long-term and short-term benefits are well worth the effort.

# References

Advice on effective curriculum transformation. (1997, Winter). *Diversity Digest,* Retrieved November 7, 2005, from http://www.diversityweb.org/Digest/W97/advice.html

Council on Interracial Books for Children. (1976). *Human and antihuman values in children's books.* New York: CIBC Racism and Sexism Resource Center.

Davidman, L., & Davidman, P. *Teaching with a multicultural perspective: A practical guide.* White Plains, NY: Longman Publishing Group. 1994

Epperson, W., Gray, L.,& Hall, M. (1999). *Strategies for reading and writing.* Dubuque, IA: Kendall-Hunt.

Gold, B. (2001, Winter). Diversifying the curriculum: What do students think? *Diversity Digest,* Retrieved November 8, 2005, from http://www.diversityweb.org/Digest/W01/curriculum.html

Helton, P. (2000, Fall). Diversifying the curriculum: A study of faculty involvement. *Diversity Digest,* Retrieved November 7, 2005, from http://www.diversityweb.org/Digest/F00/research.html

Huitt, W. (2004). Bloom et al.'s taxonomy of the cognitive domain. *Educational Psychology Interactive.* Valdosta, GA: Valdosta State

University. Retrieved February 2, 2006, from http://chiron.valdosta.edu/whuitt/col/cogsys/bloom.html.

*Norton introduction to literature*. (1977, 2004). Toronto: W.W. Norton and Company, Inc.

*Provost's task force on multicultural curriculum transformation*, (2001). Retrieved November 7, 2005, from Northern Illinois University, De Kalb, Web Site: http://www3.niu.edu/mcti/mcinfo.htm

Scott, B. (1994). Integrating race, class, gender, and sexual orientation into the college curriculum. In *A multicultural prism: Voices from the field*, J.Q. Adams and Janice R Welsch, eds., Macomb, IL: Illinois Staff and Curriculum Developers Association.

Wathington, H. (2002, Fall/Winter). Curricular transformation spurs institutional engagement with diversity. *Diversity Digest*, Retrieved November 7, 2005, from http://www.diversityweb.org/Digest/fw02/curricular.html

# Ebony and Ivory: Overcoming "the Racial Mountain" in the Classroom While Teaching Langston Hughes and the Harlem Renaissance: An African-American Perspective

## Dr. Mary Alice Trent

"What we should dream of is making our [college] campuses joyful, pioneering communities of interethnic justice and healing, as well as launching pads for social change efforts in the broader local, national, and global communities" (Gushee, 2004, p. 6). I think this opening quotation raises the academic bar in addressing intercultural competencies and racial awareness. Unfortunately, a few years ago, a former English 451 African-American Seminar student of mine, shared with me—an experience she had in a graduate literature class at a small private non-religious university. In the class of ethnically diverse students, the professor of European-American descent used the "N-word" as he was reading the literature. Needless to say, the former student of mine, who is of African-American descent, was livid! The use of the word sent chills down her body, for she could not believe that the professor would say the "N-word" in class without discussing the sensitivity of the history of the word in America. Within a year, she had moved on to another Ph.D. program at a historically black college, primarily because the opportunities were greater than at the previous institution.

**Dr. Mary Alice Trent** is Associate Professor of English at Oral Roberts University.

This illustration best serves to reiterate the truth that *race* is the last frontier that Americans, in general, elect not to discuss, even in the academy of higher learning or even in the churches across America. A long and painful legacy of Negro slavery, Jim Crow laws, public lynchings, segregation, discrimination, racial profiling, social stereotyping, and the like has made us in this day and age so sensitive among the races until we think that being politically correct means lying about the true state of race in America.

Even in the history of the arts, we have perpetuated stereotypical myths about race, particularly by European-Americans about African-Americans—myths, which were commonplace during the Harlem Renaissance. In responding to these mythical perceptions, George S. Schuyler postulates,

> Because a few writers with a paucity of themes have seized upon [. . .] the Negro rustics and clowns and palmed them off as authentic and characteristic [Afr-American] behavior, the common notion that the black American is so "different" from his white neighbor has gained wide currency. The mere mention of the word "Negro" conjures up in the average white American's mind a composite stereotype of Bert Williams, Aunt Jemima, Uncle Tom [. . .] and the various monstrosities scrawled by the cartoonists. (2005, p.97)

Some of this erroneous thinking in society, as exemplified by Schuyler, can be attributed to a lack of cultural awareness. Nearly 80 years have passed since the Harlem Renaissance, yet white and black Americans are still struggling with race, using similar stereotypes to exploit certain behavioral patterns in society. Due to the sensitivity of the race issue, the subject of *race* is a difficult one to discuss openly and honestly.

The struggle with *race* lies in our failure to embrace the truth about diversity. What is diversity? Richard Bucher argues that we have bought into the following myths about diversity: (1) diversity is limited to women and people of color, excluding white males, (2) diversity "results in standards being lowered," (3) diversity creates "divisiveness," and diversity is "to be feared" (Bucher, 2004, p. 22). Race, like diversity, must be more than just tolerated in society, as well as in the academy. Particularly, as Christians, we must be at the forefront of this issue.

Like society, in the academy of higher learning, *race* poses a challenge in the classroom, particularly for many European-American professors even more than for African-American professors—a reality to which a white English colleague of mine, who teaches Langston Hughes and the Harlem Renaissance in her American literature class, can attest. This brings us to the thesis point of this paper: In discussing the sensitivity of race in the cultural and historical context of American literature, my European-American colleague and I, who teach at a small Christian university, have discovered that there is a double standard in our pedagogical approaches to teaching Langston Hughes and the Harlem Renaissance because African-American professors can "deal" with race in a way that is not socially accepted for European-American professors.

To this end, as an African-American professor, I establish a sense of community with my students—who are mostly African-Americans, along with a small number of European-Americans and other ethnic groups— whereby they become effective readers, writers, thinkers, learners, and responsible citizens by developing mutual respect, trust, and honesty among themselves, as we dialogue about relevant issues of race in the context of the literature, so when I teach Langston Hughes in the context of the Harlem Renaissance, we celebrate him as an artist who, by defining and celebrating the new Negro, lit a candle in the darkness of racial discrimination in America during the 1920's.

In an effort to understand the racial tensions during the Harlem Renaissance, my students and I examine Hughes' own views on race as illustrated in his work, "The Negro Artist and the Racial Mountain," from *The Nation*. What the students realize is that Hughes, like many Harlem Renaissance writers, was defining and shaping his role as a "new Negro" in America according to new prescripts and standards, not by the marginalized labels of the status quo. In short, many Harlem Renaissance writers were demanding respect in a society that sought to keep blacks "in their place." Understanding this, some of my students construct workable paradigms for dealing with their own personal and social obstacles. Twenty-first Century America offers new challenges for the same groups who have historically been disenfranchised: In many ways marginalization is still front and center, as the power structure yells "reverse discrimination," but the "good ole' boy" system is still in place. Unfortunately, too many of today's young people neglect to see these issues as any concern of theirs today, as evident by their seemingly innocent yet nonchalant attitudes in the classroom.

In "The Weary Blues," African-American students, in particular, who have endured racial oppression, (and all students in general who have experienced any type of oppression) can empathize with the poet, who laments on the personal conditions of his day. Like the Negro artist in the poem, Hughes composed poetry from the depths of his soul, and the Blues was the offspring of broken promises. In his poetry, Hughes found freedom to express himself, and he cultivated it in "The Negro Artist and the Racial Mountain."

In studying "Harlem," students examine the struggle of Negroes in America around the turn of the Twentieth Century. During a period when Negroes were redefining themselves in an opposed society, Hughes' poem depicts the ongoing turmoil that many African Americans experienced. While some might argue that the poet's tone is bitter, many will say that the poet speaks to the heart of the Negro experience in America. Again, this poem gives students a great deal to discuss about the treatment of blacks during the Harlem Renaissance, as the poem presents various interpretations of what happens to dreams postponed or put off. This poem is relevant, since some of the students in the class can relate to a dream of theirs (or dream of a family member or friend) that has been aborted, and students can identify with the disappointments and heartache that may have resulted from broken dreams.

In his poem, "Goodbye Christ," students examine Hughes' ambivalence toward and distrust of orthodox religion: a religion that justified the institution of slavery, as well as the mistreatment of women. As Christopher C. Desantis suggests, Hughes in his poem explores the lack of compassion and sanctity of a religion that witnessed and/or allowed "so much suffering, so much oppression" (cited in Modern American Poetry, 2005, p. 1). In defense of Hughes, James Emanuel contends that "Goodbye Christ" is protest literature against white Christians who upheld white supremacists practices (cited in Modern American Poetry, 2005, p.3), not against God Himself. Hughes' seemingly ambivalent views on religion set the backdrop for heated debate in the classroom, particularly since a number of African-American men today have turned away from Christianity and embraced Islam. My students scrutinize the historical role that religion played in the oppression of Africans in early America, and many of the students conclude that Christianity –salvation through Jesus Christ—is the way to God and that, historically, the Christian church in African-American communities has mobilized blacks to not only seek salvation but also economical, political, and educational freedoms.

Not only do many of Hughes' poems afford students an opportunity to discuss the racial climate in America in the 1920's but also to dialogue about the racial temperature in the context of their personal experiences. Students in my Seminar often share their own personal experiences concerning race with respect to their upbringing. They confront their biases and expose their own vulnerabilities. In one particular case, one African-American student in the seminar confessed that she had bitterness, which had been stored up in her heart, toward Euro-Americans, and with tears in her eyes she released these ill feelings. In another case, a Euro-American student confessed that many whites who inflicted social oppression upon blacks were affected by their acts of oppression in such a negative way whereby making many whites spiritually and emotionally enslaved.

Increasing cultural awareness, transforming the life of students, and maximizing opportunities for cognitive and personal growth are not spontaneous but must be thoughtfully planned out by instructors. Regardless of the race of the instructor, he or she can make a difference in the lives of his or her students by challenging them to look beyond the color line to see the character of the person. We must move from tolerance to acceptance, especially those who call themselves "Christians," since we should be leading the way to greater racial harmony and cultural understanding. Our classrooms must become venues to promote acceptance and combat fear. "We should," according to David Gushee, (2004) "say first that the kingdom of God includes deliverance of the suffering, justice, peace, healing, restoration, and inclusion of outcasts and the marginalized to covenant community, and that such kingdom breakthroughs are accompanied by God's presence and great joy. So our goal in the Christian college must be to participate in the kingdom in this way" (p. 8).

Initiating and expanding intercultural interactions and competencies on college campuses must involve "administrative ownership" instead of "administrative Leadership"—i.e., the administration must partner with faculty and students to devise diversity curriculum and extracurricular activities for both short term and long term (Reed, 2005, p. 7). Transformational education promotes interactive learning whereby students are engaged in an ongoing process of learning that occurs in and out of the classroom.

While we honor the work of Harriet Beecher Stowe, Mark Twain, Langston Hughes, Cornell West, Henry Louis Gates, Michael Eric Dyson, Alice Walker, Maya Angelou and so many other white, black, red, yellow, and brown writers who have probed into racial themes in their respective works, we must take responsibility for the truth that America has not gotten to the top of the "racial mountain," which Langston Hughes speaks of. In integrating culture, Christian faith, and equality, Cornell West (1988) argues "Christian faith [. . .] requires resistance to race-base and gender-base [. . . and] class-based social hierarchies [. . . which] undermine the God-given dignity and violate the respect due to each of God's creatures" (p. 134). The words of West give us all something to ponder: If academicians can create an atmosphere that is conducive to fair play, equality, and justice for all, then in that there is healing for the mind and heart and in that the Ebonies and the Ivories, along with the red, brown, and yellow hues of skin, can co-exist the way God has intended it since the foundation of the earth.

# References

Bucher, Richard D. (2004). *Diversity Consciousness*. Upper Saddle River, NJ: Prentice Hall.

DeSantis, Christopher C. "On 'Goodbye Christ.'" *Modern American Poetry*. University of Illinois at Urbana-Champaign. 8 November 2005. www.english.uiuc.edu/maps/poets/g_l/hughes/goodbye.htm

Emanuel, James A. "On 'Goodbye Christ.'" *Modern American Poetry*. University of Illinois at Urbana-Champaign. 8 November 2005. www.english.uiuc.edu/maps/poets/g_l/hughes/goodbye.htm

Gushee, David P. "A Biblical Vision for 'Intercultural Competency.'" The Advancing Intercultural Competencies Presidential Symposium. Union University, Union, TN. 23 April 2004.

Lewis, David Levering, ed. (1995). *The Portable Harlem Renaissance Reader*. New York: Penguin.

Reed, Matthew. "Learning to Listen as We Lead." *Diversity Digest* 9.2 (2005): 6-7.

Schuyler, George. "The Negro-Art Hokum." Lewis 96-99.

West, Cornell. (1988). *Prophetic Fragments*. Michigan: Williams B. Eerdman's Publishing Co.

# Overcoming "the Racial Mountain" in the Classroom While Teaching Langston Hughes and the Harlem Renaissance: An Euro-American Perspective

## DR. KAY B. MEYERS

For the most part, I believe that people may have different packaging, but basically we are all the same, and I believe this is the way that God wants me to see myself and others. But somehow, this simple revelation is challenged by the following dilemma: When I, who am not African American, teach works by African-American writers, I must do so differently than my colleague, Dr. Mary Alice Trent, who is African American (although, like me, she would say that that is not the totality of her heritage—in fact we are both probably a mixture of many hyphens—Irish, German, English, Native American). I cannot speak from personal experience when I teach a story by Alice Walker or Toni Morrison. I do not know racial discrimination first-hand. But I can lecture up one side and down the other about the evils of racism. What I often get is affirmative nods from African-American students and eye rolls from the other students. I come off as a well-meaning but rather annoying white liberal. If Dr. Trent teaches the same writers, no one can question her insight into their lives and experiences. She doesn't need to preach. I would hope that her presence is evidence of her knowledge. However, that

---

**Dr. Kay B. Meyers** is Associate Professor of English at Oral Roberts University.

advantage can also become her disadvantage. She must be careful not to become too emotional in a discussion of race or run the risk of being called "pushy," thus alienating the very people whose hearts and minds we seek to change.

The majority of my students are 19-20 years old. They celebrate Martin Luther King Day, although I don't think most of them know why. The year I was twenty, Dr. King was assassinated. I know why that day must be celebrated. For my students, both African American and European American, 1968 is ancient history. For me, it is yesterday. Many students have seen films like *Eyes on the Prize*, which is a good thing, but films make the Civil Rights Movement seem very distant—like it was all a movie. On the other hand, I can remember daily news reports showing the police with their fire hoses and billy clubs and vicious dogs attacking men, women, and children who did nothing to deserve such treatment. My students cannot imagine going to a restaurant or a swimming pool and seeing people turned away because of the color of their skin. I cannot only imagine it, but I can visualize it from having seen it happen. Students make speeches about their right to use certain words (like the "n" word) in discussing literature because "the writer says it." Long ago I swore never to use any words that denigrate others for reasons they cannot change. I very clearly remember a college professor saying to his students that the "f" word is indeed crude and rude and shows bad taste, but the "n" word is evil and shows the blackness of the speaker's heart. He was the same professor who organized a campus-wide memorial service the day after Dr. King's death. The point is that too many students today see the issues involved in the Civil Rights Movement as having been resolved or as not affecting them. I disagree. The fact that no one wants to discuss racial matters is not necessarily a good thing. The fact that they get all nervous and fidgity when I mention racial matters is an indication of problems unsolved.

Reading works by writers of the Harlem Renaissance, particularly Langston Hughes' work, helps students open a discussion of those problems. In my American Literature II course, we look at Harlem Renaissance writers, especially Langston Hughes. Because our time is limited, I focus on Hughes' better-known works, such as "The Negro Speaks of Rivers," "I, Too," "America," "Goodbye, Christ," "Mulatto," "Theme from English B," and the split-text poem "The Colored Soldier" because they illustrate current issues and allude to historical events. I also use poems with a more "Harlem Renaissance" flavor such as "The Weary

Blues," which makes clear the influence of music on Hughes' work. The discussion of "Let America Be America Again" is especially interesting. I explain to the students that in 1936, *Esquire* published only the first fifty lines of the poem (Barnet & Bedau, 2002, pp. 802-803). We discuss the possible reasons for this, and they are asked to pretend that they are editors and explain what they would do with the poem today. Most say they would publish it all—but as a symbol of a *past* time, not because of any relevance it might have to the present. And, I add in a poem I think is especially relevant now, "Kids Who Die." Although it is highly negative, I like the poem because of its inclusive message.

The students also read excerpts from *The Big Sea*, such as "When the Negro Was in Vogue," in which Hughes discusses the relationship between whites, who "began to come to Harlem in droves" (Lewis, 1995, p. 78) and what was referred to as "the Negro literati." The student response to this work is usually positive, I think partly because it seems so distant from them. In the historical context of the rest of the course, Hughes can be seen as the descendent of Walt Whitman, as a man of importance in his own time, and as a connector between the 20s and 30s and Richard Wright's "Almos' a Man," Ellison's *Invisible Man*, Baldwin's "Going to Meet the Man," and more contemporary writers such as Alice Walker.

But this paper is not just about suggestions for teaching. It is about the responses I get to these readings—the things I have to explain, even to African-American students. For example, I have to explain the irony in Hughes' "Let America Be America Again"—for African Americans, "America" has always been a dream, not something that actually existed for them. They have to ask, "why does the boy [in Wright's story] feel he needs a gun to make himself a man?" When we look at "The Battle Royal" from *Invisible Man*, I have to explain the entire excerpt—and they don't believe me when I tell them that people actually had such stereotypical views of African Americans. In regard to Invisible Man's career difficulties, I relate stories like those of Harvey C. Russell and James Ward to illustrate the kind of world he lived in. When Russell was promoted to vice-president of Pepsi in 1962, the Ku Klux Klan organized a national boycott. In 1966, when Ward was promoted, by Bill Marriott himself, to the position of vice-president, he became the only African American in an upper management in the hotel industry. Marriott's other VPs were outraged at the idea of a black man earning as much as they did, and all threatened to quit. To keep peace, Marriott paid Ward two salaries—one on the company payroll for public display, and another out of his own personal account, so no one would know that Ward earned more than the others (Daniels, 2005, pp. 74-80).

And, on the day we read "Going to Meet the Man," most of the students come in looking nauseated and asking why Baldwin wrote such a story. Initially, they can't imagine a lynching, much less a public lynching. Then, as with *Invisible Man*, they really can't imagine any connection between sex and racial hatred culminating in violence. It is an embarrassing, yet enlightening, moment for everyone.

Now, that in itself isn't surprising—our students do live in a nicer *public* world where people don't openly say certain words or discuss certain things. It's that they won't talk about race matters at all that I find disturbing. In a class of mixed ethnicity, I fear putting my African-American students on the spot by singling them out for comments. In a class of all European-American students, when they do discuss race matters, the attitude is too often, "what's the problem?" Recently, for instance, a student asked why we want to "stir up" problems by discussing "diversity." To make matters worse, the student went on to say that he doesn't know what THEY have to be so upset about. What he didn't understand is that his use of the term "they" IS the problem. When asked why students often segregate themselves—in the cafeteria, in meetings, in classrooms—the student (with lots of head nodding from the others) explained that THEY are more comfortable together. Everyone feels better in his or her own "comfort zone." Unfortunately, that is probably true. It's just too bad that that comfort is frequently based on racial differences.

In her essay "The Civil Rights Movement: What Good Was It?", Alice Walker criticizes "white liberals" (a category into which I would probably fall) for saying that the Movement is dead since statistics say things are as bad or worse (1983, p. 120). That essay was written in 1967. Today the white liberal's question is still the same—are things really better? And, Walker's response today might still be the same as in 1967. For Walker, the importance of the Movement is its lasting effect on African Americans. She is surely correct about the legacy of the Movement, but perhaps too many of us have settled for this kind of public civility and private withdrawal from the fray without resolving anything. As a result, the underlying hope for true understanding between races—the dream of Langston Hughes and of Dr. King—has not been fully realized.

In an era when the prevailing attitude in academics (and in the culture at large) is that we have "moved on" since the racial turmoil of the Civil Rights Movement, it is important to stop and assess exactly how far we have really come. This "we have moved on" idea stems partly, in the academy at least, from the notion that "postmodernism" and its theories/ theorists recognize "marginality" and "otherness." We like to imagine we have reached the place Hughes describes in "Open Letter to the South."

Today, we, in truth, as Cornel West suggests, must "remain quite suspicious of the term 'postmodernism'" (1993, p. 393). On one hand, recognizing the achievements of women and peoples of color is quite admirable. On the other hand, however, is the unpleasant truth that, too often, labeling a group as "marginal" only results in its remaining marginal. It would be hard, for example, to imagine a more marginalized group than the African American poor of inner city New Orleans huddled together in the Superdome following Hurricane Katrina. And, here, in Tulsa, Oklahoma, a community that prides itself on its strong Christian base, the majority of the African-American population, of whom many are poor, live on one side of town—the same side of Tulsa that was burned to the ground in 1921 in the worst race riot in American history.

Studying the Harlem Renaissance as an "African American" movement does acknowledge its importance and highlights its writers, but it also can leave the impression that the Renaissance was an isolated movement, frozen in its time, place, and race, its artists without significance except in their Renaissance moment. With a writer such as Langston Hughes, this remarginalizing makes it possible for students to discuss his words as antiquated, belonging to a dead past. They can tell themselves that we have "moved on," that race relations are better now and that everyone is "equal." Unfortunately, the prediction made a decade ago by Henry Giroux is closer to the truth:

> while people of color are redrawing the cultural demographic boundaries of the urban centers, the boundaries of power appear to be solidifying in favor of rich, white, middle and upper classes. [. . .] As class divisions grow deeper, intra-class and racial tensions mask the need for collective [s]truggles for social and political justice. [. . .] As we move into a postmodern world that is progressively redrawing the boundaries established by nationalism, ethnocentrism, and Eurocentric culture, the United States appears to be refiguring its political, social, and cultural geography in a manner that denies rather than maintains a democratic community. (1993, p. 453)

As college professors, we must "[construct an] anti-racist pedagogy," which will allow us to "prepare students for a type of citizenship that does not separate abstract rights from the realm of the everyday, and does not define community as the legitimating and unifying practice of a one-dimensional historical and cultural narrative" (Giroux , 1993, p. 479). We must try, as Hughes said, to raise up a generation that will recognize the need to "let America be America again"—or, even better, a generation that will understand that "America" has never been truly "America" in the mythical sense to which Hughes refers and that they have the potential to make the myth a reality.

# References

Barnet, S., & Bedau, H. (Eds.). Langston Hughes. *Current issues and enduring questions: A guide to critical thinking and argument, with readings*. (6ᵗʰ ed.) Boston: Bedford/St. Martin's. (pp. 800-803).

Daniels, C. (2005, August 22). Pioneers: Diversity 2005. *Fortune, 72-88*.

Giroux, H. (1993). Postmodernism as border pedagogy: Redefining the boundaries of race and ethnicity. In J. Natoli & L. Hutcheon (Eds.) *A postmodern reader*. Albany: State University of New York. (pp. 452-496).

Lewis, D. L. (Ed.). (1995). *The portable Harlem Renaissance reader*. New York: Penguin.

Natoli, J., & Hutcheon, L. (Eds.). (1993). *A postmodern reader*. Albany: State University of New York.

Walker, A. (1983). The Civil Rights Movement: What good was it? *In search of our mothers' gardens*. San Diego: Harcourt. (pp. 119-129).

West, Cornel. (1995). Black culture and modernism. In J. Natoli & L. Hutcheon (Eds.) *A postmodern reader*. Albany: State University of New York. (pp. 390-397).

# Faculty Perceptions of Minority Faculty Difficulties in Orthodox Christian Institutions of Higher Learning

## DR. DONALD V. DREW

This study addresses some of the findings from research (web-based survey) initiated during the 2002-2003 academic year to capture quantitative and qualitative information regarding faculty member's work and motivations at ten Church of Christ institutions throughout the United States. These institutions fit into Robert Benne's "orthodox" category for church schools, which require a Christian vision as the organizing paradigm, 100% faculty membership requirement in the church or denomination, students required to take courses in religion, a large theology department, and a mandatory daily chapel (Benne, 2001). Benne further states,

> Orthodox schools want to assure that the Christian account of life and reality is publicly and comprehensively relevant to the life of the school by requiring that all adult members of the ongoing academic community subscribe to the statement of belief. They insist on proceeding from a common Christian commitment, meaning all the ongoing personnel are assumed to live out that commitment at the school." "This unanimous Christian commitment presumably ensures that the ethos of the college will be Christian.

**Dr. Donald V. Drew** is Professor of Management in the School of Business Administration at Oklahoma Christian University.

Survey questions were both quantitative and qualitative in nature and examined faculty demographics, lives, and motivations. A response rate of close to forty percent demonstrated a high level of interest by the schools' faculty members. While the study collected significant data regarding demographics, productivity, and motivation, it also specifically asked for narrative responses regarding perceptions of elements, which enhance and/or hinder minority faculty teaching at their university. This study focuses on these narrative responses, but also provides some supplementary analysis made available from other portions of the survey.

Most faculty (98.4%) responding to the survey list themselves as "white." According to the national survey conducted in 1999 by the Higher Education Research Institute at UCLA, institutions of all kinds, nation wide, list themselves as an average of 91.7% white (various other less reliable sources indicate this number could be as low as 86%). Because of the overwhelming number of majority participants, this research hopes to shed some light on the perceptions of primarily white Christian faculty regarding minority faculty, and identify some of the challenges that lie ahead.

The survey asked respondents to address this issue in an open-ended, narrative form: "Describe what you perceive to be the three most critical hindrances to the teaching of minority faculty and why." Despite the fact that the item could have been more clearly worded, we received a collection of rich responses. Keep in mind that due to the low number of minorities present at these schools, most responses come from white or Caucasian faculty, and are likely based on the limited experience of the writer, and may in fact be based on experience with a single minority faculty member, or even based on pure supposition on the part of the participant since they may very well work directly with no minority faculty. Nevertheless, these perceptions are valid for consideration since they reflect the cultural view of the majority in the schools studied. The responses fell into six general categories (not in any order): (1) lack of qualifications; (2) prejudice/racism; (3) the churches historical legacy of segregation; (4) lack of faculty mentors for new teachers; (5) the effect of having low numbers of minority students; and (6) competition with other schools for talented minorities. The original questionnaire asked a similar question regarding the work of female educators. This research does not, nor does not intend to, address similar issues related to female faculty members.

Due to variation in the level of detail in the responses, it was often difficult to determine exactly what faculty members meant by "lack of qualifications," a very common response. Orthodox schools hire only faculty from their own tradition, so the pool of applicants is limited by the number available and academically qualified in that population. Unfortunately, the autonomous nature of Churches of Christ makes data on the quantity and quality of this pool nearly impossible to obtain. So it could mean that there simply aren't enough minorities with academic qualifications available who are Church of Christ, or it could mean that in the determination of the respondent, those available in the pool are unqualified compared to their majority counterparts. Most responses seem to refer to the first instance; however, some suggest the second condition to be the case.

Several participants shared sentiments similar to this respondent, "(there are) not many available with proper academic credentials" (Participant 31), but in some cases were more specific, blaming an overall shortage of academically qualified minority talent who were Church of Christ.

> (T)he lack of degreed persons within churches of Christ (Participant 115), [and] Not enough denominationally-appropriate applicants in the pool . . . Applicants that are hired may not be the most outstanding available at the time (again, because of the denominational restrictions) (Participant 123).

Still others perceived a "Lack of experience" (Participant 163) and "At times, minority faculty do not come with the same set of skills and need time to develop" (Participant 170). One respondent was particularly lucid.

> Our lack of minority faculty leads to an eagerness to hire minority faculty before they are ready. I am specifically thinking of a colleague who was hired, like me, before having a good start on the dissertation. In addition to the load I face, because he is one of the very few black faculty members on campus, he has an additional burden. Many of our minority students draw heavily on his time as they seek questions on advising or, more often, seek his companionship and advice as a black role model dealing with life on a very white campus. He makes little progress on his dissertation, and as a result in his department is one of the very few (the only one?) faculty members with the potential to be tenure-track without his PhD. To one group this looks like someone under qualified was hired because he was black. Our black students

see everyone else in the department has "Dr." on their door and he doesn't and I am afraid about the conclusions that they draw. How-ever, we will not increase a minority faculty presence without hiring faculty willing to come (Participant 152).

Some blamed "a lack of serious recruitment" (Participant 73) for a shortage of qualified minority applicants. Yet when minorities are ac-tively recruited, "If less qualified minority folks are hired preferentially then the institution's academic reputation may suffer. Less qualified people come with their own hindrances and therefore there is a lower expecta-tion of them to perform at the highest level normally expected for the position" (Participant 202). Thus a formula seems to be developing. An insufficient number of available, qualified minorities, plus pressure by administrations to hire minority faculty, resulting in minority faculty being hired with (or a perception of) under developed academic qualifications. For schools without the restrictions of orthodoxy, such reasoning may be difficult to understand, but this perception appears to be well entrenched in the minds of the faculty studied.

One participant believed there exists a "lack of understanding and acceptance of their (minority faculty) cultural differences" (Participant 13), extending the issue of qualifications to a question of cultural "fit." In *The Truth About Managing People*, Stephen Robbins writes "A good fit goes a long way toward ensuring that an employee will be perceived as a high performer," and he advises, "As a manager, you should assess potential employees in terms of how well you think they will fit into your organizations culture." One of the most popular business books circulat-ing today refers to the importance of hiring high quality employees and advises that one should "get the right people on the bus, the wrong people off the bus, and the right people in the right seats" (Collins, 2001).

Using this philosophy, how does one achieve both good fit and good diversity at the same time, when diversity requires broadening one's concept of good fit? Emerson and Smith in "Divided by Faith" may provide some insight into the dilemma. According to them, white evangelicals unintentionally perpetuate division by what they term "ac-countable individualism," this being that individuals exist totally inde-pendent of organizations (Emerson & Smith, 2001). If this is correct, it would be easy to see why many white faculty place the responsibility for academic qualification solely on the shoulders of the faculty member, white or otherwise. This is further complicated by a current state of confusion amongst the professoriate as to what qualifications really are needed or required (Boyer, 1997). When schools hire faculty who are perceived to be academically under qualified with the idea of developing them, potential resentment builds from those who believe they themselves had to take personal responsibility for developing their own qualifications. The situation could be further exacerbated by the same schools having insufficient means or processes to assist under qualified faculty members, leading to the perception that underqualified faculty members are allowed to participate as a fully qualified members, based on their being a minority. The theme of qualifications is broad, and much more study needs to be done in this area to better understand how to address these issues.

The terms prejudice and racism have two distinct meanings and are not necessarily the same, but many of the participants appear to make little distinction, at least in the generally short responses provided. For this reason, this research addresses the two as a single concept. A number of faculty cited student prejudice as one of the greatest difficulties facing minority faculty. One wrote, "Some students may be prejudiced against them, especially if they don't speak clearly or with an accent" (Participant 4). Another wrote, "The students aren't used to being around minorities and sometimes say insensitive things. The reaction of students—I've been surprised with the lack of respect some students seem to show for minority faculty" (Participant 358). Many faculty use the single word "racism" to respond to the question. Others are more specific saying the "Racism of administration" (Participant 142). More often, faculty refer to a type of "passive prejudice on the part of the majority culture already in place" (Participant 17).

In 1999, the President of Abilene Christian University, one of the schools included in this study, made this announcement during the 50th anniversary Founders' Day celebration at Southwestern Christian College, a traditionally black college from the Church of Christ tradition.

> Abilene Christian University has been a Christian institution of higher education for more than 90 years. Its doors were not open to African-American students for well over half that time. We are here today to confess the sins of racism and discrimination and to issue a formal apology to all of you, to express regret and to ask for your forgiveness.

Of course, Abilene Christian University does not stand alone in their need for forgiveness. Like many churches in the United States, Churches of Christ were not immune to pervasive prejudice and racism in their past and the resulting segregation that remains in many areas of the nation today. As one participant stated, "The prejudices that exist in the church affect the thinking on campus" (Participant 116).

Murray and Clark (1990) suggest that racism manifests itself in eight ways in schools. These are as follows:

1. hostile and/or insensitive acts
2. bias in the use of harsh sanctions
3. bias in giving attention to certain types of students
4. bias in the selection of curriculum materials
5. inequality in the amount of instruction
6. bias in attitudes toward students
7. failure to hire racial minority teachers and other school personnel at all levels
8. denial of racist actions

In response to Murray and Clark's list, DJangi (1993) concludes that "insensitive students, biased teachers, skewed textbooks . . . and the psychological roots of prejudice that lie in us all have led to the rise of covert racism in educational settings." From this conclusion he raises some important questions. Are faculty trained to understand and accept other races and cultures? Do we train students to live in a multicultural society? Do administrators and faculty recognize racial tension when it occurs on their campuses? He concludes that the solution may lie in four categories: "school policies, faculty recruitment and awareness, student sensitivity, and curriculum opportunities." For Christian schools, the solutions to these issues should be relatively easy. Their mission statements and stated commitment to the Word of God are already consistent with the underlying need for respect and unity, but for most, the question is how and where to start.

Richard Hughes writes in "The Churches of Christ": "The truth is, ever since the abolition of slavery, Churches of Christ have nurtured two distinct fellowships, one white and one black." Hughes documents efforts to bridge these "two distinct fellowships" both racially and theologically over the past forty years and concludes in reference to the Churches of Christ as a whole, "Only time would tell how deeply renewal would finally run and how far the redefinition of this tradition would extend" (Hughes, 2001). Sins of the past continue to stand in the way of full fellowship for the future, and the impact can be clearly witnessed in Church of Christ schools and universities. The division is partly doctrinal: "Doctrinal conservatism of black churches at odds with progressivism of colleges" (Participant 71). Sometimes these divisions are institutional: "Institution's historical legacy of segregation" (Participant 29). Sometimes they are historical remnants which are largely invisible to the majority culture: "In a Christian environment there shouldn't be any hindrances. Perhaps only cultural attitudes due to our historical past" (Participant 72). Participant 34 synthesized all of these: "Problems between the university and black churches dating back 30-35 years. There is still some resentment among leaders in black churches in the area. Also lack of integration of churches in the area." A history of prejudice and racism resulting in segregation has created a wide gulf that continues to express itself in Church of Christ schools and adds to the problems associated with increasing diversity in Church of Christ faculty. Thus, solving the dilemma in orthodox colleges and universities may be nearly impossible without first addressing the historical legacy of segregation among the churches. There seems to be genuine interest on the part of faculty to reach beyond these impediments, but an equally genuine frustration as to the means to achieve this.

Participants specifically addressed either minority faculty as being in need of mentors or role models or demands for faculty to serve as mentors or role models. Unfortunately, none expanded on their thinking more than to say a need existed. Obviously few minority faculty make for few minority faculty mentors. While majority faculty members can and do serve as effective mentors and role models, cross-cultural mentoring relationships can possess imbedded issues which are particularly difficult for those in the relationship to readily recognize (Johnson-Bailey, Cervero, & Baugh, 2004).

If schools are to attract and retain minority faculty, Singh and Stoloff (2003) make it clear that mentoring will be key. They identify two types of relationships which they term formal and informal and conclude that an effective mentoring program must be formal, since informal mentoring relationships have been shown to develop primarily in persons similar to one another (Blackwell, 1989), thus resulting in "under-selection of minorities as protégés." Since the colleges and universities studied do not have sufficient numbers of minority faculty to effectively mentor new minority faculty members, they may find themselves having to rely on cross-cultural mentoring to achieve their aims. For this, Singh and Stoloff offer additional advice from their research. Cross-cultural mentors might remember to:

- be aware of their own beliefs, their world view, and the variables that affect their perceptions;
- be alert to cultural differences in respect to tolerances for what social scientists call power-distance;
- likewise, pay attention to cultural differences in respect to individualism verses collectivism;
- recognize and account for differences in communication styles;
- realize there are cultural differences placed on the importance of relationships and work activities; and,
- remember that differences also exist in the ways we manage conflict.

Isolation was also mentioned as an issue by study participants and it appears loosely related to the need for mentors and role models. One respondent wrote, "Isolation due to small number of minority faculty. Results in loneliness and desire to find another place of employment. Exclusion from informal social network. Results in exclusion from important information" (Participant 142). While a formal mentoring program cannot be expected to overcome minority feelings of isolation, it seems to be one that might help.

A low number of minority students (in the universities studied an average of less than ten percent) may also serve to keep minority faculty away. Current research suggests that existing diversity in an organization attracts more diverse people to join the organization. Schneider (1987) calls this process Attraction-Selection-Attrition (ASA) and suggests that organizations tend to attract, hire and retain similar types of people. Achieving diversity among both students and faculty requires intentionality to achieve real benefits.

One participant described a problem with

> The mistaken notion that students can learn from anyone. Many of our students from other co-cultures have not heard a lecture or participated in a class with someone who looks like them. It sends a message about who belongs where, and what we as an institution value. By the way, it is just as valuable for our students from the majority culture to learn from instructors of other cultures (Participant 147).

Again, back to what Participant 152 wrote:

> Many of our minority students draw heavily on his (a specific faculty member known to the participant) time as they seek questions on advising or, more often, seek his companionship and advice as a black role model dealing with life on a very white campus. He makes little progress on his dissertation, and as a result in his department is one of the very few (the only one?) faculty members with the potential to be tenure-track without his PhD. To one group this looks like someone under qualified was hired because he was black. Our black students see everyone else in the department has "Dr." on their door and he doesn't and I am afraid about the conclusions that they draw. However, we will not increase a minority faculty presence without hiring faculty willing to come.

This participant sees a colleague who is inundated with demands for attention perhaps not experienced by majority faculty, and one who apparently responds positively to this demand at considerable personal cost. But when minority faculty seek to serve the minority population of students, one participant claims that minority faculty are "self-consciousness of being a 'minority'" and "trying to promote a particular ethnic/class-based agenda" (Participant 97). Joanne Belknap (1990) in a speech to the faculty of the University of Cincinnati echoes this perception.

> It is also important to recognize that the faculty of color experience drains on their time and energy in ways that white faculty don't experience serving as role models and often advocates for students experiencing racism. While I attempt to make myself a person to whom students would feel comfortable discussing racism and other forms of harassment and discrimination, it is obvious that my African-American colleagues are much more likely to have to respond to racism occurring to students . . . not to mention responding to the racism they themselves or other faculty of color experience.

Finally, one participant citing the "relatively small number of minority students in our institutions" stated "These are conditions that exist, and therefore require aggressive action on the part of Administration." Just how administrations' aggressive actions will solve a shortage of minority students on their campuses is unclear, but it seems that increased minority faculty diversity and increased minority student diversity will arrive "hand in hand" or not at all.

The sixth and final category addresses the reality that all the schools surveyed must compete with other institutions for talented faculty of all types. One participant articulated a common theme among faculty responses, "Universities with money and power will attract minority faculty away from smaller universities where they might make the most impact" (Participant 51). This is an oversimplification since money itself plays a relatively low role in faculty motivation compared to more intrinsic factors (see the motivational factor analysis under Supplemental Analysis); however, schools with more "power" can provide opportunities small schools cannot, making "opportunities elsewhere . . . more appealing" (Participant 151).

There are other considerations as well. One participant believes that tight budgets in their school result in faculty with "excessive work load in and out of classroom," a "decreasing emphasis upon academics on campus," and an "increasing complexity of requirements and programs" (Participant 332). Such an atmosphere could be unattractive to any potential faculty member, regardless of race or ethnicity. Another participant saw the problem as an inability to attract the "brightest and best with graduate degrees and luring them to small, low-paying university jobs when they can get triple pay and prestige elsewhere" (Participant 350).

In addition to the lessons learned from the narrative responses, we should consider some of the major findings from the rest of the study. A landmark study by Bowen and Sosa (1989) postulated that by 2007 there would be only eight candidates for every ten open faculty assignments. Competition among institutions of higher learning for qualified faculty would become increasingly fierce. Small, private colleges and universities with special faculty requirements such as the "orthodox" schools in this study would find it increasingly more difficult to attract faculty due to competition with better funded private independent and state universities. While the state of such competition in 2005 is somewhat anecdotal, the universities studied seem to be experiencing at least some difficulty overall in attracting and retaining faculty, and definite difficulty in the area of attracting and retaining minority faculty. One of the main purposes of this study was to help leadership of small, private universities enhance their ability to attract and retain qualified faculty by better understanding what motivates academicians of all races in their life and work.

Every few years, the Higher Education Research Institute at UCLA queries faculty members at colleges and universities throughout the United

States in regard to demographics, work life, and motivations. The 1999 study collected faculty members' personal goals noted as very important or essential. At number one with 98% was to "be a good teacher." This was followed by "being a good colleague," "develop a meaningful philosophy of life," "raise a family" and "help others who are in difficulty." On the low end were "influence political structure," "be involved in programs to clean up the environment," and "be very well-off financially." As for reasons noted as very important in the decision to pursue an academic career, respondents listed intellectual challenge, intellectual freedom, freedom to pursue scholarly interests, teaching opportunities, and autonomy as most significant. This study sought to identify the most important themes affecting Christian faculty's motivations and provide some additional thought as to how understanding these motivations may enhance faculty attraction and retention.

In addition to the narrative response portion of the survey used to collect the faculty responses addressed earlier, the study also used a modified questionnaire with 36 attitudinal statements originally developed by Sylvia and Hutchison and later modified by At-Twaijri and Al-Khursani, and Pinto and Pulido. The Q-Sort technique was used asking respondents to rate responses for each item on a scale from 1 (never) to 7 (always).

Factor analysis was used as the prime analytical model. The goal of the analysis was to identify factors that underlie the variables. The principle components method of extraction with varimax rotation was used, five factors were extracted, and a scree plot obtained of the Eigen values. Factors extracted were based on latent root criteria that required Eigen values to be in excess of 1 to be considered significant. Factors less than 1 were discarded.

The research resulted in identifying five factors that affect faculty motivation. These factors are as follows:

1. The importance of relationships with colleagues and academic leadership.
2. The role of intrinsic motivators related to personal accomplishment.
3. The impact of financial and other extrinsic benefits.
4. The need for personal control and academic freedom.
5. The impact of workload on performance.

The first and apparently most important motivational factor, the importance of relationships with colleagues and academic leadership, sheds the most light on our understanding of the narrative responses. This factor indicates the respondents' overall satisfaction with academic leadership and high value for a collegial environment, and we can conclude that confidence in and trust for others to act as professionals takes high priority in academic life. Looking at the items contained in that factor, we can also conclude that it is very important for faculty to perceive that others are doing their work and are competent, that the faculty member is able to contribute to group decision making, that the member is recognized for his or her contributions, and that he or she be able to work in and maintain a collegial atmosphere.

These are powerful concepts, particularly when considered in light of the most often mentioned narrative concern, lack of qualifications. Whether considered within the context of minority faculty or not, concern for the qualifications of others and themselves takes a high priority as a faculty motivator. One could also create a logical link between competence and personal development with the narrative concern with a lack of mentors for new teachers. What we might learn from this is that these two narrative concerns are as universal as they are racial.

If these schools are to successfully address the challenges of an increasingly multicultural America, they will have to come to terms with all six of the following areas of concern while maintaining their unique characteristics as Christian institutions of higher learning. First, academic qualifications must not be sacrificed at the alter of diversity, but neither should it be an excuse for failing to identify existing qualified faculty, and when necessary, developing the qualifications of minority faculty members. Faculty concern for others and themselves to be adequately "qualified" is an important motivator. Second, racism and prejudice must not find a home at Christian colleges and universities. Administrators, faculty, students, and all other stakeholders must drive out the ignorance upon which racism and prejudice feed. Third, historical segregation cannot continue as an excuse for maintaining the "status quo." Fourth, a lack of faculty mentors in the present cannot stop these schools from taking positive steps to train existing, experienced faculty for this role. Fifth, a lack of minority students will continue unless students see these colleges and universities taking positive steps to recognize the accomplishments of minority scholars by adding them to their faculty roles. Last, competition for minority faculty will continue, so colleges and universities must learn how to successfully compete. In order to attract and retain minority faculty, orthodox schools will need to develop a diversity mindset that is intentional, integrated, and inclusive.

Diversity becomes intentional when it is considered as part of the organization's strategic planning enterprise. Intentionality provides a framework for action, which imbeds the importance of diversity development within the minds of university stakeholders. Such a process may be pragmatic at its origin, building a "business case" for diversity, and building towards more advanced forms of integrated diversity as the process matures (Wilson, 1997). Wilson recommends that strategic goals consist of seeking to actively remove inequalities in the systems; creating a strong advocacy for cultural differences and resulting processes; proactively including diverse members on key teams wherever and whenever possible; providing mentoring based on individual needs; and taking proactive measures to prevent harassment and discrimination.

In addition, an acceptance of diversity will require more integrated thinking on the part of all university stakeholders. In order for perceptions to change in both majority and minority faculty, all must become convinced that a more equitable job situation will lead to increased job satisfaction for all and will result in increased faculty commitment. Schools must ask "What impedes minority faculty from being able to do their jobs effectively, and what must be done to remove these impediments?"

Finally, in order for a positive diversity environment to become a reality, it must include all members of the school community. "A complex strategy-making process penetrates all layers of management and utilizes organization members' skills and abilities from all levels providing a firm with a strategic resource that is difficult to imitate" (Snyman & Drew, 2003). Include everyone in the process, tell everyone the results, try again . . . and again . . . and again.

# References

Abilene Christian University Press Release (1999, November 22). ACU president apologizes for past racial discrimination; civil rights attorney Fred Gray formally accepts apology. ACU News [On-line], Available: www.acu.edu/events/news/991122-apology.html

At-Twaijri, M.I., Al-Khursani, S.A. & Odah, A.M. (1994). Motivational factors in academia: The case of a large university in the Arabian Gulf, European Journal of Engineering Education, 19, 475-484.

Belknap, J. (1990). Racism on campus: Prejudice plus power. Vital Speeches of the Day, 57 (10), 308-313.

Blackwell, J.E. (1989). Mentoring: An action strategy for increasing minority faculty. Academe, 75 (5), 8-14.

Benne, R. (2001). Quality with soul. Grand Rapids, MI: Eerdmans

Bowen, W.G. & Sosa, J.A. (1989). Prospects for faculty in the arts and sciences: A study of factors affecting demand and supply, 1987-2012. Princeton, NJ: Princeton University Press.

Boyer, E.L. (1990). Scholarship reconsidered: Priorities of the professoriate. Princeton, NJ: The Carnegie Foundation for the Advancement of Teaching. Collins, J. (2001). Good to great. New York, NY: Harper Collins.

DJangi, A.R. (1993). Racism in higher education: Its presence in the classroom and lives of psychology students. Paper presented at the annual meeting of the American Psychological Association. Ontario, Canada, August 23, 1993.

Drew, D.V. (2001). An examination of collective expectancy and team performance at work in a complex organization, Submission to the 2001 Oklahoma Christian University Colloquium, Edmond, OK.

Drew, D.V. (2002). Enhancing collegiality: A new strategy for faculty and administrators of Christian universities. Submission to the 2002 Oklahoma Christian University Colloquium, Edmond, OK.

Drew, D.V. (2002). Keeping faculty at the Christian university: The roles and limits of intrinsic motivation. Presentation to Christian Scholar's Conference, Oklahoma Christian University, Edmond, OK., July 18, 2002.

Edelson, M. (1992). The complicated job of finding faculty, American Demographics, 14, 12, 16-18.

Ehrenberg, R.G. (2002). Studying ourselves: The academic labor market, On-line posting: http://www.nber.org/papers/w8965.

Emerson, M.O. & Smith, C. (2001). Divided by faith: Evangelical religion and the problem of race in America. Oxford, England: Oxford University Press.

Higher Education Research Institute, University of California Los Angeles (1999). Faculty attitudes and characteristics: Results of a 1998-1999 survey. Chronicle of Higher Education (46/2).

Hughes, R.T. (2001). The churches of Christ. Westport, CT: Praeger

Johnson-Bailey, J., Cervero, R.M., & Baugh, S. (2004). Mentoring in black and white: the intricacies of cross-cultural mentoring. Mentoring & Tutoring: Partnership in Learning, 12 (1), 7-21.

Murray, C.B. & Clark, R.M. (1990). Targets of racism. The American School Board Journal, 177 (6), 22-24.

Pinto, G. & Pulido, E. (1997). Motivation of faculty members at a Latin American university: A case study, European Journal of Engineering Education, 22, 4, 421-426.

Robbins, S.P. (2003). The truth about managing people: And nothing but the truth. Upper Saddle River, NJ: Prentice Hall

Singh, D.K. & Stoloff, D.L. (2003). Mentoring faculty of color. Paper presented at the Annual Meeting of the American Association of Colleges for Teacher Education, New Orleans, LA.

Snyman, J. & Drew, D.V. (2003). Complex strategic decision processes and firm performance in a hypercompetitive industry. Journal of American Academy of Business, Cambridge, 2 (2), 293-298.

Sylvia, R.D. & Hutchison, T. (1985). What makes Ms. Johnson teach? A study of teacher motivation, Human Relations, 38, 841-856.

Wilson, T. (1997). Diversity at work: The business case for equity. Etobicoke, Ontario, Canada: Wiley

# Acknowledgments

I would like to thank my original research partner, Jackie L. Halstead of Abilene Christian University, Oklahoma Christian University for providing the grant necessary to conduct this research, and the 369 participating faculty who took time to provide honest comments on this often difficult subject.

# Why Engineers Make Good Apologists

## DR. DOMINIC M. HALSMER

Since the fall of 2004, faculty and students in engineering and the sciences at Oral Roberts University have been reaching out to the Tulsa community in an effort to provide answers to skeptics of the Christian faith, especially with regard to science. This outreach is consistent with the university mission to raise up students to go into every person's world with healing for the totality of human need. The effort focuses on reaching an important people group: the analytically-minded, who are generally familiar with modern science. Faculty and students interact with skeptics during dinners, apologetics-related presentations, and friendly sports competitions. Presentations emphasize evidence from the sciences for a master design engineer for the universe. Cross-cultural relationships develop which improve mutual understanding and facilitate acceptance of the Gospel.

This outreach activity has prompted reconsideration of how well the Engineering, Physics, and Physical Science Department at Oral Roberts University in Tulsa, OK, is accomplishing its mission. The mission statement of the department is as follows:

> The Engineering, Physics, and Physical Science Department seeks to provide students with the knowledge, skills, and experiences that will

---

**Dr. Dominic M. Halsmer** is a liscensed Professional Engineer in the state of Oklahoma and Chair of the Engineering, Physics, and Physical Science Department at Oral Roberts University.

prepare them to enter directly into professional practice as Christian engineers, or into advanced studies in engineering, or other professional areas. This training equips students in the application of science and mathematics for the improvement of the physical world, and enables graduates to enter the engineering and scientific communities, and contribute to the healing of the human condition. The department supports the overall university mission by the development of analytical thinking and problem solving in science and engineering, and promotes understanding and reconciliation between the fields of science and theology.

First and foremost, the goal of the department is to produce engineering and science graduates who are academically excellent, enabling them to make a positive impact in the technical field of their choice after graduation. This is a critically important step that ensures that our graduates have credibility in the industrial or academic communities where they serve. The technical expertise of our graduates affords them opportunities to contribute to the healing of the human condition in several different ways. They provide creative technical solutions in many diverse fields through the application of science and mathematics for the betterment of humanity. However, as *Christian* engineers and scientists, they should also be prepared to give an answer to everyone who asks them to give the reason for the hope that they have. As exhorted in 1 Peter 3:15, this should be conducted with gentleness and respect. This preparation should result in the improvement of the human spiritual condition, as those who are seeking answers to life's biggest questions are drawn toward the hopeful life of their Christian colleague. This preparation should also result in opportunities to promote understanding and reconciliation between the fields of science and theology. The important question, which needs to be addressed, is: "How should engineering and science graduates be prepared, in order that they might successfully handle such opportunities?"

To begin answering this question, one must consider the group of people who predominantly populate the communities where the graduates will be working. It is expected that graduates will mainly be interacting with other engineers and scientists. This people group is significantly different from the normal population. According to Samuel C. Florman, who has written extensively on the engineer, people tend to think of engineers as practical, analytical, and nonemotional.[1] Think of Spock on the original *Star Trek* television program to get an extreme view of this personality type. Florman also quotes results from five psychological studies of the engineering personality, which seem to justify generalizations about this people group.

> These five studies yield a high consistency insofar as the character traits which engineers have in common are concerned. This is the more remarkable because these authors studied engineers in different fields and by different methods and techniques. It is therefore probable that unlike many other occupations where it is impossible to demonstrate any consistent trend as far as personality traits are concerned, the engineering profession—with the exception of research, administration, and sales specialties—is composed of a homogenous group of men with a fairly narrow range of temperamental variation.[2]

Engineers and scientists are interested in the pursuit, realization, and utilization of truth, especially truths that can be discovered through use of the scientific method. Hence, they tend to be very methodical and careful in their work, so that their results might be utterly dependable. The first and most critical canon of the Code of Ethics of the National Society of Professional Engineers (NSPE)[3] is that "engineers, in the fulfillment of their professional duties, shall hold paramount the safety, health and welfare of the public." Florman contends that "The resolve to be dependable is another essential element of the engineering view."[4] This view of their work, and the world in general, would tend to make anyone more skeptical of purported truths, even beyond what skepticism might have already existed before the start of such a career. Engineers and scientists have been trained to establish a high degree of certainty before embracing the veracity of engineering solutions or scientific findings.

It follows that engineers and scientists would require more than the average amount of evidence, and possibly from a broader range of sources, to be convinced of any particular proposition. They also lend more credence to evidence that is scientifically verifiable. Concerning Christian apologetics, this would explain why many engineers and scientists don't consider evidence or arguments from Scripture to be particularly compelling. Does this imply that they will never believe? The special revelation of Scripture is only part of the manner in which God has revealed himself to humanity. Wouldn't evidence and arguments from the general revelation of nature be much more compelling to such a people group?

The special revelation of Scripture does suggest that much can be known about God through an understanding of the universe. Paul's letter to the Romans speaks of God's invisible qualities, his eternal power and divine nature, being clearly seen and understood by everyone, from what has been made (Romans 1:20). According to Paul, this has been evident from the creation of the world, but the last hundred years has seen many scientific discoveries that effectively support Paul's assertion. As an example, consider Einstein's extensively-tested Theory of General Relativity. This theory implies that all matter, energy, space, time, and the information content inherent therein, came into existence at a point in history. Such a beginning for the universe suggests a creator with the divine attribute of being transcendent of our dimensions of space and time. This would help to explain the apparently supernatural capabilities of such a creator, from our point of view in the four-dimensional created realm. Thus, Christians graduating in engineering or science should be familiar with the scientific evidence for a creator. They should be able to help people see God's eternal power and divine nature in the created order of the universe. Lee Strobel's new book, entitled *The Case for a Creator*,[5] which came out last year, does an excellent job in this regard. Although it does not discuss much about the identity of the creator, this too can be inferred to some degree by evidence from nature. One of the powerful messages of the book of *Job* is that Job was able to discern the existence of a personal redeemer to rescue him from his fallen human condition.

As skeptics consider the evidence for a creator, they may become more open to the idea that this creator would desire to communicate with the creation in a reliable manner, such as inspired writings. It may be helpful to point out consistencies between general and special revelations, such as the expansion of the universe. This recently-discovered characteristic of our universe is mentioned several times in Scripture by multiple authors. They consistently claim that God is responsible for stretching out the heavens like a tent. Interestingly, scientists are currently hard-pressed to explain the mysterious force, currently known as "dark energy," which is allegedly accelerating the expansion of the universe.

Why is it that science and theology appear to contradict one another? These occurrences are not surprising and, in fact, should be expected. If science is defined as man's interpretation of the facts about nature and theology is defined as man's interpretation of the facts about God, then a comparison of the two will undoubtedly produce contradictions since man's interpretations tend to be flawed. It makes sense, however, that there would be no contradictions between the facts concerning nature and the inspired Word of God since God has authored both revelations.[6]

Florman also states that most engineers tend to be pragmatists, rather than ideologues.[7] They are interested in what works. When dialoging with an engineer, an apologist should point out that eternal separation from the Creator is not a very pragmatic option. Humans reach their full potential while in close intimate relationship with their Creator. To ignore that all-important relationship just doesn't work for human beings. They are not designed to operate outside of that relationship. Humans were designed to be in relationship with God. It is their purpose. Engineers are very familiar with the concept of design for a purpose. This suggests a new category of powerful evidence to be considered by engineers and scientists: that of intelligent designs found in nature. From studies of the very large, i.e., astronomy, to studies of the very small, i.e., biochemistry, the universe is replete with examples of design for a specific purpose. Consider the tiny bacterial flagellum, a highly efficient molecular motor that serves as the propulsion system for many bacteria. It is made up of the same kind of parts that human engineers use to make larger motors. This molecular design can have an interesting effect on engineers who view it for the first time, as Lee Strobel recounts in the following story.

> Drawings of the flagellum are, indeed, very impressive, since they look uncannily like a machine that human beings would construct. I remember a scientist telling me about his father, an accomplished engineer who was highly skeptical about claims of intelligent design. The dad could never understand why his son was so convinced that the world had been designed by an intelligent agent. One day the scientist put a drawing of the bacterial flagellum in front of him. Fascinated, the engineer studied it silently for a while, then looked up and said to his son with a sense of wonder: "Oh, now I get what you've been saying."[8]

However, God is not only involved in engineering the universe in a material sense. More importantly, he is engaged in "spiritual engineering" for our benefit, as seen in 2 Samuel 14:14: "Like water spilled on the ground, which cannot be recovered, so we must die. But God does not take away life; instead, he *devises* ways so that a banished person may not remain estranged from him." God is an engineer, both in his awesome creation of this beautiful universe, and in his design of our redemption, through the obedient sacrifice of his son, our Lord Jesus Christ. Part of this design involves the calling of believing engineers and scientists to participate with God in spiritual engineering, providing gentle and respectful answers to questions raised by skeptics, especially in the area of science.

God has placed in humanity a curiosity for the world and how it works, as well as the ability to discover scientific truth. He's also placed evidence for his existence and his nature within His creation to be found by those truth-seekers who will look for him. Proverbs 25:2 (NIV) reflects this strategy which God has put in place to woo us back to Himself: "It is the glory of God to conceal a matter; to search out a matter is the glory of kings," or in The Message version: "God delights in concealing things; scientists delight in discovering things." The following modern proverb relates this idea to engineering: "Amusement park engineers design wild, spinning rides so that people can lose their senses for a few moments. God has designed this wonderful, spinning ride we call earth in the hopes that we come to our senses for all eternity." Engineers and scientists may find evidences and arguments from nature to be particularly compelling. Good stewardship of the creation includes being prepared to share this knowledge with those who need it the most.

Adam and Eve (and all their progeny) were banished from the presence of God after they chose to disobey, but God has made available a magnificent means of reconciliation which is intimately tied up with His creation of the material world. In the greatest of mysteries, God would become a part of His creation and engage in a daring rescue mission, which would reveal the divine depth of His love for us. The universe itself has been designed to draw us back to our creator, and to help us accept and return His love. As proclaimed by the writer of the Psalms,

The heavens declare the glory of God;
the skies proclaim the work of his hands.
Day after day they pour forth speech;
night after night they display knowledge.
There is no speech or language
where their voice is not heard.
Their voice goes out into all the earth,
their words to the end of the world.[9]

Those who honestly study aspects of the cosmos can't help but discover the information that the psalmist so beautifully describes. Our minds are inherently inquisitive. Children naturally take things apart to see how they work. This kind of behavior is actually associated with another engineering-related field known as reverse engineering. Reverse engineering is simply the process of extracting knowledge or design information from anything that has been engineered. As an example, consider the development of the Tu-4 long-range bomber by the Soviet Union toward the end of World War Two. The United States Air Force got a big surprise when the Tu-4 was unveiled at a 1947 air show, since the plane appeared to be nearly identical to the United States B-29 Superfortress. With the release of newly declassified documents in 2001, the Smithsonian Institution's National Air and Space Museum revealed that the Soviets had, in fact, copied the Superfortress virtually part for part; all 105,000 of them. They were able to do this by completely dismantling and studying one of three B-29s that were forced to make an emergency landing in southeastern Russia after a mission over Japan in 1944. Unfortunately for the Soviets, the Tu-4 inherited the same problems as the B-29: notoriously unreliable engines, which tended to catch fire just as readily as the American version.[10]

A significant amount of our latest and greatest technologies have arisen through reverse engineering of the biological systems that we find so prevalent in our world. This relatively new field, which is known as biomimetics, is thoroughly surveyed in a brand new book, edited by Yoseph Bar-Cohen of Jet Propulsion Laboratories, called *Biomimetics: Biologically Inspired Technology*.[11] Currently, concepts in reverse engineering have been found to be extremely useful in deciphering computer software and hardware systems, as described in *Reversing: Secrets of Reverse Engineering*[12] by Eilam. Here we see a fascinating parallel between the organization of computer instructions and the chemistry of life. Physicist Paul Davies contends that life involves more than just "self-organization."[13] According to Davies, "Life is in fact *specified*— i.e., genetically directed—organization. Living things are instructed by the genetic software encoded in their DNA (or RNA)."[14] Like design specifications, which define how an engineered product will meet performance requirements, complex information is specified at the fundamental level of life to provide what is needed for growth to maturity and the fulfillment of purpose.

For centuries now, scientists and engineers have reveled in the fact that our world is a wonderland of discovery, and that our minds are well equipped to unravel the mysteries of the cosmos. We tend to take this situation for granted, but Albert Einstein understood that, aside from the wisdom of a creator, there is no compelling reason when things should have worked out this way. He described the situation well when he said, "The most incomprehensible thing about the world is that it is comprehensible!" Astronomer Guillermo Gonzalez and Philosopher Jay W. Richards have compiled a detailed description of the uniqueness of planet Earth in this regard. In *The Privileged Planet: How Our Place in the Cosmos is Designed for Discovery*, "They demonstrate that our planet is exquisitely fit not only to support life, but also to give us the best view of the universe, as if Earth were designed both for life and for scientific discovery."[15] Our planet is not the only element of creation that exhibits this characteristic. The fields of science and engineering flourish at all levels and in many different venues. Our curiosity for how things work appears to be insatiable, and yet we are continually satisfied with an endless supply of riddles from nature that seem to be designed especially for us to unravel.

From the very beginning, we were made in God's image and given authority to subdue and rule over creation. "So God created man in his own image, in the image of God he created him; male and female he created them. God blessed them and said to them, 'Be fruitful and increase in number; fill the earth and subdue it. Rule over the fish of the sea and the birds of the air and over every living creature that moves on the ground.'"[16] Bearing the image of God, we were also given the creativity and ingenuity to devise solutions to problems that would enhance the quality of life and lift the human spirit. When Henry Ford realized the great potential of an affordable automobile, he said, "I will build a motor car for the great multitude . . . so low in price that no man . . . will be unable to own one—and enjoy with his family the blessing of pleasure in God's great open spaces."[17] Of course, along with this God-given authority and inventiveness comes the responsibility of good stewardship. Did Henry Ford also realize the enormous potential for injury and death resulting from automobile accidents that would quickly increase at alarming rates? And yet, few would argue that the automobile should never have been built.

Engineers recognize the high priority of ensuring safety in their designs. The first of the fundamental canons of the Code of Ethics of the

National Society of Professional Engineers (NSPE) is that "Engineers, in the fulfillment of their professional duties, shall . . . hold paramount the safety, health and welfare of the public."[18] Although the entire NSPE Code of Ethics is somewhat lengthy, the Engineer's Creed, which was adopted by the NSPE in 1954, provides a more concise statement of the commitments of professional engineers:

> As a Professional Engineer, I dedicate my professional knowledge and skill to the advancement and betterment of human welfare.
> I pledge:
>
> * To give the utmost of performance.
> * To participate in none but honest enterprise.
> * To live and work according to the laws of man and the highest standards of professional conduct.
> * To place service before profit, the honor and standing of the profession before personal advantage, and the public welfare above all other considerations.
>
> In humility and with need for Divine Guidance, I make this pledge.[19]

Engineers are concerned with more than just safety. They have committed to dedicate their God-given (and hard-earned) abilities to the advancement and betterment of human welfare! *Spiritual* engineers not only recognize the obvious significance of the last line of the Engineer's Creed, but also recognize the underlying implications of the first line, in light of the spiritual estrangement inherent in the human condition. Such engineers seek to engage in enterprises that contribute to the improvement of all aspects of human welfare, including the spiritual condition.

Spiritual engineers understand that stewardship of creation means more than just taking good care of the environment and making good use of natural resources. It recognizes that everything belongs to the Lord, and hence we must seek His purposes for how everything is to be used for His glory. This includes personal stewardship over the time, energy, gifts, and information that have been entrusted to us. In general, engineers are gifted with the wisdom and ability to combine information and technical skills with available resources to develop products, processes, and systems that benefit other people. Spiritual engineers look to do this in a way that lifts people's spirits and encourages them to soar to the great heights for which they were created.

# References

1. Samuel C. Florman. (1994) *The Existential Pleasures of Engineering.* New York: St. Martin's Press.

2. *A Profile of the Engineer: A Comprehensive Study of Research Relating to the Engineer,* prepared by Deutsch and Shea, Inc., issued October 1957 by Industrial Relations Newsletter, Inc., p. II-8.

3. http://nspe.org/ethics/eh1-code.asp.

4. Florman, p. 180.

5. Lee Strobel. (2004) *The Case for a Creator.* Grand Rapids, MI: Zondervan.

6. Hugh Ross of *Reasons to Believe* (www.reasons.org)

7. Florman, p. 181.

8. Strobel, pp. 205-206.

9. Psalm 19:1-4

10. CNN: How Soviets copied America's best bomber during WWII (http://archines.cnn.com/2001/US/01/25/smithsonian.cold.war/)

11. Yoseph Bar-Cohen. (Ed.). (2006). *Biomimetics: Biologically Inspired Technologies.* Boca Raton, FL: CRC Press.

12. Eilam, Eldad. (2005). *Reversing: Secrets of Reverse Engineering.* Indianapolis, IN: Wiley.

13. Funck, Larry L. (2005). The Creation of Life: Charting When, Where, and How? in *Not Just Science* (pp. 218-219). Grand Rapids, MI: Zondervan.

14. Eilam, Eldad. (2005). *Reversing: Secrets of Reverse Engineering.* Indianapolis, IN: Wiley.

15. Gonzalez, Guillermo and Richards, Jay W. (2004). *The Privileged Planet: How Our Place in the Cosmos is Designed for Discovery.* Washington, D.C.: Regnery Book Jacket.

16. Genesis 1:27-28

17. Beakley, George C. and Leach, H.W. (1982). *Engineering, an Introduction to a Creative Profession* (p. 480). New York: Macmillan.

18. http://nspe.org/ethics/eh1-code.asp

19. http://nspe.org/ethics/eh1-cred.asp

# Culture, Cultural Pluralism, and Multiculturalism: A Biblical Analysis of Diversity

Dr. Timothy D. Norton
Prof. Darlene P. Gaskill
Dr. Gwetheldene L. Holzmann

In the understanding of culture, cultural pluralism, and multiculturalism, a Biblical Worldview regarding society comes into focus. These three terms, symbolizing a renewal in philosophical thought over the past four decades (Gutek, 1997), have been interchangeably used to inculcate concepts that endeavor to strengthen diversity. Rather than being seen as similar, these distinct terms, each with its own variation and relevance, are best viewed from a foundational understanding of the term culture.

Culture, as a concept, incorporates two acknowledged meanings. The first implies an understanding of a body of knowledge representative of humankind's noblest ideas. This definition, stemming from the Western idea of culture, presumes universality in scope. The second meaning places culture in a flexible mode, which can incorporate both a universal and singular emphasis. This definition sees culture as a whole way of life. It presents for analysis the entire framework of a given society or

**Timothy D. Norton** is Associate Professor in the Graduate School of Education at Oral Roberts University, **Darlene P. Gaskill** works in the Art Department at Oral Roberts University, and **Gwetheldene L. Holzmann** works in the School of LifeLong Education at Oral Roberts University.

comprehends the individual groupings within that society. As such, it can evoke an understanding of the intellectual, spiritual, and material life of the entire people or encompass the history, language, and traditions of a particular sociological community within that society (Hobbs & Rush, 1997).

Cultural pluralism exists when "various cultures and ethnic groups within a nation maintain their own identities" (Banks as cited in Hobbs & Rush, 1997, p. 202). Banks implies that identities can have numerous means of expression. These identities can be seen in lifestyles, religion, language, and geographical locations. The identities are considered legitimate insofar as they do not conflict with the overall values of the host society. He further points out that in order for the legitimacy of the identities to be maintained, the society must be "both democratic and committed to pluralism" (p. 202).

England (1992) sees pluralism as a state where "groups maintain participation in the development of their traditions and special interest while cooperatively working toward the interdependence needed for a nation's unity" (p. 1). Banks' idea of legitimate identities is seen by England as those traditions and interests that join together to create the model for national identity.

Multiculturalism is a "philosophical concept built on the ideas of freedom, justice, equality, equity, and human dignity" (National Association for Multicultural Education, 2003, p. 1). By means of democratic principles, multiculturalism serves to challenge discrimination based on diversity. Its emphasis is that of preparation for participation in an interdependent world. Its focus is to inform regarding the "histories, cultures, and contributions of diverse groups" (National Association for Multicultural Education, 2003, p. 1).

From these definitions, one can see that culture places emphasis upon a society or upon a particular group as demonstrating an entire way of life. Cultural pluralism then segments the groups within the society and legitimizes their identities within the national identity. Multiculturalism facilitates experiences that further highlight the individual diversities and, while acknowledging their interdependent world, serves as a means of eliminating oppression and injustice within that world. Its focus then moves from a personal cultural mindset to that of a universal identification with histories, cultures, and diverse groups. With an understanding of diversity terminology, it becomes necessary to examine the biblical framework upon which each term rests.

The Bible indicates that God was the fashioner of humankind and that man was made in His own image (Genesis 1:26). This human race was commanded to increase and multiply to the point that it would establish many nations upon the earth. These nations were to function as co-laborers in the earth to both subdue it and replenish it. This admonition, given first to Adam and Eve, was to be fulfilled by their progeny from one generation to the next (Genesis 1:24). In so doing, God provided the means for the establishment of mankind as equals in His creation of them and as caretakers of this world. Man's corruption of the purpose of this command reached its zenith in the edifice of the Tower of Babel. Here, the people of the world were as one and desired to reach unto the heavens to make a name for themselves. God, in order to restrain them from their imaginings, confounded their language and scattered them abroad (Genesis 11:4-8). It is at this point in history that one nation and one people become many nations of many people. The replenishing of the *entire* earth had now begun.

Various cultures then began to develop through this dispersal of mankind throughout the earth. As each group migrated into geographical areas and became established, collective concepts and beliefs manifested themselves (Sowell, 1994). These cultures, which came into existence through the act of God, have increased over the centuries as men have acted on their own needs and desires. Entire cultures have been established through natural disasters and man's suppressions. People groups have moved across continents as conquering hordes; some have been forced to migrate for various reasons, while others may have been taken to foreign lands as slaves (1994).

This infusion of different people into the culture of others allowed for the development of cultural pluralism. An example of this can be seen in God's dealings with Israel. In Joshua 22: 4-5, God commanded Israel that when they went into a foreign land they were to keep his commandments. By this, God established the manner in which Israel was to maintain their own culture as they lived within the culture of other people. They were to dwell with others and to actively participate in their nation. This blending of cultures was not to result in the acceptance of all of their cultural differences, but only those that did not compromise their covenant with God. The history of the Jewish people exemplifies a separate existence within their adopted cultures. The Diaspora (mandatory removal from their ancestral homeland) in 70 A.D. further illustrates

their need to maintain their cultural pluralism in the face of their reloca-
tions (Sowell, 1930).

In contrast to culture and cultural pluralism, multiculturalism is not
the result of supernatural or natural phenomena. There are no biblical
examples of multiculturalism because it is a philosophical creation of the
human mind. As such, it does not have a Biblical foundation. It instead
relies upon the tenets of naturalism in its justification that all cultures are
"morally equivalent" (Colson, 1999, p. 21). Relying upon the Word of
God for truth, biblical reasoning does not allow for the justification of
multiculturalism as a basis for diversity and its validation in society.

Multiculturalism has become the primary focus of education in the
postmodern age. As Elkind (as cited in Walling, 2001) states, "in the
postmodern period, which we now occupy, we value the articulation of
sociocultural differences rather than linear social progress, cultural particulars rather than universals, and the irregular as being 'as legitimate
and as worthy of exploration as the regular'" (pp. 4-5). This emphasis
has led to an abandonment of the tri-partite foundation of the definition
of diversity. Culture and cultural pluralism have now been incorporated
into multiculturalism. This enveloping of the three elements into one
may be perceived as the natural course of societal evolution. However,
can the three be represented in the one and still maintain diversity?

Banks (as cited in Gorski, 2000) points out that "an individual's
strong national identification is essential to his/her development of a global identity" (p. 3). To abandon the usage of "culture" as part of an
integral, yet complementary, aspect of the landscape of diversity awareness may eliminate "the cultivation of one's intellect through acquiring a
body of knowledge that compresses civilization's noblest ideas" (Hobbs
& Rush, 1997, p. 202). This body of knowledge, though considered
universal, has its roots in Western civilization.

Hobbs and Rush (1997) see this redefining of diversity as
multiculturalism's rejection of Western culture and of its impression of
Western culture as "at best, wanting, at worst, destructive" (p. 206).
They feel that to categorize Western culture this way is to ignore several
important aspects of current cultural study. Primarily, the fact that Western culture is studied and considered attractive to other cultures, particularly Asians, is noteworthy. The increasing number of concert musicians
in the United States who are Asian-Chinese, Indian, Korean, and Japanese and the number of Asian-American teachers of instrumental music

within American universities is to Hobbs and Rush one of the indications of the acceptance of Western culture as an appropriate diversity study.

England (1992) points out the conflict between cultural pluralism and multiculturalism when she indicates that pluralistic processes are often put "under the name of multiculturalism issues and concerns; frequently the use of the term pluralism is avoided" (p. 1). It is within the sphere of cultural pluralism that the following question can be examined and answered: "How should cultures be compared or treated in relation to one another?" (J. Paul Getty, 1997, ¶ 1). By looking at diverse ethnic, racial, religious, and social groups, respect can be given for one's individuality; and yet, through the means of interdependence and cooperation, a nation's unity can be created and maintained. In dialog and participation, communities are exercising cultural pluralism. These practices help to "guarantee that authentic cultural translation" (J. Paul Getty, 1997, ¶ 2) is achieved. In cultural pluralism, individuals can be seen as members of a larger society, a subgroup, or as individuals free to explore possibilities beyond any group. In this sense, the concept of diversity does not function as a means of separation but rather as one that serves to enlighten and enlarge one's human experience (England, 1992).

However, "the underlying goal of multicultural education is to affect social change. The pathway toward this goal incorporates three strands of transformation: the transformation of self; the transformation of schools and schooling; and the transformation of society" (Gorski, 2000, p. 2). This transformational approach to education is the primary purpose of multiculturalism. It is to be a progressive approach that leads to the alteration of education so that it critiques holistically and uncovers shortcomings, failings, and practices that are discriminatory. Multicultural education sees the school as the avenue for the metamorphosis of society by eliminating oppression and injustice (Gorski, 2000, p. 2). This process of elimination presents itself through a naturalistic philosophical approach. As such, multiculturalism's focus is on cultural relativism, moral relativism, and postmodernistic thinking.

Because different cultures and societies view moral behavior differently, multiculturalists see the moral behaviors of all cultures as relative, believing that they should not be judged by those outside of the culture and that "one's behavior may not be judged even *within* one's own culture" (Schmidt, 1997, p. 4). In moral relativism, nature is all that there is, and therefore, there is no transcendent source for truth. In this framework, the individual is free to "construct morality on their own" and

"Every principle is reduced to a personal preference" (Colson, 1999, p. 21). With postmodernism, being that all truth is subject to the individual and is culturally or socially constructed, both cultural relativism and moral relativism find a secure base for their expression. In fact, Schmidt sees multiculturalism as " the marriage of cultural relativism with postmodernism" (p. 4).

As previously mentioned, the intent of multiculturalism is to critique holistically and to uncover shortcomings, failings, and practices that are discriminatory based on diversity. The question, then, is whether multiculturalism's means of measuring these conditions is centered in a framework that allows for the biblical expression of truth. Considering its philosophical attachment to naturalism, it would appear to be unreasonable to expect the multiculturalists to follow a transcendent idea of truth in the evaluation of justice within a culture or society.

In conclusion, one can see that both culture and cultural pluralism have beginnings that mirror biblical realities. However, multiculturalism, with its naturalistic philosophical roots, does not. The Christian educator, in rejecting multiculturalism, can be confident in his/her presentation of diversity as seen within a Biblical framework of culture and cultural pluralism.

# References

Colson, C., & Pearcey, N. (1999). *How now shall we live?* Wheaton, Illinois: Tyndale House.

England, J. T. (1992). Pluralism and education: Its meaning and method. *ERIC Digest.* Retrieved September 20, 2004, from http://www.ericdigests.org/1992-2/method.htm

Gorski, P. (2000). *A working definition of multicultural education.* Retrieved September 19, 2004, from http://www.edchange.org/multicultural/initial.html

Gutek, G. L. (1997). *Philosophical and ideological perspectives on education.* Boston: Allyn and Bacon.

Hobbs, J. A., & Rush, J. C. (1997). *Teaching children art.* New Jersey: Prentice Hall.

J. Paul Getty Museum. (1997). *Discipline-based art education and cultural diversity.* Retrieved September 22, 2004, from http://www.getty.edu/bookstore/toc/dbaecudi_toc.shtml

National Association for Multicultural Education. (2003, February 1). *Multicultural education.* Retrieved September 19, 2004, From http://www.nameorg.org/resolutions/definition.html

Schmidt, A. J. (1997). *The menace of multiculturalism.* Westport, Connecticut: Praeger.

Sowell, T. (1981). *Ethnic America.* New York: Basic Books.

Sowell, T. (1994). *Race and culture.* New York: BasicBooks.

Walling, D. R. (2001). Rethinking visual arts education: A convergence of influences *Kappan Professional Journal, 82,* 626-631.

# A Study of the Relationship between Student Satisfaction and Ethnicity at a Private, Non-Denominational Midwestern University

## Dr. Wendy G. Shirk
## Dr. Mary Lou Miller
## Dr. Cal Easterling

The largest group of prospective students contributing to enrollment growth during the next 15–20 years will likely come from increasing populations of minority students (LaFore, 2001). Even though these minority populations in higher education have been growing at a rapid rate, not enough attention has been given to the recruitment of these groups. According to Person and Christensen (1996), poor race relations have characterized American society, and higher education institutions have suffered from the effects of America's ethnocentrism.

Gonzalez (2000) noted that ethnic minority students who attended predominantly Anglo institutions were likely to experience marginalization and alienation; however, minority students, especially African American students, have had a significant representation in these institutions since 1954 (Flemming, 1984). According to Hauser and Anderson (1991),

**Dr. Wendy G. Shirk** is employed at Oral Roberts University, Dr. Mary Lou Miller works in the Computer Science/Mathematics Department at Oral Roberts University, and **Dr. Cal Easterling** is in charge of Institutional Research at Oral Roberts University.

college enrollment for minority students decreased in the middle 1980's but has gradually increased since that time. The declining trend in college enrollment in the middle 1980's was especially evident among African-American and Hispanic students, who exhibited the highest tendency to drop out of school (Sewell & Hauser, 1980). Porter (1990) illustrated this in a study he conducted in 1980. He revealed that African-American students were 22% more likely to drop out of school than were their Caucasian peers, and Hispanic students were 13% more likely to drop out of school than their Caucasian peers.

Porter (1990) further found that the decrease in the number of minority students in college directly correlated with the increase of student loans and the decrease of student grants. Olivas (1985), Mortenson and Wu (1990), and Mortenson (1989) noted that, compared with Caucasian students, both African-American and Hispanic students were less willing to finance their college education and go into debt to pay for their education. Ekstrom (1991) stated that students who were willing to go into debt to pay for their college educations had higher retention rates; African-American and Hispanic students were less willing to go into debt and were therefore more at risk for attrition. Somers (1996) examined the influence of financial aid and the price of education as factors that have contributed to the retention of students; Somers' Price Response Theory asserted that, to a degree, extra financial aid attracted students.

The University of Georgia utilized HOPE Scholarships for many of its minority students. For the recipients in the state of Georgia, these scholarships paid all tuition and fees at public institutions for high school minority students with at least a "B" average, and $3,000 a year for minorities who attended certain private institutions (Retention Rates Drop for Georgia's HOPE Scholars, 1999). In 1999, Georgia's largest public institution of higher education was the University of Georgia, which also "had the highest HOPE retention rate at 56%" (p. 10). These findings have suggested that HOPE Scholarship recipients exhibited higher grade point averages and more college credits, and they also exhibited lower attrition rates (Towns, 1997). Conversely, the findings of a study by Hu and St.John (2001) suggested that among minority groups, financial aid did not appear to be the source of attrition/retention; the findings from this study "pointed to the importance of improving student college grades and college experiences, particularly for African Americans and Hispanics, as a means of improving opportunity to persist among racial/ethnic groups" (p. 275).

Shifts in the racial composition of higher education populations have caused concern for institutions of higher learning (McDaniel & Graham, 2001). According to Liu and Liu (1999), the national effort to provide racial minorities access to higher education institutions over the last three decades has greatly improved minority access to higher education on many levels. Pincus (1980) concluded that race greatly affected social stratification and attrition rates. Levin and Levin (1991) reported that academic preparedness, enrollment in college preparatory courses, commitment to educational goals, and adaptability were all characteristics that had the greatest impact on minority students who were at risk for attrition. Nettles, Thoeny, and Gosman (1986) noted that African-American students typically had "significantly lower levels of pre-college preparation than white students, [were] less academically integrated, had less satisfaction with their universities, experienced more interfering problems, and had less well-developed study habits" (p. 309) than did their Caucasian peers. In a Harvard Law School study, Latino students as well as African-American students were more dissatisfied than were other students (Bandler, 1999). Richardson and Bender (1987) found that black students held lower occupational and educational goals than did other students. Smitherman and Carr (1981) concluded that African-American students sought faster entry into the job market than did their Caucasian counterparts.

Although many researchers have stated that academic issues have contributed to whether or not minority students persisted in college, other researchers have disagreed. Tracey and Sedlacek (1984, 1985, & 1987) found that students' self-concepts and abilities to cope with racism were determining factors of student satisfaction and persistence. Most institutions have been unaware of these factors and of the multicultural nature of the pool of students making application for admission (LaFore, 2001). LaFore noted that students of color also needed curriculum relevance, shared experiences, social inclusion, and culture-affirming experiences in order to persist in higher education. She asserted that it was the collective efforts of the Admissions office, the Financial Aid office, the Student Services office, the faculty, and the president and trustees to commit to the recruitment and satisfaction of minority students. Minority students and alumni who had positive experiences while attending college have been the best recruiters of other minority students.

C. Ford (1996) and LaVant, Anderson, and Tiggs (1997) asserted the need for mentoring and empowering minority students. One program highlighted in Richardson's (1997) review of C. Ford's work was the University of Georgia's program that successfully targeted black freshmen and sophomores through peer counseling, advising, mentoring, tutoring, study skills, and financial aid. This program proved to be highly successful at the University of Georgia.

The U.S. Census Bureau has defined Hispanics as people who have claimed Latin American background. Historically, Hispanic people have preferred to be referred to as "Latino," "Latina," or "Mexican American" (Aguilar, 1996). According to Aguilar, the dropout rate among Latinos has had far-reaching consequences, and Mexican Americans have traditionally had high attrition rates in high school (Davalos, Chavez, & Guardiola, 1999; U.S. Department of Education, 1992) and in higher education. Attinasi's (1989) study involving Mexican-American youth found that "getting ready" behaviors were associated with college persistence. These behaviors involved learning more about colleges and then forming expectations regarding college experience. In a study of Hispanic women conducted by Aguilar, "Nearly one-half (48.8 percent, n = 41) of the respondents indicated that they experienced sexism. Some respondents felt that they experienced dual and conflicting expectations from within and outside their culture" (p. 150). From within their own culture, these Hispanic women reported feeling little support for women, but instead only expectations to be wives and mothers. From outside their culture, these Hispanic women felt that they had few role models and they always had to prove themselves. According to Aguilar, teachers and administrators would witness a drop in the attrition rates of Hispanics if these students were affirmed and involved in activities that removed social and structural barriers in education.

Rendon, Jalomo, and Nora (2000) stated that working-class Latino students were less likely to get involved socially and academically in higher education compared with their Caucasian counterparts. Rendon et al. explained engagement as getting involved in social clubs and regularly meeting with faculty. Historically, engagement has been more difficult for working class students, yet it has been essential in maintaining student persistence.

The number of African Americans in the overall American population has increased, yet the number of black students in predominantly white institutions has not directly correlated with America's shifting demographics (Person, 1994; Simpson & Frost, 1993; Frost, 1999). Historically, African-American students have expressed concerns about their ability to succeed academically at predominantly white institutions (Murtaugh, Burne, & Schuster, 1999). Increasing numbers of African-American students have chosen to attend predominantly Caucasian institutions in the past several decades (Leach, 1987). Liu and Liu (1999) found that, for African American students who attended Anglo colleges, there was a tendency to experience marginality and isolation. In this study, 45% of African-American students reported that they did not feel involved in their universities' general campus life. Social maladjustment, discrimination, cultural alienation, and disconnected relationships with predominantly Caucasian faculty members were among the issues of concern named by the surveyed students. Gardner (1998), who studied Christian colleges, stated that the number of nonwhite faculty has been small, forcing Christian colleges with limited budgets to compete with larger institutions for nonwhite faculty and students. These larger institutions have historically had the means to pay higher salaries in the recruitment of nonwhites. To compete, many Christian higher education institutions have turned to minority recruiters for help.

The racial climate at predominantly white institutions has been a determining factor for whether minority students persisted until graduation. Nora and Cabrera (1996) asserted that a negative racial climate, or perception of prejudice, lowered the satisfaction level and persistence rate of minority students who attended predominantly white institutions. Both non-minority and minority students reported that they perceived a negative campus climate and discriminatory views held by faculty. They also reported in-class racially-oriented experiences. In each of these measures, minority students reported higher perceptions of prejudice and discrimination than did whites (Nora & Cabrera). Conversely, according to Flemming (1985), African-American students who attended African-American institutions communicated greater satisfaction with academic life and relationships with faculty members. The 1998 CSS results for the CCCU indicated that 89.5% of students who participated in the 1998 studies were satisfied with their overall college experience; however, only 39.8% of students were satisfied with the ethnic diversity of students, and only 35.3% of the students were satisfied with the ethnic diversity of the faculty (Burwell, 1998). Asian American students have also faced feelings of alienation in higher education (Koyama & Lee, 1989). Even though minority students have been targets of discrimination on college campuses, they have shown a history of being able to adjust in predominantly Caucasian institutions (Nora & Cabrera, 1996).

According to Tinto (1993), retention programs should be committed to the education of all students, not just some. "Advertising, recruiting messages, and publications designed to address the concerns [of minorities at predominantly white institutions] have been favorably received in qualitative testing" (Murtaugh, Burns, & Schuster, 1999, p. 368).

According to Sanders and Burton (1996), environmental factors needed improvement in order to strengthen minority student satisfaction. These environmental factors included providing a sense of belonging and providing the perception of equal opportunity. These factors have proven to be more satisfying or dissatisfying to minority students than social factors such as maintaining meaningful relationships with peers. According to Fralick (1993), programs designed to increase retention for the general population have also been helpful in retaining minority students.

The targeted population of this study consisted of the students of the institution being studied. This institution was a private, non-denominational, midwestern university with a student body of approximately 5,300 credit and non-credit students. The sample for this study consisted of approximately 225 of the 500 graduating seniors of the institution.

This study examined in detail the problem of attrition in higher education. Although postsecondary participation has significantly increased during the past twenty-five years, the proportion of students graduating with degrees has remained somewhat constant (Gladieux & Swail, 2000). In 1993, over 800,000 freshmen withdrew from higher education institutions in the United States before their sophomore years; almost 50% of students who entered two-year institutions and 28.5% of students who entered four-year institutions decided not to return after their freshmen years (American College Testing, 1993; Snyder & Hoffman, 1995; Tinto, 1993). In private, non-denominational institutions, 47% of freshmen historically dropped out before their sophomore years (Gardner, 1998). For many years, scholars have sought explanations for attrition and student dissatisfaction, and college and university administrators have desired to reduce their attrition rates (Braxton, Milem, & Sullivan, 2000).

This study specifically investigated the degree to which student satisfaction and ethnicity were related. First, the statistical coding and the frequencies and percentages of the variables were indicated. Second, the results of the correlational analysis were examined to determine the degree to which overall student satisfaction and ethnicity were related. Third, the results of the correlational analysis reported the degree to which all of the sub-areas of student satisfaction (found on the College Student Survey) and ethnicity were related.

The following sub-areas of student satisfaction (CSS, 2001) were listed below the directions which read, *Please rate your satisfaction with your current (or more recent) college on each of the aspects of campus life listed below*:

- General education or core curriculum courses
- Science and mathematics courses
- Humanities courses
- Social science courses
- Courses in your major field
- Relevance of coursework to everyday life
- Overall quality of instruction
- Laboratory facilities and equipment
- Library facilities
- Computer facilities
- Quality of computer training/assistance
- Availability of internet access
- Sense of community of campus
- Tutoring or other academic assistance
- Academic advising
- Career counseling and advising
- Student housing
- Financial aid services
- Amount of contact with faculty
- Opportunities for community service
- Job placement services for students
- Campus health services
- Class size
- Interaction with other students
- Ability to find a faculty or staff mentor
- Leadership opportunities
- Recreational facilities
- Overall college experience (p. 2)

The following possible choices on the CSS were available to respondents concerning the 28 sub-areas of student satisfaction listed above: "Very Satisfied;" "Satisfied;" "Neutral;" "Dissatisfied;" or "Can't Rate/No

Experience." Because the CSS only accommodated a "Dissatisfied" response and *not* a "Very Dissatisfied" response, unlike the two available choices for satisfaction, the examiner grouped the responses "Very Satisfied" and "Satisfied" together and coded them as "Satisfied." The investigator used the following numerical codes to statistically score the data:

1. Can't Rate/No Experience
2. Dissatisfied
3. Neutral
4. Very Satisfied or Satisfied

The following response choices regarding ethnicity (CSS, 2001) were listed below the directions, which read, *Are you: (Mark **all** that apply)*:

- White/Caucasian
- African American/Black
- American Indian
- Asian American/Asian/Pacific Islander
- Mexican American/Chicano
- Puerto Rican American
- Other Latino
- Other (p. 2)

There were seven cases for which there were either no responses or multiple responses for the question on ethnicity. The survey respondent who did not indicate a response on the question of ethnicity was omitted from the survey results and the multiple responses were placed in the most appropriate categories. The researchers limited the coding of the "ethnicity" variable because the representation of ethnic groups other than "White/Caucasian" or "African American/Black" was extremely limited. Ergo, the investigator determined that, for sampling and statistical reasons, the following limited coding be assigned:

1. White/Caucasian
2. African American/Black
3. Other (which included American Indian; Asian American/ Asian/Pacific Islander; Mexican American/Chicano; Puerto Rican American; Other Latino; and Other)

According to McGrath and Braunstein (1997), because studies have concluded that so many variables have influenced student attrition, individual higher education institutions have historically conducted their own research in order to allow faculty and administrators to better understand the problems within their own cultures and communities. Concerning making generalizations in this discussion, the data for this study were collected by and from a single, medium-sized, non-denominational institution located in the Midwest. The graduating seniors at the university studied were more likely to have been exposed to similar conditions, which controlled for several threats to internal validity. These students were exposed to these conditions in regard to laboratory facilities and equipment; tutoring or other academic assistance; career counseling and advising; amount of contact with faculty; campus health services; interactions with other students; and their ability to find faculty or staff mentors.

Based on the results of the analysis, African-American students and other students of color reported dissatisfaction with their interaction with other students on campus more than did their Caucasian counterparts. These findings were consistent with a study reported by Liu and Liu (1999). They reported that there was a tendency to experience marginality and isolation among African-American students who attended Anglo higher education institutions. In this study, 45% of African-American students claimed that they did not feel involved in their university's general campus life. Similarly, Nora and Cabrera (1996) and Gonzalez (2000) found that students of color often believed that their school environments were discriminatory, and LaFore (2001) noted that students of color needed shared experiences, social inclusion, and culture-affirming experiences in order to feel satisfied and persist in higher education.

Based on the results of the study, African-American students and other students of color reported dissatisfaction with their ability to find faculty or staff mentors more than did their Caucasian peers. LaFore (2001) supported these findings and asserted that faculty members should be active in the recruitment of, commitment to, and availability to minority students. C. Ford (1996) and LaVant, Anderson, and Tiggs (1997) argued the need for mentoring and empowering minority students, which included the need for increased faculty availability to minority students.

The researchers verified the support of previously reported research, as well as verified the present findings, to the contribution of the already-existing body of knowledge. Retention models have revealed that when college students' expectations were met, the students expressed higher levels of satisfaction and were more likely to be retained (Braxton et al., 1995; Bank & Biddle, 1992). The extensive retention research by Levitz and Noel (2001b) indicated that even though moderately dissatisfied students may remain at their institutions, these same students may urge their acquaintances not to enroll. Because most institutions have historically recruited from the same neighborhoods and high schools each year, this dissatisfaction may have had a large impact on the recruitment of students.

Based on the findings of this study, the following recommendations have been suggested for administrators, faculty, and staff at the university studied as well as other similar higher education institutions:

1.  Because the largest group of prospective students contributing to enrollment growth during the next 15–20 years will likely come from increasing populations of minority students (LaFore, 2001), more attention should be given to minority student populations. African-American students and other students of color reported dissatisfaction with their interaction with other students on campus more than did their Caucasian counterparts. LaFore noted that students of color needed shared experiences, social inclusion, and culture-affirming experiences in order to feel satisfied and thus persist in higher education. Administrators and educators should make sure these students of color are involved in general campus life. It is also recommended that students of color at the university studied be allowed to freely express their uniqueness within the confines of the university's honor code and culture. Additionally, administrators and educators at the university studied, as well as others in higher education, should, to a greater degree and more intentionally, celebrate ethnic holidays and freely discuss multicultural issues in their classrooms and elsewhere.

2.  Faculty members should be active in the recruitment of, and the commitment and availability to their students of color. Faculty members should be willing to mentor and empower all of their students, being careful not to exclude their students of color. Because students of color reported dissatisfaction with their ability to find a faculty or staff mentor more than did their Caucasian peers, faculty members should

make attempts to be overtly available through the use of clear verbal and nonverbal directions as to their office hours and their willingness to mentor their students. Attention should be given to students of color through peer counseling, as well as effective advising, mentoring, and tutoring. It is also recommended that administrators provide faculty and staff members with training regarding sensitivity toward diversity and the understanding of multicultural issues.

3. The university studied consists of approximately 26% non-Caucasian students, 10.4% non-Caucasian faculty members, and 21% non-Caucasian staff members. Faculty and staff demographics should more closely approximate student demographics because students naturally gravitate toward mentors of like ethnicity with similar backgrounds. It is recommended that qualified faculty and staff of color be actively recruited to fill positions as they become available. In addition to the demographic argument for actively recruiting qualified staff and faculty members of color, another educational reason is that diversity on campus lends a more robust exchange of ideas and a variety of perspectives to the campus community (C. Easterling, personal communication, March 7, 2002).

4. It is recommended that all faculty members at the university studied invite qualified guest speakers from varied ethnic backgrounds to be directly involved in campus life; this would help satisfy the need for an increased number of experiences for all students, but especially students of color.

5. It is recommended that all faculty members at the university studied assess their curricula choices to determine their relevance to multicultural issues. Furthermore, faculty members should intentionally show films and videos depicting people from varied ethnic groups and utilize examples in literature that include multicultural awareness.

6. Faculty should be willing to engage in meaningful, connected relationships with students (Pascarella et al., 1986; Rosenthal et al., 2000; Tinto, 1993; Noel, 2001). Research has suggested that frequent contact with faculty members has been an important element of student persistence and satisfaction (Pascarella & Terenzini, 1979; Pascarella & Wolfle, 1985;

Stage, 1989), and such contact has been especially effective when it has gone beyond classroom contact into informal settings (Stage, 1989). It is recommended that faculty members be encouraged to invite student groups into their homes and participate in student activities such as retreats, sporting events, and fine arts programs.

7. Future research is recommended in the area of trend analysis at the university studied. Trend analysis could be conducted utilizing a series of College Student Survey results since the university studied has results from 1998, 2001, and more recently, 2002. This analysis could reveal trends in the variables in this study: student satisfaction and ethnicity.

8. Future research is recommended in the area of ethnicity at the university studied. When examining the ethnicity variable, the researchers did not ascertain the difference in responses between the American students of color and the many international students of color who attend the university studied. Furthermore, ethnic groups other than Caucasian and African American should be further researched due to their small representation in this study. When measuring student satisfaction levels, future research should isolate the ethnicity variable and break it down further.

# References

Anderson, E. (2001, July). *The force field analysis of college student persistence.* Paper presented at the National Conference on Student Retention, New Orleans, LA.

Astin, A. W. (1970). The methodology of research on college impact, part 1. *Sociology of Education, 43*(3), 243-254.

Astin, A. W. (1975). *Preventing students from dropping out.* San Francisco: Jossey-Bass.

Astin, A. W. (1993, September 22). College retention rates are often misleading. *The Chronicle of Higher Education,* 1-5.

Attinasi, L. C. (1989). Getting in: Mexican Americans' perceptions of university attendance and the implications for freshmen year persistence. *Journal of Higher Education, 60,* 274-277.

Baker, S., & Pomerantz, N. (2000). Impact of learning communities on retention at a metropolitan university. *Journal of College Student Retention, 2*(2), 115-126.

Bandler, J. (1999, September 22). Students give Harvard law their wish list. *Wall Street Journal,* p. NE1.

Bank, B. J., Biddle, B. (1992). What do students want?: Expectations and undergraduate persistence. *The Sociological Quarterly, 33*(3), 321-329.

Bernal, M. E., Saenz, D. S., & Knight, G. P. (1991). Ethnic identity and adaptation of Mexican American youths in school settings. *Hispanic Journal of Behavioral Sciences, 13,* 135-154.

Braunstein, A., & McGrath, M. (1997). The retention of freshmen students: An examination of the assumptions, beliefs, and perceptions held by college administrators and faculty. *College Student Journal, 31*(2), 188-200.

Braxton, J. M., Milem, J. F., & Sullivan, A. S. (2000). The influence of active learning on the college student departure process. *The Journal of Higher Education, 71,* 569-90.

Braxton, J. M., Vesper, N., & Hossler, D. (1995). Expectations for college and student persistence. *Research in Higher Education, 36*(5), 595-611.

Cabrera, A. F., & Nora, A. (1996). College students' perceptions of prejudice and discrimination and their feelings of alienation. *Review of Education, Pedagogy, and Cultural Studies, 16,* 384-409.

Davalos, D. B., Chavez, E. L., & Guardiola, R. J. (1999). The effects of extracurricular activity, ethnic identification, and perception of school on student dropout rates. *Hispanic Journal of Behavioral Sciences, 21*(1), 6-77.

Easterling, C. (2000). ORU students compared with CCCU and other private universities: From 1998 College Student Survey. *ORU Institutional Research:* Tulsa, OK.

Edwards, M., & Cangemi, J. P. (1990, Fall). The college dropout and institutional responsibility. *Education, 111*(1), 107-117. [On-line]. Available: Academic Search Elite: Item #: AN: 9108193090. ISSN: 0013-1172.

Ekstrom, R. B. (1991). *Attitudes toward borrowing and participation in post-secondary education.* Paper presented at the annual meeting of the Association for the Study of Higher Education, Boston, MA.

Endo, J. J., & Harpel, R. L. (1982). The effect of student-faculty interaction on students' educational outcomes. *Research in Higher Education, 16,* 115-135.

Farnum, T., & Williams, B. (2001, July). *The role of faculty in institutional efforts to improve retention.* Paper presented at the National
Conference on Student Retention, New Orleans, LA.

Flemming, J. (1984). *Blacks in college: A comparative study of students'
success in Black and white institutions.* San Francisco: Jossey-Bass
Publishers.

Flemming, J. (1985). *Blacks in college.* San Francisco: Jossey-Bass Publishers.

Ford, C. A. (1996). *Student retention success models in higher education.* Tallahassee, FL: CNJ Associates, Inc.

Fralick, M. A. (1993). College success: A study of positive and negative
attrition. *Community College Review, 20*(5), 29-39.

Frost, W. L. (1999). It takes a community to retain a student: The trinity
law school model. *Journal of College Student Retention: Research,
Theory, & Practice, 1*(3), 203-224.

Gardner, C. J. (1998). Keeping students in school: Christian colleges
seek to improve retention rate. *Christianity Today, 42*(10), 34. [On-
line]. Available: Academic Search Elite: Item #: AN: 1015885. ISSN:
0009-5753.

Gay, L. R. (1992). *Educational research: Competencies for analysis and
application* (4th ed.). NY: MacMillan Publishing Company.

Gibson, J., Ivancevich, J., & Donnelly, J. (2000). *Organizations: Behavior, structure, and processes* (10th ed.). Boston: McGraw Hill.

Gladieux, L. E., & Swail, W. S. (2000, May). Beyond Access: Improv-
ing the Odds of College Success. *Phi Delta Kappan, 81*(9), 688-673.
[On-line]. Available: Academic Search Elite Item: AN: 3078356,
ISSN: 0031-7217.

Gonzalez, K. P. (2000). Toward a theory of minority student participation in predominantly white colleges and universities. *Journal of College Student Retention, 2*(1), 69-91.

Hauser, R. M., & Anderson, D. K. (1991). Post-high school plans and
aspirations of black and white high school seniors: 1976-86. *Sociology of Education, 64,* 263-277.

Higher Education Research Institute (2001). *Cooperative Institution Research Program.* Los Angeles: University of California.

House, J. D. (1999). The effects of entering characteristics and instructional experiences on student satisfaction and degree completion. *International Journal of Instructional Media, 26,* 423.

Hu, S., & St. John, E. P. (2001). Student persistence in a public higher education system: Understanding racial and ethnic differences. *The Journal of Higher Education, 72*(3), 265-286.

Johnson, J. L. (1997). Commuter college students: What factors determine who will persist and who will drop out? *College Student Journal, 31,* 323-332.

Johnson, J. L. (2000). Learning communities and special efforts in the retention of university students: What works, what doesn't, and is the return worth the investment? *Journal of College Student Retention: Research, Theory, & Practice, 2*(3), 219-238.

Johnson, J. L., & Romanoff, S. J. (1999). Higher education residential learning communities: What are the implications for student success? *College Student Journal, 33*(3), 385-399.

Killingsworth, B. L., Hayden, M. B., & Dellana, S. A. (1999). Total quality involvement in the classroom: Integrating TQM in a systems analysis and design course. *College Student Journal, 33*(3), 465-467.

Koyama, J. T., & Lee, Y. T. (1989, May). *Asian Americans at Berkley. A Report to the Chancellor.* Berkley, CA: University of California.

Kue, G. D., & Love, P. G. (2000). A cultural perspective on student departure. In J.M. Braxton (Ed.), *Reworking the Student Departure Puzzle* (pp. 196-212). Nashville: Vanderbilt University Press.

LaFore, V. J. (2001, July). *Recruiting students of color.* Paper presented at the National Conference on Student Retention, New Orleans, LA.

LaVant, B. D., Anderson, J. L., & Tiggs, J. W. (1997). Retaining African American men through mentoring initiatives. *New Directions for Student Services, 80,* 43-53.

Leach, B. (1987). How to retain black students on predominantly white campuses. *Black Issues in Higher Education, 4*(7), 36.

Levin, J. R., & Levin, M. E. (1991). A critical examination of academic retention programs for at-risk minority college students. *Journal of College Student Development, 32,* 323-334.

Levitz, R., & Noel, L. (2001b, July). *The earth-shaking but quiet revolution in retention management.* Paper presented at the National Conference on Student Retention, New Orleans, LA.

Liu, E., & Liu, R. (1999). An application of Tinto's model at a commuter campus. *Education, 119*(3), 537-541.

McGrath, M., & Braunstein, A. (1997). The prediction of freshmen attrition: An examination of the importance of certain demographic, academic, financial, and social factors. *College Student Journal, 31*(3), 396-408.

Mortenson, T. G. (1989). Attitudes toward educational loans. *Journal of Student Financial Aid, 19,* 38-51.

Mortenson, T. G., & Wu, Z. (1990). *High school graduation and college participation of young adults by family income backgrounds: 1970-1989.* Iowa City, IA: American College Testing Program.

Murtaugh, P. A., Burns, L. D., & Schuster, J. (1999). Predicting the retention of university students. *Research in Higher Education, 40*(3), 355-371.

Noel, L. (2001, July). *Reaching the next level of excellence in recruitment and retention.* Paper presented at the National Conference on Student Retention, New Orleans, LA.

Noel, L., & Levitz, R. (2001). *National Student Satisfaction Report.* USA Group Noel-Levitz, Inc.

Nora, A., & Cabrera, A. F. (1996). The role of perceptions of prejudice and discrimination of the adjustment of minority students to college. *Journal of Higher Education, 67*(2), 119-148.

Olivas, M. A. (1985). Financial aid packaging policies: Access and ideology. *Journal of Higher Education, 56,* 462-475.

Pascarella, E. T., Duby, P. B., & Iverson, B. K. (1983). A test and reconceptualization of a theoretical model of college withdrawal in a commuter institution setting. *Sociology of Education, 56,* 88-100.

Pascarella, E. T., Smart, J., & Ethington, C. (1986). Long-term persistence of two-year college students. *Research in Higher Education, 24*(1), 47-71.

Pascarella, E. T., & Terenzini, P. T. (1977). Patterns of student-faculty informal interaction beyond the classroom and voluntary freshmen attrition. *Journal of Higher Education, 5,* 540-552.

Pascarella, E. T., & Terenzini, P. T. (1979). Interaction effects in Spady's and Tinto's conceptual model of college dropout. *Sociology of Education, 52,* 197-210.

Pascarella, E. T., & Wolfle, L. (1985). *Persistence in higher education: A nine-year test of a theoretical model.* Paper presented at the annual meeting of the American Educational Research Association, Chicago, IL.

Person, D. R. (1994). Black and Hispanic women in higher education. In F. Rivera-Batiz (Ed.), *Reinventing urban education* (pp. 303-326). New York: IUME Press.

Person, D. R., & Christensen, M. C. (1996). Understanding black student culture and black student retention. *NASPA Journal, 34,* 47-56.

Pincus, F. (1980). The false promise of community colleges: Class conflict and vocational education. *Harvard Educational Review, 50,* 332-361.

Porter, O. F. (1990). *Undergraduate completion and persistence at four-year colleges and universities.* Washington, DC: The National Institute of Independent Colleges and Universities.

Rendon, L. I., Jalomo, R. E., & Nora, A. (2000). Theoretic considerations in the study of minority student retention in higher education. In J.M. Braxton (Ed.), *Reworking the Student Departure Puzzle* (pp. 127-156). Nashville: Vanderbilt University Press.

Retention rates drop for Georgia's HOPE Scholars. (1999). *Black Issues in Higher Education, 16*(6), 10-11.

Richardson, R. C. (1997). A review of the book: Student retention success models in higher education. *Black Issues in Higher Education, 13,* 46-47.

Richardson, R., & Bender, L. (1987). *Fostering minority access and achievement in higher education.* San Francisco: Jossey-Bass.

Robbins, T. L., & Fredendall, L. D. (2001). Correlates of team success in higher education. *The Journal of Social Psychology, 141*(1), 135-136.

Rosenthal, G. T., Folse, E. J., Alleman, N. W., Boudreaux, D., Soper, B., & vonBergen, C. (2000). The one-to-one survey: Traditional versus non traditional student. *College Student Journal, 34,* 315.

Sanders, L., & Burton, D. (1996). From retention to satisfaction: New outcomes for assessing the freshman experience. *Research in Higher Education, 37,* 555-567.

Seymour, E. (1993, April 10). *Why are the women leaving?* Lecture presented at the NECUSE Conference.

Sewell, W., & Hauser, R. (1980). The Wisconsin longitudinal study of social and psychological factors in aspirations and achievements. In A. Kerckhoff (Ed.), Research in the sociology of education and sociology of education and socialization. Greenwich, CT: JAI Press.

Simpson, R. D., & Frost, S. H. (1993). *Who goes to college and why? Inside college: Undergraduate education for the future.* New York: Insight Books/Plenum Press.

Smitherman, H. O., & Carr, L. L. (1981). Persistence patterns of non-curricular students in community college. *Community/Junior College Research Quarterly, 5,* 367-375.

Smitherman, C. E. (1997). Implications of considering students as consumers. *College Teaching, 45,* 122.

# Part Two

Religion, Diversity, and Culture

# Two Faiths, Both Alike in Dignity: An Assessment of Muslim and Hindu Paradigms of the God–World Relationship

## Dr. Randall B. Bush

"Two households, both alike in dignity, In fair Verona where we lay our scene. . . ." Thus begins the prologue to Shakespeare's immortal play, *Romeo and Juliet*. The tale of unflagging enmity and relentless strife between two households is familiar and universal. Wherever the differences between people-groups are exaggerated to the point that life's passion is spent fueling the hatred and demonizing of the other, the story is repeated. Furthermore, what is true of households on the small scale is often true of larger households of culture and faith. Religions may have rich traditions—and in that respect may possess great dignity—but how often does that dignity plummet to ignominy where worldviews propel cultures and peoples toward hellish Armageddons of their own making?

If a place exists where I might first lay the scene of conflict between two great households of faith, then that place could very well be the Kashmir on the border between Pakistan and India in the aftermath of the partitioning of India in 1947. The bloodbath that ensued between Muslims and Hindus after that dreadful event is one of the sadder chapters of human history. There, we find a place where the image of God, reflected

---

**Dr. Randall B. Bush** is Professor of Philosophy and Christian Studies, and he is the Director of Interdisciplinary Honors at Union University in Jackson, TN.

in the human family, has been fragmented and distorted almost beyond recognition, and a place where the Logos of reconciliation that the Christian faith knows to be revealed in Jesus Christ scarcely can be found.

The religious and political conflicts that plague this densely populated region of our planet have also spilled over into places to which people from that region have immigrated—Great Britain and the United States among others. The 7 July 2005 London bombings, committed by young Pakistani males, could have as easily occurred in New York City, which, according to the 2000 United States Census, saw the Pakistani population increase by 154% over the decade of the '90s—from 13,501 in 1990 to 34,310 in 2000—the largest increase of any Asian population in that ten year period (Census Profile, 2000, n.p.).[1] Of all Asian groups, the Pakistani population was poorer, less literate, and featured more persons residing per household. Many have come to Western societies like the United States seeking refuge from conflict only to find microcosms where the conflict continues. According to Prema Kurien, the conflict between Indians of Muslim and Hindu descent, far from abating after immigrating to the United States, has intensified over political issues of what it means to be Indian. This is due to a variety of factors such as the effects upon their identity of marginalization by the larger society and the growing importance that religious identity and ethnicity plays for them because of such marginalization (Kurien, 2001, p. 265). If one adds to this already volatile mix of native hostilities the clash between traditional Islamic or Hindu values, and the opposite course charted by America's open culture and socio-economic system, then one can better understand how these conflicts can be projected into, and reenacted in, new arenas.[2]

In order to see the larger picture, one needs to understand how worldviews fostered by belief-paradigms affect cultural and political realities that boil over into horrific cultural conflicts. In the cases of Islam and Hinduism, there could hardly be two more diametrically opposed religious belief systems. My purpose in this paper will be to delineate some of these differences before attempting to demonstrate how a Christian Trinitarian paradigm may help us understand exactly how the Christian faith can be inclusive of the best aspects of the world's cultural diversity. By attempting to understand the larger picture, I hope to provide a more adequate Christian worldview out of which Christian practitioners of the social sciences can operate more effectively.

First, what is the Islamic conception of God, and how does that conception influence geopolitical and cultural realities? In Islam, the ideal of raw power is elevated to universal status and for the most part characterizes what is meant by the proposition "God." However, from a Christian standpoint this proposition must be deemed deficient in content insofar as Allah's wisdom fails to be grounded in an adequate conception of Allah's inner nature.[3] Since Allah's nature is utterly inscrutable, his exercise of power appears to be arbitrary.[4] Furthermore, while the distinction in Judaism and Christianity between God's inner nature on the one hand, and His disposition and actions toward human beings (i.e., His will) on the other, translates into the believer's confidence that he/she can know and discern the will of God with a high degree of confidence and trust in God's goodness, this is not equally true of Islam.[5] Since Allah has no constant nature in which his will is anchored, the believer can only respond with acts of blind submission.[6] Such acts of submission have no other rational basis than that of the believer's helplessness in the face of Allah's superior and overwhelming might.[7] Indeed, "might-makes-right" serves as the ultimate rational basis for the believer's acts of submission.

"*Allabu Akbar*"—"God is most great" is the cry that resounds from minarets and mosques. Yes, God is great, but is He good? While the goodness of God in Christian and Hebrew belief is a dimension of the constant reality of his inner nature, in Islam, the goodness of Allah is made completely relative to the power category. One is reminded of the following *non causa pro causa* paradox: Is good only good because God wills it, or does God will something because it is good. In Islam, the former card trumps the latter. In Christianity, the discussion of how best to conceive of the relationship between God's will and His nature came to a head in the debate between the Thomists and the Scotists in the thirteenth century. The followers of Thomas Aquinas emphasized the priority of the Divine Intellect over the Divine Will (Aquinas, trans. 1972, *Summa Theol.* I. q. 19, a. 1 & ad. 2), while the followers of Duns Scotus emphasized the priority of the Divine Will over the Divine Intellect (Scotus, trans. 1997, *On the Will and Morality*, pt. 4. 16); however, neither of these schools went so far as to allow one of these emphases to obliterate the other. Even among the Medieval Nominalists where the doctrine of God's absolute potential (*potentia absoluta*) was stressed, God's power of ordination (*potentia ordinata*) was equally stressed. This latter distinction became the basis for the Nominalists' affirmation that

God could be trusted despite his ways of acting appearing sometimes to the human observer as arbitrary and inexplicable. By contrast, while Islam has a doctrine of the divine *potentia absoluta*, its doctrine of the *potentia ordinata* lacks the level of consistency found in the Jewish and Christian versions of this doctrine.

The Islamic understanding of Allah and the nature of the Muslim's relationship to Allah translate into politics and culture in significant ways. Islam's brand of monotheism has been labeled totalitarian, and certainly totalitarian cultural and political thinking have been more endemic to Islam than to Christianity or Judaism.[8] The correspondence between divine totalitarianism and human totalitarianism is expressed in the *Shahada*, or the recitation of the creed, "There is no God but Allah, and Mohammad is the prophet of Allah." The One God corresponds to the one prophet, and the one prophet, to the One God. Therefore, what is true concerning Allah tends also to be true concerning his prophet.[9] The power of God knows no restraint; the power of the prophet knows no restraint except that placed on him by Allah. What this restraint exactly entails is often unclear. The prophet with unfettered tongue utters the words of the Qur'an freely in the original holy language of Arabic. He becomes the sole mouthpiece of Allah, and whoever disputes this claim is deemed an infidel. There are no plurality of witnesses, no myriad of voices, no tedious process of canonization of the Holy Scriptures, and no checks and balances as one finds in both Jewish and Christian traditions concerning Scriptures' canonization.[10] The word of the one prophet is final and indisputable. Mohammad does not sum up the voices of the past; he negates them and replaces them. Because all other voices are rendered mute, the Qur'an, unlike the New Testament which depends upon the Hebrew Scriptures for the explication of its fuller meaning, needs no other Scripture to support it. Indeed, the Hebrew and Christian Scriptures are considered to be corrupt and unworthy of the least amount of attention so that for the Islamic scholar there is no other reason to study them than to refute them (Watt, 1991, p. 33).[11]

One finds as well an understanding of the role of the prophet in Islam that is quite different from that found in Judaism and Christianity. In Judaism, the prophetic and kingly roles do not merge as they do in Islam. In fact, the opposite is true. The prophets of the Hebrew Scripture, especially in the period before the Babylonian exile, contested the presumptions of kingly power. Saul knew his Samuel (1 Sam 15:1-28), David, his Nathan (2 Sam 12:1-15), and Ahab, his Elijah (1 Kings 18:16-45).

This conflict between prophetic wisdom and royal power was also extended into Christian thought in a significant way. Even though New Testament writers portray Jesus both as a prophet and a king, these aspects of His work are kept separate.[12] Evidence of this exists in the so-called Messianic Secret Motif first recognized by Wilhelm Wrede (Cranfield, 1962, vol. 3, p. 273), but which he also misconstrued.[13] What was Jesus' reason for enjoining His disciples to tell no one that He was the messiah? (Mark 8:29-30). The reason must be that the meaning of the word "messiah" in first century Judaism was laden with all kinds of political innuendos that Jesus wanted to avoid. Most Jews of the first century desired the coming of a political messiah who would throw off the yoke of Roman domination. The Sicarii or Zealots, one sect of Judaism at the time, wished for a return to the days of the Maccabees when the Jews had known independence from foreign oppressors. Jesus did, of course, go on to die a martyr's death, and in this respect, He suffered the fate of a prophet. In fact, the kingly designation could only properly be attributed to Jesus when viewed through the lenses of His resurrection. The gospel of Mark makes this especially clear. This distinction between Christ's prophetic role and His kingly role became extremely influential in the Christian tradition. Even during times when popes and emperors overstepped this theological boundary, voices of prophetic protest arose within Christendom that countered the abuse of power.

Unfortunately, Islam neither shares with Christianity and Judaism this understanding of the prophetic role, nor does it appreciate the importance of maintaining the separation of the prophetic function from the political function. Mohammad was not only a prophet; he was also a military leader. In this respect he was more like a king than a prophet in the Judeo-Christian sense. In fact, the merging of the prophetic and kingly functions in the person of Mohammad set a dangerous precedent in Islamic politics that extends across history to the present day. After the division of the Islamic world into the Sunni and Shiite factions that transpired because of the martyrdom of al-Husayn and his family in C.E. 680, the Islamic world lost its hope of achieving a unified religion under one God and one prophet (Esposito, 1999, p. 663). Now, the long succession of Caliphs in Sunni Islam is countered by the succession of Imams among the Shiites (Ayubi, 1991, pp. 1-10). Neither group accepts the other as legitimate; however, the ideal of one God, one prophet, still captivates the Muslim imagination (Vatikiotis, 1991, p. 67).[14] This is without question the ideal to which such groups as al-Qaeda and the

Islamic Brotherhood wish to return, and the main objective of their campaign of terror against the West is to rid Muslim lands of all traces of Western influence and interference (Brooke, 2004, n.p.) including the very idea of nationalism, which is viewed by radical Islamists as a Western construct inimical to Islam (Vatikiotis, 1991, p. 62). However, their vision of this ideal pristine totalitarian unity has taken an extremely nihilistic turn,[15] as Roger Scruton (2002) observes,

> It rejects the modern state and its secular law in the name of a "brotherhood" that reaches secretly to all Muslim hearts, uniting them against the infidel. And because its purpose is religious rather than political, the goal is incapable of realization. The Muslim Brotherhood failed even to change the political order of Egypt, let alone to establish itself as a model of Koranic government throughout the Muslim world. Where Islamists succeed in gaining power—as in Iran, Sudan, and Afghanistan—the result is not the reign of peace and piety promised by the Prophet, but murder and persecution on a scale matched in our time only by the Nazis and the Communists. The Islamist, like the Russian nihilist, is an exile in this world; and when he succeeds in obtaining power over his fellow human beings, it is in order to punish them for being human (Scruton, n.p.).

The jockeying for power among Islamic political aspirants strangely resembles the immortals in the Sci-Fi movie Highlander, where one immortal, in order to hold on to his immortality, must decapitate his immortal competitor. "In the end, there can be only one" goes the refrain. This is a sad exaltation of the individual human ego—and the male more than the female ego—to a position that rivals the prerogatives Allah himself.

Another way in which Islam's totalitarian paradigm is expressed in Islamic religion and culture is in the pervasiveness of Islamic *sharia* law, which governs the minutest aspects of Muslim life. Because the rationale for "submission" to Allah, as described above, is grounded not in his inner nature but in his arbitrary and inscrutable Will, obedience to his laws ceases to be a means toward an end and instead becomes an end in itself. This understanding of law is, from the majority of Christian standpoints, one-dimensional and absolutist. All laws are given equal importance, so that regulations governing eating and human cleanliness are as equally binding as those governing familial and social relations. "The all-embracing nature of Islamic Law can be seen from the fact that it does not distinguish between ritual, law (in the European sense of the word), ethics and good manners" (Totalitarian nature of Islam, n.d., n.p.). The elevation of trivial legal minutiae to a position of ultimate significance creates a disadvantage for the Muslim mind in that it is habituated not to see distinctions between what may be deemed of greater or lesser importance. Because the Muslim mind is conditioned from birth to see all things in terms of black and white and is prone to exaggeration and hyperbole, it often fails to recognize and appreciate the subtleties and ambiguities of life (Vatikiotis, 1991, p. 69). In this respect, Islamic *sharia* law resembles in a very remarkable way that legalism of Pharisaic Judaism which Jesus continually challenged. Christianity understands that God's intention in giving the law was not to exact from His people sheer obedience for the sake of obedience but was a means of reaching a higher apprehension and appreciation of God's reality. For this reason, early Christians radically rethought how they would relate to Jewish regulations such as circumcision and dietary practices.

As in Pharisaic Judaism, Islam's emphasis on sheer obedience for the sake of obedience can curtail human freedom, stunt human development, inhibit human creativity, and interfere with humanity's recognition of its need for grace and forgiveness. In the end only one—the prophet, the caliph, the imam—can be free. The duty of all others is to submit without question. The truncating of human freedom, development, and creativity—and not the capitalistic aspirations of the West—is the major reason for the loss of vitality in the Islamic world and the backward-looking focus of its present course. Where repentance and the acceptance of divine forgiveness can provide the Christian the opportunity for reformation of character and improvement, the lack of this emphasis in Islam can cause qualities and acts of humility, introspection, and repentance to give way to pride, blame, and resentment.

Hinduism represents such a diverse group of faiths that the American Academy of Religion a number of years ago changed its program to read "Hinduisms" to reflect its pluralistic nature (AAR online program book, 2001, n.p.). Hindus are admittedly more pluralistic than Muslims, a fact that no doubt has contributed to the Muslim categorization of Hinduism as a polytheistic religion against which jihad should be waged. Truly, Hinduism could hardly be more opposite in its understanding of the God-world relation than Islam. Where Islam is at its heart exclusive of all those who do not follow its beliefs and practices in the most formal way, Hinduism is inclusive and tolerant of virtually every path to God.

Furthermore, where Islam elevates the ideal of raw power to an ultimate universal status, Hinduism elevates to this status the category of sublime wisdom. This stress on God as sublime wisdom helps one understand why Hinduism is more philosophical and reflective in character than Islam. However, where Allah in Islam is the principle that *determines and directs* every aspect of reality, Brahman, the highest expression of deity in Hinduism, remains detached and separate from the phenomenal world. Brahman is not a God of power like the Yahweh of the Hebrew Scriptures, or Allah of the Qur'an, but is *laissez faire* in his relation to the world. Brahman (the highest expression of God) functions as an *inspiring ideal* of transcendent wisdom that persuades those souls that have become separated from Brahman to return to Brahman. Unlike the Hebrew God, whose power and will is manifested concretely and tangibly throughout history, Brahman's power does not extend beyond Brahman's reality into the world of human affairs in any discernibly purposeful way. Although Brahman's wisdom does become accessible to human beings through the incarnations of Vishnu, the lack of a focus on the power principle does help explain why the worldview of Hinduism is a-historical. History, time, and the physical world possess no positive ontological value. As a result, their significance in the scheme of things is devalued. The absence of the idea of a God of direction and determination also explains why the Holy Scriptures of Hinduism, the *Vedas*, the *Upanishads*, and the *Bhagavad Gita* are mythological and/or philosophical rather than of an historical nature.

Of the myths that describe the creation of the world and of humankind, the Rig-Vedic myth of the sacrifice of Cosmic Man or Parusha stands as the most important for the way that Hindu society was traditionally structured. From the sacrifice of Purusha, the four principle castes of Hinduism were believed to have been derived—the Brahmin (priestly) from his head, the Kshatriya (princely) from his arms, the Vaisya (worker) from his legs, and the Shudra (slave) from his feet (*Rig Veda*, trans. 1966/1979, 10. 90. 10-13). These castes were hierarchically arranged in a chain of being ranging from the noble to the base. The original doctrine of *varna* or color privileged the light-skinned *Aryans* over the dark-skinned *Dasas* whom they had conquered upon migrating into the Indian subcontinent about 2000 B. C. E., though the literal meaning of *varna* does not have the bearing on caste today that it once did. (Noss & Noss, 1994, pp. 86-87) The hierarchical arrangement of society, however, does place greater value and importance on higher castes than on lower ones, and the paradigm fits neatly with the schema of sin, punishment, and salvation that constitutes the central meta-narrative of Hindu religion. One version of this meta-narrative is found in the *Bridhadaranyaka Upanishad* where the flame and smoke of the sacrificial fire are related to ideas of karmic law and the cycle of rebirth (*samsara*). The smoke of the sacrificial fire symbolizes this cycle: The smoke ascends to heaven to make the clouds which return to earth as rain and feed the vegetation that is eaten by physical beings. It is finally offered up as semen in the act of copulation, resulting in conception and birth (or rebirth). The fire of the sacrificial altar, by contrast, symbolizes the uniting of souls with the sun in its long journey northward. The souls proceed from there to the world of the *Devas* (gods) and ultimately to the world of Brahman from whence they will not return (*Bridhadaranyaka Upanishad, Adhyaya*, trans. 1884/1989, *Adhyaya* 6, *Brahmana* 2: 9-16).

One sad result of the Hindu belief in karma and reincarnation has been the entrenchment of systemic injustice created and perpetuated by the caste system, which still persists in modern India despite efforts of the Indian government to abolish it. Because the physical world—the world of *maya* or illusion—serves as a kind of purgatory in which souls are punished for sins committed in previous incarnations, there is very little incentive on the part of higher castes to improve the lot in life of those at the bottom of the social ladder.[16] Indeed, one could argue that to help someone improve one's status in the physical world is to interfere with justly deserved divine retribution. This outcome is true despite the fact that one of the central doctrines of Rig-Vedic Hinduism is *tat tvam asi* (that are thou) the belief that all living beings are sacred and share a spiritual unity with Brahman (*Chandogya Upanishad*, trans. 1900/1988, *Prapathaka* 6, *Khandas* 8-11). The Hindu respect for the sanctity of life does not, however, rise to the level of active compassion for the poor and oppressed such as one finds in the prophetic tradition of Judaism or in pristine Christianity but expresses itself instead as benign indifference.

On one front, benign indifference can be observed in lax attitudes towards the pursuit of pleasure (*kama*) by less enlightened peoples (Smith, 1991, pp. 14-15) as well as the explicit sexual imagery used by those who worship gods of sex and procreation such as Shiva and Shakti, whose symbols are, respectively, the lingum (phallus) and the yoni (vagina) (Noss & Noss, pp. 137-40). The attitude of more enlightened Hindus toward the worship of gods of sex and procreation is not to condemn but to tolerate it. Active moral directives, prohibitions, or taboos against human sexual excess are therefore discouraged. One cannot help but think that tolerance towards such excess placed those engaging in it at a disadvantage when the AIDS crisis first emerged. Such a lack of precaution might cause one to forfeit one's life before one was even able to think about curbing one's behavior. In retrospect, one might ask if those who were more enlightened might have been kinder if they had been less tolerant of such excess.

On another, more philosophical, front, the great Hindu scholar Sarvepalli Radhakrishnan issued his opinion concerning the superiority of Hinduism to Christianity when he claimed that the Christian religion represents a lower level or less developed stage of enlightenment than what philosophical Hinduism has obtained. Radhakrishnan's argument was that Christianity is inferior to Hinduism because it emphasizes a personal God who becomes incarnate in a particular man, Jesus Christ (Neill, 1961, pp. 83-84). Radhakrishnan's emphases upon the impersonal nature of Brahman, and upon the eclectic and universal character of his own Hindu faith, led him to deem Christianity, with its excessive emphasis on particularity, as inferior. However, in the light of what I have just noted about Huston Smith's characterization of Hindu attitudes toward the pursuit of pleasure and sexual excess, one might question whether the emphasis on particularity which Radhakrisnan viewed as a weakness is really as much of a weakness as he claimed. May not this weakness be viewed from another vantage-point as Christianity's strength, as the Apostle Paul argues in 1 Corinthians 1:18-28 concerning the wisdom of the cross which the Greeks count as foolishness? Repeated emphases on particularity in Christian theology—its doctrine of a good creation, its affirmation of the personal involvement of God with his people, its doctrine of the Incarnation and servant-hood of God in Jesus, and its focus upon the Cross—do in fact seem to offer not a less inclusive understanding of universality than the one Radhakrishnan espoused, but a more inclusive one. Christianity's brand of inclusion is more universal precisely because the universality espoused by philosophical Hinduism is, at its very base, exclusive of particularity and therefore elitist. Where in Christianity universality embraces particularity in order to redeem it, in philosophical Hinduism, the universal excludes the material world and deems particularity as merely illusory.

The attitude of benign indifference I have just referred to has, of course, been modified in India, but this only occurred because of the work of the great social reformer, Mohandas Gandhi, who himself, being a Vaisya, defied the wishes of the *Modh Bania* of his caste and was made an outcast when he traveled to England to study (The caste system, n.d., n.p.). As a person of color, Gandhi was a victim of the racial discrimination, which characterized South African society at the time. His experiences there led to his engagement in the kind of social activism that was to characterize the rest of his life. Upon returning to India, Gandhi's family managed to get him reinstated into his caste, but Gandhi was forever changed by his experiences in England and South Africa. The Mahatma engaged in the work of untouchables and insisted that others under his authority, including his wife, do so as well. Through his Satyagraha movement, he did more to raise the status of untouchables in India than any other Hindu leader since his time.

I do not think, however, that one can support the view that Gandhi's Satyagraha initiative was grounded wholly in his native Hindusim as he himself so often claimed.[17] Other sources figure as influences on his thought—for instance, the writings of Leo Tolstoy and Christian artist and socialist John Ruskin's book, *Unto This Last* (Neill, 1961, pp.80-81). To be sure, Gandhi was unimpressed with inauthentic forms of Christianity practiced during the late Victorian era; hence his famous assertion, "I like your Christ, I do not like your Christians. Your Christians are so unlike your Christ." At the same time, however, he enthusiastically embraced the egalitarianism and simplicity of life that characterized Tolstoy's and Ruskin's versions of Christianity.

I wish at this point that I could assert that Christianity historically has held to a more attractive alternative than that offered by Hinduism's wisdom model of God, but this has not always been the case. Forms of Christianity that emerged during the third to the fifth centuries were themselves indebted to Indo-Aryan philosophical ideas, most notably to those of Plato and the Neo-Platonists concerning how society should be ordered. One finds the predilection for the class system in Plato's Republic, albeit Plato's classes were not as rigidly fixed as those historically found in the Hindu caste system. Plato, after all, did make allowances for both upward and downward migration between higher and lower classes (Plato, *Republic*, trans. 1930, 3. 415a). Still he approved of slavery, and this sets him at odds with New Testament perspectives (see Paul's epistle to Philemon). Plato's hierarchical notion of government would exert an immense influence on both secular and sacred forms of social organization in the Christian West and would linger in some enclaves up to the present day. Perhaps this is the reason that one of the most multicultural and egalitarian treatises ever written, which appears in the New Testament, strikes many Westerners even today as idealistic. I refer to Luke's second treatise to Theophilus, better remembered as the Acts of the Apostles. In this treatise, that Person of the Holy Trinity known as the Holy Spirit, does not remain an inspiring ideal aloof from the world but descends in power upon the church (Acts 2:1-13). Anyone who has studied inter-biblical and rabbinic Judaism knows that the Spirit (Heb=*ruach*, Gk=*pneuma*) was a cognate idea with Hebraic concepts of wisdom (*hokmah*), word (*memra*), and Torah. The Holy Spirit was not therefore merely associated with enthusiasm as often seems to be the case in recent times. The descent of the Holy Spirit on the Jewish festival of *Shavu'ot* (Weeks or Pentecost) brought to the minds of the earliest Jewish Christians the event of the giving of the Torah to Moses on Mt. Sinai, for Pentecost was a celebration of that event. One rabbinic source mentions that the Torah went forth at that time in the seventy languages of the world.[18] The unknown languages at Pentecost, which were actually existing languages in the world at that time because those present understood in their own tongue, signaled a reversal of the confusion of languages at the Tower of Babel.

The Pentecost event also inaugurates a human equality movement unparalleled in the history of the world up to that time. This emphasis on equality is already found in first-century Judaism because of the role played by the book of Ruth at the Pentecost festival. The Christian Pentecost, however, went a step further. Earlier forms of organization—the insistence for example that there be twelve apostles to correspond numerically to traditional Israelite tribal organization (Acts 1:23-26)—were replaced by non-traditional forms. The Risen Christ elected Saul of Tarsus, the great persecutor of the church, as the thirteenth apostle (Acts 9:1-7), and, in doing so, burst the old wineskin that was the earlier organizational form. Divisions between race and culture were eradicated through the work of the Holy Spirit as Jew and Gentile now supped together, not on standard kosher Jewish cuisine, but on what must have been—from Peter's perspective at least—foods of the most disgusting and indigestible sort (Acts 10:9-13). The rigid divisions between rich and poor were blurred as the early Christian community agreed to share all things in common (Acts 2:43-45). The male-over-female model of authority was also undermined as a teacher of the feminine variety such as Priscilla taught the young Apollos "a more excellent way" (Acts 18:24-

26). Now not only sons, but daughters also would prophesy or preach (Acts 2:17).

A parallel between the Greek text of the Book of Acts and the Greek translation of the Hebrew Scriptures, the Septuagint, reveals that Luke's treatise is a counterpart to the Book of Joshua in the Old Testament.[19] Ideas of conquest are reflected, but the conquest is of a different sort—not conquest realized by means of holy war, but conquest realized through the willingness of martyrs to lay down their lives and to do so without taking hosts of innocent people with them as they go (Acts 7:59). Furthermore, the settlement-of-the-land theme is echoed, not a settlement that eradicates previous inhabitants by the sword,[20] but a settlement that provides a means for the inclusion all peoples, cultures, and languages. This radically differs from Islam, where power is most often executed by force, and from Hinduism, where the highest wisdom remains unattainable for vast numbers of people. Still, the blight upon early Christian communalism by the likes of Ananias and Sapphira who lie to the Holy Spirit about revenues from the sale of their property (Acts 5:1-3) reflects the blight in the Book of Joshua of Achan, who sinned by taking spoils of war in the aftermath of the Battle of Jericho (Joshua 7). Ananias and Sapphira serve as a reminder to us that Christianity is not just to be believed; it is also to be practiced. Certainly we can learn something about our own practice of faith from Gandhi on this count.

When speaking about Islam, I referred to the roles of prophet and king, but Hinduism does not utilize these, at least not in a way identical to Islam. In Hinduism, the important human persona is the *priest* whose main purpose is to offer *sacrifice* (the *agnihotra*) on the fire altar. Priestly and sacrificial rituals constitute the essence of Hinduism from the earliest historical strata of that religion, and this is why the class of priests still occupies the highest place in Hindu society. However, just as the roles of prophet and king *converge* in Islam in a way that is antithetical to Christianity, so do the roles of priest and sacrificial victim remain *wholly separate* in Hinduism in a way that is antithetical to Christianity. I support this claim by pointing out that the priest in Hinduism is concerned above all with issues of purity and detachment from the world of *maya* or illusion. How can the dark weight of matter be expurgated in order that the *atman* (soul) may reunite with Brahman? This is the chief question the Brahmin priest undertakes to answer. The attempt to dispel all darkness and cleanse all matter from the *atman* also explains why a member of the Brahmin caste cannot even look upon an untouchable without contracting ritual pollution. Similar ideas concerning priestly purity and ritual pollution can be found in Judaism (e. g., Lev 5:2-3; 7:21); however, in exilic and post-exilic Judaism the identification of Israel with the "servant of God" led to a convergence and identification of the roles of the servant of God and the sacrificial victim. Isaiah 53, for instance, contains an excurses on vicarious suffering—the suffering of the innocent who were taken into captivity along with the guilty and who suffered vicariously on their behalf.[21] Of course this passage became vastly important as an apologetic for first century Christians as they sought to prove to their fellow Jews that the Old Testament Scriptures taught the concept of a suffering messiah.

The way that priestly and sacrificial imagery are applied to Jesus in the writings of the New Testament is quite different from that which we find in Hinduism. According to the New Testament, the light at the top of the chain of being embraces and redeems those who are in darkness at the bottom of the chain. The Hindu Brahmin priest would view this idea as anathema. The Christian doctrine of the Incarnation, that God became man in Jesus Christ, also teaches the utter identification of God with the lowest of the low. This identification goes well beyond the Hindu concepts of the incarnation of Vishnu as a fish or even as the god Krishna. Krishna is portrayed as an amorous god who seduces as many as six-thousand *gopis* (milkmaids), and according to one Bengali sect, makes love forever with his consort Radha (Noss & Noss, pp. 143-44). Such incarnations lack the moral depth and the intensity of identification with victims of social degradation and oppression such as one finds in the Gospel accounts of Jesus' encounters with poor, outcast, and sinful human beings. Jesus identifies with such and offers them grace, forgiveness, and the prospect for real improvement in the present world, and not just in the world to come. This focus radically differs from that found in Hinduism where so often the lower castes have been sacrificed for the sake of the higher. Where a disconnection exists in Hinduism between the priest and his sacrifice, in Christianity, the Great High Priest *is* the vicarious sacrifice (Heb 4:14-15; 9:11-12). In Christianity there is identification between the two roles.

Because Jewish and Christian conceptions of God and God's relation to the world have continually wrestled with the nature and mystery of the power-wisdom dialectic, these conceptions offer the greatest hope for remediation of cultural perspectives trapped by deficient notions of Deity. I shall proceed to argue here that a paradigm based on a Christian

Trinitarian understanding can offer the best theoretical and practical hope for such remediation.

First, the Christian emphasis on God the Father, which has its roots in the Hebrew understanding of Yahweh's relationship with his people Israel, contains a corrective to the Islamic model of God where raw power is exalted to the status of a universal. At the same time, the Christian emphasis supplements the Hindu view which is wholly lacking the concept of a God who directs and determines the course of creation. Old Testament accounts of manifestations of Yahweh's power may seem arbitrary insofar as one is inside what Ernst Bloch called "the darkness of the lived moment" (Bloch, 1938-1947/1986, vol. 1, p. 287). A retrospective analysis, however, reveals that the *potentia absoluta* and the *potentia ordinata* are dialectically related from the very beginning, although the convergence of the two may not be fully apparent until one has gained the clarity of perspective made possible through reflection over the long haul. Yahweh is not portrayed by the whole of the Hebrew Scriptures, as Carl Jung opined, as an amoral and irrational life-force who somehow learns wisdom from his creature, Job (Jung, 1953-1979, vol. 11, p. 405). When one takes the Hebrew Scriptures as a whole, it is evident that the Wisdom that directs the *potentia ordinata* is fully present from the beginning. Of course, from our perspective this Wisdom appears to be unfolding through the expression of God's inexhaustible potentiality in terms of God's manifestation of his actual power. This manifestation of actual power is in the final analysis not arbitrary but is characterized by a voluntary self-limitation on God's part—what could be called a gradual *kenosis* or self-emptying for the sake of the other. Beginning with the Person of God the Father, this self-limitation is first manifested with the episode of creation and is deepened in God's covenanting with his people Israel in which he pledges unconditional love toward them. Continuing with the Person of God the Son, this self-limitation is further deepened in the Incarnation and reaches its greatest depth in the suffering and death of Jesus upon the Cross. One cannot help but notice the radical contrast between God's vivid displays of power on Mounts Sinai (Exod 19:17-19) and Carmel (1 Kings 18:38), and the silence of God at Mount Calvary (Matt 27:46). Nevertheless, if one compares Sinai or Carmel with Calvary, one must say that the greatest manifestation of God's power is not at the former, but at the latter, place. The kind of coercive power that can move individuals and societies behaviorally without changing the human heart, gives way at Calvary to the kind of persuasive power that can transform the human heart from within and proceed from there to transform whole societies. This is a Power that, though from our perspective seems to be disjoined from Wisdom, is, from the perspective of eternity, forever thoroughly interpenetrated by Wisdom.

God's direction and determination of the course of his world does, of course, link up more to sociological than to psychological categories, and for this reason to some extent bears a resemblance to the Islamic belief about Allah's determination of the world. But the difference lies in the way in which God glorifies Himself through His creation. For Islam, Allah's "ego" is all in all, and the others to whom he relates resemble pawns in the great chess match of life that Allah shall win. The Christian understanding, by contrast, connects the fullness of God's manifestation to the cross where Jesus, being lifted up, is glorified (John 12:32). Here the glorification of God comes through God's sacrificial love. God glorifies Himself through creation, not at the expense of creation, but through the redemption and enrichment of creation made possible by God's loving sacrifice and utter self-giving.

Second, the Christian emphasis upon God, the Holy Spirit, contains a corrective to the Hindu idea of a transcendental divine ideal of wisdom which inspires souls in their development through life but which tends to do so in an uneven and inequitable manner. At the same time, the Christian understanding of God as Spirit supplements the Islamic view of God, which on the whole lacks this concept. Because of the doctrines of reincarnation, karma, and caste in Hinduism, the relationship between God and the world tends to be too inward and psychological at the same time that this relationship tends to ignore or deem as unimportant human external conditions or to recognize how external conditions can hamper the progress of individual souls through this world. In the Christian faith, by contrast, the manifestation of the Holy Spirit always has significance for the physical as well as the spiritual wellbeing of individuals in society, and for the social, as well as for the psychological, dimension. Though the work of God as Spirit begins in the psychological dimension, it does not remain there but immediately extends as well to the social dimension. In Islam, an opposite problem is apparent: Here the relationship between God and the world tends to focus on external conditions and stresses justice and equality, but Islam does not sufficiently deal with the need of the individual soul to develop its powers of reflection and creativity. This lack of emphasis on psychological development may help explain the anti-progressive tendencies characteristic of so many Islamic societies. This is the point at which the doctrine of the Holy Spirit in Christian theology can provide a way out of the psychological stagnation that plagues Islamic society and the social inequity that plagues Hindu society. The Holy Spirit signals a process opposite to, and yet complementary with, the process of eternal *kenosis* mentioned in connection with the doctrine of God the Father. The Holy Spirit's work signals the idea not of *kenosis* (emptying) but of *plerosis* (filling up) as the Divine Wisdom ever guides the increase of glory's manifestation in the tangible world of particulars and lifts that world of particulars towards full participation in the Transcendent Meaning of all things. Episodes in this process of *plerosis* begin with the Resurrection and Ascension of Christ, and are continued with the coming of the Holy Spirit on the day of Pentecost and the subsequent expansion and sanctification of the church, which culminates at the Second Advent of Christ.

One sees as well how the Spirit proceeds from the Father not only in eternity but also in time. Put in another way, the eternal *plerosis* or filling-up proceeds from the eternal *kenosis* or self-emptying. On the level of particular human experience, this is summed up by such statements as Christ's words concerning his life, "I have power to lay it down, and I have power to take it up again" (John 10:18) or his words to his disciples "Whoever finds his life will lose it, and whoever loses his life for my sake will find it" (Matt 10:39), and again "many that are first shall be last, and the last shall be first" (Matt 19:30).

Third, Christianity maintains that the divine Logos, the Second Person of the Trinity, became incarnate in Jesus of Nazareth (John 1:14). Islam seriously objects to the doctrine of the Incarnation, insisting that Jesus was a prophet and only a prophet (Qur'an 4:171; 5:75; 43:59, 63-64), albeit a prophet with political power more in the vein described above than a prophet as traditionally understood in Jewish and Christian thought. Hinduism has a lesser problem with the idea of incarnation, since it affirms that there are numerous incarnations of the God Vishnu. Here, however, it is not merely a question of whether incarnation is possible or not, but a question of *who* the god is who is incarnated. The incarnation of Vishnu as Krishna lacks the moral force that accompanies the Christian conception of the Incarnate Logos. The words, teachings, and actions of Jesus form the content of that Logos, and in this respect the Logos that became incarnate in Jesus Christ differs in content from that principle of deity, which became incarnate in Krishna.

When referring to the work of the incarnate Christ, John Calvin spoke of the *munus triplex*—the threefold work of Christ as prophet, priest, and king (Calvin, trans. 1960, *Institues* 2. 15. 1-6); however, I should like to extend this into a *munus quadraplex*, and add to Calvin's three categories the work of Christ as *sacrificial victim*. The prophet-king dialectic then links the incarnate Christ more to the reality and work of God the Father, while the priest-sacrifice dialectic relates Christ to the reality and work of God the Spirit.[22] This Christological link cannot become a pure abstraction that is distilled from Christ's actual and tangible work as prophet, king, priest, and sacrifice, but must retain the concreteness and quality of engagement that characterized the person and work of Christ in his Incarnation as Jesus of Nazareth. What then becomes incumbent upon us is first to understand how the universal Wisdom-Power paradox that is ascribed by us to the transcendent God comes to be expressed 1) as the wisdom-power dialectic evident in the work of the economic trinity, and 2) which especially as the wisdom-power dialectic evident in the person and work of the incarnate Christ. The story of Jesus provides us with the clues of how this dialectic works in the realm of concrete particulars. Through his incarnation, death, burial, resurrection, and ascension, Jesus the Christ as the eternal Logos reveals the link between the eternal *kenosis* of the Father and the eternal *plerosis* of the Spirit. Here also is the place at which the Christian church, as the heirs of the New Covenant, and as the Body of Christ on earth, reflects and participates in the *kenosis-plerosis* dialectic. The church represents the extension of the incarnation into the temporal-spatial continuum. This extension of the theoretical into the realm of the practical cannot degenerate into forms of sheer pragmatism on the one hand, or be inflated into extreme ideologies on the other. Because sheer pragmatism is reductive, it ultimately short-circuits and produces failure. Sheer pragmatism is of the same species as the Trinitarian heresy of modalism where the Father becomes the Son and the Son becomes the Holy Spirit. Sheer pragmatism, like modalism, lacks a comprehensive and multi-dimensional understanding of the God-world relationship. Ideologies, on the other hand, tend to be Unitarian rather than Trinitarian. I am amazed at how often academics in their ivory towers resemble Hindu Brahmins to the degree that they have lost touch with the concrete world of particulars, while some fundamentalist preachers are so engaged with particularity and so eschew the emphasis on universality that they oddly begin to resemble ayatollahs, imams, and mullahs. Whether overly inclusive or overly exclusive—whether at the extreme left or the extreme right—ideologies will ultimately fail to provide lasting solutions to real human dilemmas. Indeed, they always will do so because of their inherent lack of dynamism and their inflexibility in coping with the anomalies and dilemmas that emerge in the concrete world. An adequate Trinitarian view, on the other hand, will always see the need for both/and as well as either/or in thinking about the God-world relationship. It will always underscore the importance of the behavioral and moral aspects of human life as well as the free and vital aspects. Moreover, an adequate Trinitarian view will always strive to bring justice where there is injustice, and to inspire human creativity where there is apathy, psychological stagnation, and hopelessness. The both/and I am referring to is implied in the doctrine of the immanent Trinity—the Trinity as it is in itself—while the either/or is implied in the doctrine of the economic Trinity—the Trinity in its relation to the world. To hold to both in such a way that an emphasis upon one does not eclipse the emphasis on the other means that our focus on the theoretical always must inform our focus on the practical at the same time practice must inform theory. Insofar as the church, as heirs of the New Covenant and as the body of Christ on earth, can provide a bridge between divergent perspectives and between the individual and the collective, I believe that it also provides the best place where this could be done.

# References

AAR Online program book (1991). Retrieved September 23, 2005 from http://www.aarweb.org/Annualmeet/2001/pbook/pbook.asp?ANum=&DayTime=&KeyWord=Hinduisms&B1=Submit.

Ayubi, Nazih (1991). *Political Islam: Religion and politics in the Arab world*. London & New York: Routledge.

Aquinas, Thomas (1972). *Summa theologica*. In Mary Clark (Trans. & Ed.), *An Aquinas reader: Selections from the writings of Thomas Aquinas* (pp. 155-156). New York: Fordham University Press.

*The Bhagavad Gita* (1986). Barbara Stoler Miller (Trans.). New York: Bantam Books.

Bloch, Ernst (1988). *The Principle of Hope*. 3 vols. Neville Plaice, Stephen Plaice, and Paul Knight (Trans.). Oxford: Basil Blackwell. (Original work published 1938-1947).

*Bridhadaranyaka Upanishad* (1989). In Max Mueller (Trans. & Ed.), *The sacred books of the East* (Reprint ed.) (vol. 14, pt. 1, pp. 72-228). Delhi: Motilal Banarsidass. (Translated and published 1884 by Oxford University Press).

Brooke, Peter (2004). The Salafiyyah movement. In *Islam and politics. Brecon political and theological group programme*. Retrieved September 23, 2005 from http://web.ukonline.co.uk/ pbrooke/bptdg/ programmes/julnov04/list.

Bruce, F. F. (1988). *The Book of the Acts*. Grand Rapids: William B. Eerdmans.

Bush, Randall (2005), A tale of two scriptures: Jewish-Christian and Islamic paradigms of scripture and their impact on culture. *Christian Scholars Review, 34,* 309-326.

Calvin, John (1960). *Institutes of the Christian religion*. 2 vols. Ford L. Battles, Trans. John T. McNeill. Ed. Philadelphia: Westminster Press.

Camarota, Stephen (2002). Immigrants from the Middle East: A profile of the foreign-born population from Pakistan to Morocco. *Center for immigration studies*. Retrieved September 23, 2005 from http:// www.cis. org/articles/2002/back902.html.

The caste system and the stages of life in Hinduism (n.d.). Retrieved September 15, 2005 from http://www. friesian.com/caste.htm.

*Chandogya Upanishad* (1988). In Max Mueller (Trans. & Ed.), *The sacred books of the East* (Reprint ed.), (vol. 1, pt. 1, pp. 1-144). Delhi: Motilal Banarsidass. (Translated and published 1900 by Oxford University Press).

Census profile: New York City's Pakistani American population (2000). Retrieved September 23, 2005 from http://www.asianamerican federation.org/cic/briefs/pakistani.pdf#search = 'Pakistanis%20in%20 New%20York%20City'.

Cranfield, C. E. B. (1962), Mark, Gospel of. In George A. Buttrick (Ed.), *The Interpreter's Dictionary of the Bible*. (vol. 4, pp. 267-277). New York & Nashville: Abingdon.

Esposito, John L. (1999). Contemporary Islam: Reformation or revolution? In John L. Esposito, (Ed.), *The Oxford history of Islam* (pp. 643-690). Oxford & New York: Oxford University Press.

Fuller, Graham (2003). *The future of political Islam*. New York: Palgrave Macmillan.

Jung, Carl G. (1953-1979). *Collected Works*. R. F. C. Hull (Trans.) 19 vols. London: Routledge & Kegan Paul.

Jackson, Paul (2001). Background studies and New Testament interpretation. In Alan Black & David S. Dockery (Eds.) *Interpreting the New Testament: Essay on methods and issues* (pp. 188-208). Nashville: Broadman & Holman.

Kurien, Prema (2001). Religion, ethnicity, and politics: Hindu and Muslim Indian immigrants in the United States. *Ethnic and Racial Studies*, 24, 263-93. Retrieved September 23, 2005 from http://www.clas.ufl.edu/users/kenwald/pos6292/kurien.pdf#search = 'Hindu%20immigrants%20to%20the%20United%20States'.

*The laws of Manu* (2001) In Max Mueller (Ed.) & G. Bueler (Trans.), *The sacred books of the East* (Reprint ed) (vol. 23). Delhi: Motilal Banarsidass. (Translated and published 1886 by Oxford University Press).

Neill, Stephen (1961). *Christian faith and other faiths: The Christian dialogue with other religions.* London: Oxford University Press.

Noss, David & Noss, John (1994). *A history of the world's religions* (9th ed). New York: MacMillan.

Plato, *Republic* (1930). Paul Shorey (Trans.) In *The Loeb classical library* (Reprint ed., 1982). Vol. 5. Cambridge: Harvard University Press.

Qutb, Sayyid (n.d.) The cause of god. In *Milestones.* Retrieved September 23, 2005 from http:// www.youngmuslims.ca /onlinelibrary/ books/milestones/hold/chapter_4.asp.

*Rig Veda* (1966/1979). R. C. Zaehner (Trans.). London. J. M. Dent. In Barbara C. Sproul (Ed.), *Primal Myths* (pp. 180-181). San Francisco: Harper.

Robinson, H. Wheeler (1964). *Corporate personality in ancient Israel.* Philadelphia: Fortress Press.

Scotus, Duns (1997). *On the Will and Morality.* Allan B. Wolder (Ed.) & William A. Frank. (Trans.). Washington: Catholic University of America Press.

Scruton, Roger (2002). The political problem of Islam. *Intercollegiate review.* Retrived September 15, 2005 from http://s2read.tripod.com/.

Scruton, Roger (2003). The West and the rest: On terrorism and globalization. *National Review online.* Retrieved September 23, 2005 from http://www.nationalreview.com/comment/comment-scruton 092302.asp.

Smith, Huston (1991), *The world's religions: Our great wisdom traditions.* San Francisco: Harper.

Smith, Wilfred Cantwell (1957). *Islam in modern history*. London: Oxford University Press.

Taheri, Amir (1987). *Holy terror: The inside story of Islamic terrorism*. London: Hutchenson.

*Targum Pseudo-Jonathan on Genesis* (1992). Michael Maher (Trans.). Collegeville, MN: The Liturgical Press.

The totalitarian nature of Islam (n.d.). *Institute for the secularization of Islamic society*. Retrieved September 16, 2005 from http://www.secularislam.org/humanrights/totalitarian.htm.

Vatikiotis, P. J. (1991), Islam and nationalism: The problem of secularism. In Andrew C. Kimmens (ed.), *Islamic politics* (pp. 61-73). New York: H. W. Wilson.

Wagner, William (2004). *How Islam plans to change the world*. Grand Rapids: Kregel.

Warraq, Ibn (1995). *Why I am not a Muslim*. Amherst, New York: Prometheus Books.

Watt, William Montgomery (1991). *Muslim-Christian encounters: Perceptions and misperceptions*. London and New York: Routledge.

Zwemer, Samuel (1905). *The Moslem doctrine of God*. New York: American Tract Society.

# Notes

1. This is not only true of New York but of most of large metropolitan areas of the United States. The number of Pakistani immigrants living in the United States in 2000 reached 269,831(Camarota, 2002, n.p.)

2. See, for example, the chapter entitled, "The politics of sex and the family, or the 'collectivity' of Islamic morality," in Ayubi, 1991, pp. 33-47. Ayubi observes that the Islamic practice of regulating sexual desire in males by means of the veiling of women do not and cannot work for young Islamic males living in sexually open Western societies. As Islamic regulations governing sexual relations remain unchanged and binding, economic pressures delay the marriageable age for Muslim men. As a result, the sexual frustration felt by young Muslim males fuels resentment toward the culture that throws explicit sexuality in their face at the same time that it makes their own sexual fulfillment seem an almost impossible dream. Pent up hostility surfaces in resentment and rage against the culture that is the obstacle to sexual fulfillment.

3. Islamic debate on the nature of God was pretty much quelled when al-Gazali, in the 10th century C.E., rejected the Mu'tazilites' attempts to speak of

God using philosophical reasoning. Al-Gazali rejected Avicenna's effort to speak in terms of God's essence and existence. Al-Ashari, having himself trained as a Mu'tazilite, sealed their doom when he used their own logical arguments against them. Al-Ashari insisted that Qur'anic language concerning Allah be taken literally. One could indeed speak of Allah sitting upon a throne. However, one could never know the mode of Allah's sitting, it being beyond human comprehension (Noss, 1994, pp. 610-11).

4. For instance, some *suras* in the Qur'an speak of Allah as beneficent and merciful (1:1, 3, 163; 2:37, 54, 128, 143, 160, 173, 182, 192, 199, 218) or as Oft-forgiving (2:192) while others portray him as deliberately leading people astray (2:7, 17) or as refusing ever to forgive those who disbelieve (4:168-9).

5. One *locus classicus* for this idea appears in Exod. 3:13-15 where two aspects of the Divine Name are revealed to Moses. "I am that I am" (*ehye asher ehye*) better translated "I will be who I will be" points to the mystery and inscrutability of the Divine Name. The words "I am the God of your fathers, the God of Abraham, the God of Isaac, and the God of Jacob" point to the manifestation and trustworthiness of the divine name.

6. The word "Islam" means "submission."

7. Samuel Zwemer notes that the terrible attributes of Allah are more numerous than the glorious attributes and that the former are emphasized more than the latter (Zwemer, 1905, p. 47). "Through fear of death and terror of Allah's mighty power the pious Moslem is all his life subject to bondage" Zwemer, 1905, p. 45.

8. For the compatibility of Islam with democracy and democratic ideals, see Esposito, 1999, pp. 675-689 and Fuller, 2003, pp. 40-65.

9. As Roger Scruton observes, "Apart from the caliphate—the office of 'successor to' or 'substitute for' the Prophet—no human institution occupies such thinkers as Al-Ghazali, Ibn Taymiya, or Saif Ibn 'Umar al-Asadi for long. Discussions of sovereignty—*sultan, mulk*—tend to be exhortatory, instructions for the ruler that will help him to guide his people in the ways of the faith" (Scruton, 2002, n.p.)

10. For a fuller discussion of this subject see my article in *The Christian Scholar's Review* (Bush, 2005).

11. Verses in the Qur'an supporting this doctrine are in *suras* 2:75, 79; 3:78; 4:46; 5:13; 5:41. Bishop Stephen Neill quotes Wilfred Cantwell Smith, "The present writer knows no book by a Muslim showing any 'feel' for the Christian position; nor indeed any clear endeavour to deal with, let alone understand, the central doctrines. The usual Muslim attitude is not to take the central doctrines seriously at all. That is, they do not recognize that Christians take them seriously; and that however absurd they might seem to outsiders (to Muslims they appear both stupid and blasphemous) the Trinity, the Deity and Sonship and Crucifixion of Christ, and the like are affirmations deeply mean-

ingful and precious and utterly integral to the Christian faith" (Smith, 1957, p. 104, n.1, quoted by Neill, 1961, pp. 61-62).

12. One important basis for this can be found in Jesus' words, "Render therefore unto Caesar the things which are Caesars, and unto God the things that are God's" (Matt 22:21).

13. Cranfield states that Wrede supposed that the features of this motif "were the invention of the primitive church read back into the story in order to get over a dogmatic difficulty (the alleged fact that Jesus neither claimed to be Messiah during his life nor was recognized as such by his disciples . . .)" (Cranfield, 1962, vol, 3, p. 273).

14. According to Vatikiotis, "It is through this romantic version of the past and the fathers that militant Islamic movements today try to appeal to and attract recruits, especially when the idealized past contrasts so favourably with the rotten and corrupt condition of the *umma*, the Islamic nation" (Vatikiotis, 1991, p. 67).

15. One major source of nihilism in modern Islamic political thought was Sayyid Qutb (1906-1966), whose study in the United States brought him into contact with nihilist themes in the thought of Heidegger, Nietzsche, and Sartre (Ayubi, 1991, pp. 134-42). In *Milestones*, Qutb writes, "Mankind today is on the brink of a precipice, not because of the danger of complete annihilation which is hanging over its head, this being just a symptom and not the real disease, but because humanity is devoid of those vital values which are necessary not for its healthy development but also for its real progress." In another place, he states, "In short, to proclaim the authority and sovereignty of God means to eliminate all human kingship and to announce the rule of the Sustainer of the universe over the entire earth" (Qutb, n.d., n.p.).

16. The *Chandogya Upanishad*, trans. 1900/1988, mentions that those of pleasant conduct will enter a pleasant womb, either of a Brahmin, a Kshatriya or a Vaisya, But those who are of stinking conduct will enter the womb of a dog, a swine, or an outcast (*Prapathaka* 5. *Khanda* 10. 7). The *laws of Manu* go into detail about the types and number of rebirths (Laws of Manu 12. 1-126. trans. 1886/2001. pp. 483-513). If a Brahmin steals gold from another Brahmin, the culprit will pass a thousand times through the bodies of spiders, snakes, lizards, aquatic animals, etc. (*Laws of Manu* 12. 52, trans, 1886/2001, p. 496).

17. For one, the doctrine of *ahimsa* (non-injury), which Gandhi adopted from Jainism, is contradicted by the *Bhagavad Gita* when Krishna tells the warrior Arjuna, "Conquer your foes and fulfill your kingship! They are already killed by me. Be just my instrument. The archer at my side!" (*Bhag. Gita* 11:32-33, trans. 1986, p. 104).

18. *Midr. Tanhuma* 26c states, "the Ten Commandments were promulgated with a single voice, yet it says, 'All the people perceived the *voices* (Ex. 20:18); this shows that when the voice went forth it was divided into seven voices and then went into seventy tongues, and every people received the law in its own

language" (cited by Bruce, 1988, p. 54). This tradition of the seventy languages is also found in *Targum Pseudo-Jonathan* (trans. 1992, p. 50) of Gen 11:7-8 in connection with the Tower of Babel. The one language of Babel, the "language of the Sanctuary" in which the world was created in the beginning, is confused by the seventy angels that stand before God.

19. Paul Jackson (2001, pp. 196-197) notes that Greek word for embezzled, *nosphizomai*, which is used in both texts, is a rare word used in only one other New Testament passage (Titus 2:10).

20. The Islamic practice of expansion by means of the sword is still held up as an ideal in the Muslim world. William Wagner quotes the Ayatollah Khomeini, "Those who know nothing of Islam pretend that Islam counsels against war. Those who say this are witless. Islam says, 'Kill all the Unbelievers' just as they would kill you. Islam says, 'Kill in the service of Allah.' Whatever good there exists is thanks to the sword, and the shadow of the sword. People cannot be made obedient except by the sword. The sword is the key of Paradise, which can only be opened for Holy Warriors" (Wagner, 2004, p. 23). Also quoted by Warraq, 1995, pp. 11-12 and Taheri, 1987, pp. 226-227.

21. H. Wheeler Robinson makes the case that the servant poems of Isaiah contain examples of "corporate personality." According to this interpretation, the servant in Isaiah 53 originally referred to Israel, and the suffering of Israel in captivity is a sacrificial offering through which the nations can approach Yahweh (Robinson, 1964, p. 17).

22. This also helps to bridge the Antiochene and Alexandrian Christological traditions. The Antiochenes stressed the distinction between the human and divine natures in Christ, while the Alexandrians emphasized the unity of the two natures.

# Indian and Pakistani Christian Families: Challenges of Diversity in 21st Century America

## DR. ESTHER BARKAT

For the last three decades, the Asian-American population in America is growing rapidly. The four major groups of Asian American are East Asian, such as Chinese, Japanese, and Korean; Pacific Islander; Southeast Asian, such as Thai and Vietnamese; and South Asian, such as Indian and Pakistani. They represent more than 29 distinct subgroups that differ in language, religion, and customs (Pang, 1990). Each group has its own distinct challenges. There are several hundred studies done on Asian communities and the challenges they face in United States. There are several books written by scholars regarding Asian children and their families. However, there are very few if any research articles or books available on the Christian community that has come from India and Pakistan and the challenges they face in United States. Therefore, this author has chosen to focus attention on Christian immigrants from India and Pakistan and the challenges they are facing in 21st centaury. The overall goal of this paper, therefore, is to discuss the historical/ cultural background of Indian and Pakistani Christian immigrants, to understand the challenges they face each day, and how they can be helped.

India and Pakistan became independent separate countries in 1947 after years of direct British rule. The Indian subcontinent was partitioned

---

**Dr. Esther Barkat** is Assistant Professor of Social Sciences at Waynesburg State College, Waynesburg, Pennsylvania.

on the basis of the greater concentration of Muslims in Pakistan and Hindus in India.

The Republic of India is a country in South Asia, which comprises most of the Indian Sub content. India shares its borders with Pakistan to the west, China, Nepal, and Bhutan to the northeast, and Bangladesh and Myanmar on the east. The Islamic Republic of Pakistan is a country located in South Asia and borders India, Afghanistan, Iran, China, and the Arabian Sea. The name India is derived from the river Indus. The Indus Valley civilization covered most of what is now Pakistan (Dharmaraj 2005).

The leading religion of Pakistan is Islam, which is the faith of about 97 percent of the people. About four-fifths of the Muslims are Sunnite, and about one-fifth are Shiite. Hinduism and Christianity are the leading minority religions; other religious groups include the Sikhs, the Parsees, and a small number of Buddhists (Encarta '97 Encyclopedia). Government figures tell us that Christians number 2.5-3 million out of a population of about 135 million. The leading religion of India is Hinduism. India has diverse religious groups some of them include Buddhism, Jainism, Sikhism, Hinduism, Islam, and Christianity. The majority of citizens are Hindu and speak Hindi, 14 major Indian Languages are also spoken, along with hundreds of rural dialects (Brammer 2004).

Indian and Pakistani Christians live in a society, which is religiously and culturally diverse. Their theology is formed in the context they live in and is free from western influence. This context includes diverse religions/cultures, classes, races, and diversity of languages, and various economic statuses. Indian and Pakistani faith is based on the fundamentals of Christian teaching and is very literal unlike western faith that is based on metaphoric speculations (Dharmaraj 2005).

According to the information presented by the "Explore India Millennium Year," Christianity arrived in the Indian sub continent, especially in South India with Saint Thomas, one of the apostles of Jesus Christ who later died in South India. However, others believe that the first missionary to arrive in the country was Saint Bartholomew.

Historically, Saint Francis Xavier in 1541 started a missionary movement in India. Later he was followed by Portuguese missionaries as well as missionaries from other countries like Denmark, Holland, Germany and Great Britain. Throughout the 18th and 19th centuries these missionaries preached Christian doctrines in India and also made important contributions to the social improvement and education in India.

Roman Catholic Church work goes back to Mughal times. Catholic, European Christianity came to the Indian sub continent when Vasco de Gamma sailed into the Indian Ocean in 1498. However, Anglican and Protestant church work began in the 19th century. This work began, when the Parliament of India allowed missionaries to work in areas controlled by the East India Company. Today there are about 27 million Christians in India (Samuel, 2004)

Most of India's missionary work, initially, was directed towards winning educated and high caste people. The results of these efforts were virtually unknown. Also, the affluent Hindus and Muslims did not find the message of hope appealing to them. Therefore, the majority of the Christians who were converted to Christianity by missionaries were from the low caste of Hindu. Some Hindus from higher caste may have converted to Christianity; however, they were not very verbal and did not come out and let others know that they are from higher caste because of the family name and the fear for their lives. That includes my own maternal grandparents.

The message of hope that Christianity gives appealed to masses that were under caste. They were called Dalit or scheduled-caste Hindus, formerly known as untouchables. The Dalit is a Sanskrit word meaning burst, split, broken, crushed, or destroyed but, since the nineteenth century, often taken to mean downtrodden and is used in reference to Untouchables (Harijans), outcastes, Scheduled Castes and others living in a reduced social state.

The other term, which was used, for the early Christian church in India, especially, in west Punjab was chuhra caste. The chuhra caste was associated with the people whose main job was to sweep the bathroom and remove human excretion. So for a long time, the Christian movement was used interchangeably with the term chuhra movement, and the mission most involved was called chuhra mission. This transposition of the chuhra caste into the Christian church has inevitably made the Christian community the natural inheritor of the chuhra heritage. In 1964, Alfred Allaud-Dean Asimi, in his dissertation, wrote "Sociologically, therefore, even though the present Christian community may disavow any adherence to the chuhra traditions; the characteristic features of the chuhra caste will stand as its social, cultural, and religious background." Unfortunately in the 21st century Indian-Pakistani Christians are still facing the same challenges, and the stigma of low caste has not completely washed away. Bishop Munawar Rumalshah of the Diocese of Pashawar

(1998) in his presentation at "Hear the Cry: Standing in Solidarity with the Suffering Church" Conference stated, "This does not mean that at present time the quality of Christian life is questionable; but it does mean that their desire to reach out to others is very much hampered by such a social handicap. It is for this reason also that church continues to feel itself to be isolated."

Historically, the Aryan invaders established the caste system. Aryans invaded the original inhabitants of the Indus River Valley in 1500 BC. The fair-skinned Aryans arrived in India from south Europe and north Asia. In order to secure their status, the Aryans resolved some social and religious rules, which only allowed them to be the priests, warriors and the businessmen of the society. Aryan invaders with that in mind created the caste system by dividing society into four major castes based on the colors or Varnas (Var NAAS). These castes were supposedly created from God's own body: The Brahmin (priestly caste) castes were created from God's mouth, the Kshatriya (warriors and rulers) from his arms, the Vaishyas (traders and calf people) from his thighs, and the Shudra (those who serve the other three castes) from God's feet. There were however, other people as well who were completely outside these four-caste systems. They were called untouchable, who are called Dalits, a people broken to the core by the system of social arrangement (Dharmraje 2005). That group of missionaries was most successful in spreading the gospel and converting people from other religions to Christianity.

At present, the caste system is outlawed in India and is not practiced in Pakistan. However, the caste system prevails in varying degrees in practice. Since it is believed that masses of Christians came from the lower caste, the stigma of being from the lower caste stayed with the Christian community in India and Pakistan. Though over the years the Christian communities have succeeded in advancing to a high place in the community and have the same standing economically as Muslims and Hindus, the majority of Christians in these countries are still being discriminated against due to the history of Dalit, their past jobs, and their past status in the society.

The other reason for discrimination of Christians in India and Pakistan by the Muslim community is their misinterpretation of the Quran. Many Muslims believe that they are not to have fellowship with Jews and Christians. This misinterpretation, along with the stigma of being from lower caste, creates difficult situations for Indian and Pakistani Christians.

The Third reason Hindu and Muslims shy away from making close contact with Christians is the widespread misconception that Christianity is a western religion. The most common conception among Hindus is that Christians want to convert everyone to Christianity. These factors create problems for Christians in India and Pakistan. The discrimination against Christians in both of these countries is very openly practiced and is a constant concern of Christians. Constitutionally, minorities have equal rights in both countries; however, the discrimination of Christians in both countries is practiced in varied forms. For example, in India the government has a program of reservations for jobs and university education. This program gives preference to people of the lower castes and those below caste. To qualify for these programs, one has to declare his or her caste. Many Christians would not put themselves in any category of caste because they have denounced the caste system. Unfortunately, many Christians in India who did come from these castes do not take advantage of the program, which was designed for them (Samuel, 2004).

In Pakistan, the manifestations of Islamic way of life are experienced through **Shariah** (Islamic Law) that means living under the Islamic laws rather than common laws, as obedience to the sovereignty of God. The Shariah creates difficulty for Christians. The only way Christians are protected and acknowledged is to pay Jizziah (tax for the conquered non-Muslim as a guarantee for their protection), since Christians and other minorities were not conquered in Pakistan; this makes a complicated situation for these minorities. Currently Shariah is being practiced selectively (Rumalishah, 1998). The political system of separate electorates compelled Christians (and other religious groups) to vote in elections for their candidates only. This has isolated them from the political mainstream.

The **blasphemy law**, which prescribes a mandatory death penalty for insulting the Prophet of Islam, has been widely abused. Private citizens have mainly used it as a weapon to settle old scores and to take out vendettas. The victims have almost always been Christians. 90 percent of such cases never reach court of law, and even if one does, the witness of a Christian is not admissible (Rumalishah, 1998). In 1998, the death of Bishop John Joseph as a result of the blasphemy law created unrest in Pakistan Christian community. The Pakistani Christian community was devastated and was afraid of physical harassment and insecurity.

Another challenge Christians in these countries face is the neglect from other Christian countries. The majority of the time, Christians living in the western world have no idea how Christians are treated in India and Pakistan. It is a common consensus that the western world does not care what happens to Christians in India and Pakistan or for that matter in other Muslim countries. It is believed that the western world acts like Christians in India and Pakistan don't even exist.

Despite minority status, discrimination, and any stigma attached to Christian heritage, Christians in both countries are seen as leaders in all kind of fields. Christians in India and Pakistan have progressed tremendously. Christian hospitals, school, and other institutions have given the Christian community opportunities to flourish and make progress. The international community's awareness and recognition of religious persecution in Pakistan and India especially, after September 11, 2001, is creating a subtle yet profound positive effect on the plight of the Christian community.

Whatever the reason for migration, the families do not leave their struggles behind. They face a brand new set of problems and challenges. This creates psychological burdens for these families and in turn creates burdens for the American communities they live in. Christians from both India and Pakistan come to America with a very fundamental understanding of Christianity. They have serious difficulty with western views about religion that is based on metaphoric speculations. They also have difficulty dealing with lack of commitment to marriage, easy divorce, premarital sex, homosexuality, women's place on the pulpit, and child rearing.

Though these parents want their children to become successful in schools and careers, they don't want their children to follow the American views of religion, moral values, and family life styles. However, their desire to transfer their strong cultural and religious values from one generation to the next generation faces difficulty as the children begin to develop their own identities, own worldview, and their own place in the society.

While the Indian and Pakistani children develop their own worldview based on their own experiences in society, their parents continue to hold on to their homeland worldview about religion, family, and culture. This sharp difference between parents and children's worldviews creates serious difficulty within families. The family connectedness and conformity to role expectations that are considered the virtues of Indian and Pakistani culture clash with American emphasis on autonomy—following and choosing one's own path.

An increasing number of young Indian and Pakistan people are finding that there is a wide gap between what they learn from home and what they are learning from peers, school, colleges, work places, and even churches. Many find it difficult to follow the cultural and religious traditions of their parents' homeland. The young Indian and Pakistani Christians are entering into the mainstream of American society with a mixed sense of identity. Many young South Asians are shying away from the old school teachings of traditions as well as Christianity. The older generation follows the cultural and religious values rigidly, where as the second generation is either searching for the spirit of the culture and Christianity or has abandoned it altogether. They have either developed their religious and culture identity or are totally confused. They have either internalized their ethnic identity and are ready to incorporate elements from other cultures or have rejected their own cultural identity and have accepted the "white" identity. "White identification" means incorporation into "white" culture and rejection of the values of one's ethnic culture (Kim 1985).

On the other hand, South Asian parents—who are more loyal to their own group, like authoritarianism, have a rigid view of life, limited education, infrequent contact with other cultures, and are unable to view others and their culture in a manner that is outside of their own cultural background—are facing their own challenges. The South Asian parents who view the world through their own cultural filters become disoriented, uncomfortable, paranoid, and disheartened when they see that children are choosing their own path and are not fully connected to their parents' worldview. When children express their own independent thinking, the parents consider their children as rebellious and a shame to their society and family. They become torn between what is expected of them as a part of their community and what their children are demanding.

As the children become older, the gap between the parents' worldview and children's worldview widens, and conflicts between children and parents increases. This situation creates many psychological burdens for parents, as well as for children, and in turn creates many mental health issues. The conflict between parents and children weakens the family structure and bond, and children turn to their peer and in some cases to deviant peers that may result in drug and alcohol abuse. This type of family conflict between parents and children often lead to deviant behavior and alcohol, tobacco, and other drug (ATOD) use by these children.

Another problem, which makes Indian and Pakistani families dys-functional, is their emphasis on *gender-specific roles*. Since Indian and Pakistani families come from the society, which emphasizes patriarchy, they continue to expect females to maintain a subordinate role and not assume decision-making power. The ancient tradition of the dependence of a women on her father while unmarried, first, then brother, then husband and then on son has been passed down by patriarchy and inter-nalized by women (Dharmaraj 2005). The women who comply with this notion and accept their position are highly valued. The Christian com-munity justifies this notion by using the Paul's letters to church of Corinth. For example verse 3 of chapter 11 of 1 Corinthians states "the head of the woman is the man" vs 8, "the man is not of the woman but the woman of the man." In another letter to Ephesis, Paul says, "Therefore as the church is subject to Christ, so let the wives be to their own hus-bands in every thing. A woman submitting to men is considered very biblical/religious/cultural and a very essential part of Indian and Paki-stani Christian family structure. However, when people from India and Pakistan come to America, they face another kind of teaching, which in their view contradicts biblical and cultural teaching. American culture encourages women to be independent and develop their personal identity and social independence. These two separate messages create problems for children and parents and in turn further weaken the family harmony. This is not to say that Indian and Pakistani girls, while in their perspec-tive homeland, don't get education and have their own careers or when they come to America, they don't chose their own path of life and be-come independent thinkers. The problem is that when girls, who chose their own path of life, become independent thinkers and become self-sufficient, they face a different set of cultural difficulties. For example, in many cases a young male would rather go back and choose a wife from his parents' homeland because these women will comply with the notion of submission and dependence on men. If a girl goes back to her parents' homeland and gets married to an Indian or Pakistani man, the Indian or Pakistani man may have difficulty adjusting to the lifestyle of an American born and raised girl who is an independent thinker and is self-reliant. Also, Indian and Pakistani men appear to have a double standard for women in their families. It is easier for them to accept the feminist ideals of European-American women then to accept the feminist ideals of their wives and daughters. They expect their wives and daugh-ters to accept the traditional submissive roles.

*Dating* is another issue that creates a problem for Indian and Pakistani families. The children growing up in American culture see dating as a part of American society Their Indian and Pakistani parents usually had arranged marriages. They want to pass on to their children the same tradition. Children being raised in American society hate the idea and, therefore, rebel against their parents. They date secretly. They even get into relationships which are unhealthy and abusive.

The gap between *Educational aspiration* of parents and children creates some family conflicts as well. Research indicates that in Asian families parents explicitly give messages to their children about their duties and responsibilities which also include doing well in school and enhancing family pride and prestige (Kim, Coletti, Williams, & Hepler, 1995). The studies show that on average Indian and Pakistani people, along with other South Asians, tend to express the highest educational aspirations (Brammer, 2004). When children don't or are unable to achieve these expectations of the families, more than any other group, Asian-American students turn to drugs when their grades go down (Ellickson, Colins, & Bell, 1999). Drug abuse is not the only problem; these children and teenagers are highly prone to depression and anxiety. To top it off, the Indian and Pakistani families, along with other Asians, shy away from getting counseling. Typically, Asians will turn to a trusted friend, spiritual leader, or physician when they are unable to resolve mental health issues with the family (Brammer, 2004).

Yeh (2001) identifies several factors as possible reasons for the underutilization of mental health services:

1. lack of familiarity with counseling services;
2. misconceptions about *counseling*;
3. cultural stigma and shame over mental health problems;
4. availability of alternative resources to traditional *counseling;*
5. linguistic barriers;
6. teachers and other *school* personnel unawareness of how to recognize Asian-American mental health problems to facilitate appropriate referrals.

Yeh (2001) concludes after identifying these factors that "these factors do not point to a lack of need for mental health care among Asian-American students; rather, they highlight the unique barriers to the use of mental health services among this population."

One of the major reasons for not searching for professional help is the stigma attached to admitting that one has mental health problems. The studies show that Asian Americans have greater stigmatizing beliefs than do whites. This perceived shame of seeking help leads to many husband and fathers preventing families from seeking professional help.

It should be noted that there is a generation gap between older Asian Americans' and younger Asian Americans' views of counseling. The younger generation of Asian Americans is more acculturated than the older generation of Asian Americans, and the younger ones are more apt to seek professional help for mental health issues. Their experience while in American schools and communities allows them to feel comfortable discussing mental health issues with not only friends and coworkers but with mental health professionals; however, their parents shy away from sharing their mental health issues with outsider.

Indian/Pakistani Christian children and youth not only experience racial discrimination like any other Asians but also face neglect from other non-Christian South Asians. Christians continue to be treated as such by their non-Christian South Asian counterparts. While working with South Asian communities, two reason for this discrimination came to surface. First reason was that the Indian/Pakistani immigrants who were born and raised in India and Pakistan and who came to America with a well-rooted understanding of caste system and religious discrimination have difficulty interacting with the Christian community and making friends. On the other hand, the stigma of being from poor and deprived situations creates a social handicap for Christians, and therefore, it is difficult for them to reach out to non-Christian south Asians. Secondly, the Christian immigrants who lack education and work blue color jobs tend to have their own view of religious separateness and have difficulty making friends with people from other religions. They live in South Asian communities with self-imposed isolation. Due to these two scenarios, the Indian/Pakistan Christian children/youth feel alienated and neglected. The feeling of alienation leads them to immerse themselves in the white American society. They begin to consider themselves as "adopted whites." They try to adopt the mainstream values and traditions. However, they don't fit fully in those groups either. The lack of understanding of religious/political persecution on the part of the western world, in general, and America, in particular, creates additional burden for Indian and Pakistani Christians. They feel marginalized the same way as they felt marginalized in their homeland. This sense of isolation and rejection brings them back to their own ethnic groups. However, they come back to their own ethnic group with the feelings of anger and resentment towards mainstream culture. The dream of coming to America to overcome religious discrimination becomes shattered and leads to a sense of isolation and low self-esteem. The feeling of low self-esteem, the prevalence of racism in American society, lack of emotional support from parents, teachers, and peers, and lack of understanding on the part of the American community about Indian/Pakistani Christians living in America create additional burdens and in turn mental health issues for these children. The sense of alienation and lack of sense of belonging create depression and anxiety in these children, as well as their families.

The well-educated professionals who reside in suburban cities and are well acculturated into mainstream society will go to mainstream churches and find alternatives to adjust to new communities without worrying about South Asian non-Christian communities' attitudes and stereotyping. However, the poor, working class and uneducated who struggle to adjust into mainstream society any way will feel alienated, depressed and broken just as they felt in their homelands. As a result, they will further isolate themselves from mainstream America.

In America all Asian Americans, including Indian and Pakistani Christians, are generally stereotyped as a successful and high achieving minority. They usually are considered model minorities and looked upon as smart kids and problem free (Feng 1994). This image of "Whiz Kids" creates false images and masks the need for individual differences and reality. The "Whiz Kids/Model Minority" notion has created some serious problems. First, the notion that all minority kids are whiz kids is false. There are educational, social, economic, and political differences among all Asian families that can have an effect on children's ability or aspirations. The studies show that children who come from wealthy and educated families have different experiences than the children who come from poverty-stricken families. Children whose parents do not speak English will have different school experiences than the children whose parent speak fluent English. Children who are called "Uptowners" have different educational experiences than the ones who are called "Downtowners."

The studies show that the notion of whiz kids creates false expectations from these children by the school system and teachers. These kinds of expectations from schools and teachers create an unnecessary burden for children, which in turn create a sense of failure and a sense of incompetence in children. This type of stereotype also has led teachers and school systems to neglect the importance of developing student services and support system for Asian Americans who are undereducated and have low socioeconomic status (Lee & Yeh, 2002). This type of notion also creates false expectations from parents. Children's inability to do well in school is attributed to laziness rather then academic problems. Usually Indian and Pakistani parents' solution is to force their children to develop better will power and spend more time at home away from peers. Not only that, the "Whiz Kids" notion creates a false image in Asian children, and in turn they shy away from seeking help when they face academic difficulties. This leaves them feeling depressed and isolated (Lee, 1996). Unfortunately, the stereotypical image of Asian Americans as the model minority makes it difficult for these Asians to seek support from the larger society.

Finally, the "Whiz Kids" notion suggests that Asian Americans should feel good that they are not lumped with other minority groups who are considered the "less model minority," but are fully accepted in mainstream culture, especially when affirmative action is debated. This characterization has a negative effect on the relationship between Asians and other minorities. Rathod (2004) states that this type of thinking misrepresents Asian Americans' success as proof that America provides equal opportunities for those who conform and work hard. In reality, Asian Americans experience racism, like all other minority groups.

The issues related to the dynamics of South Asian families present great challenges for the professionals and educators who work with them. Mainline denominations, colleges, universities, and other organizations are recognizing that it is a very crucial and important challenge to be undertaken. To meet the needs of these communities, several strong programs are surfacing. To name a few, the General Board of Global Ministries of the United Methodist Church has started "the Asian American Language Ministry Study." The purpose of the study is to assist ministry among a spectrum of Asian ethnic groups that have developed ministries among immigrant populations in the United States. The key areas of interest are new congregations, community ministries, clergy and lay leadership training, and resource development (Rathod, 2004). Under the umbrella of this ministry, a new youth ministry "South Asian Youth (SAY)" ministry has emerged. The mission of SAY is to reach today's youth and help them develop their healthy Christian identity. South Asian American Leaders of Tomorrow (SAALT) is another new emerging pro-

grams to empower minority communities in their struggle. There are
other churches and denominations that are establishing programs to meet
the needs of South Asian Christian communities. However, the harvest
is plenty, and there is much more work that needs to be done.

The following are some of the suggestions to meet the need of In-
dian/ Pakistan Christian families:

1. The most important aspect of working with South Asian Christian families is:

- To familiarize oneself with the values, traditions, and customs related to the Indian and Pakistani Christian Culture.
- To understand that all cultures are valid and have great value
  to offer.
- Have a great appreciation for diversity.
- Along with appreciation for diversity, one should also have
  understanding of the power of culture to shape people's
  behaviors.

2. Under the new church development programs of mainline domi-
nations, separate congregations are being built for Indian/Pakistani Christian communities. There are hundreds of Indian and Pakistani churches
in United States. Some are independent of mainline denominations, and
others are part of mainline denominations. These churches basically are
full of members who are blue color workers and people of low socioeconomic status. These church members are the ones who want to recreate
the homeland culture in United States. Though these churches are a good
source for fulfilling the needs of the people who continually want to be
connected with their own people, yet these churches are not necessarily
meeting the needs of the young generation. The studies indicate that the
new generation is spiritually hungry and are satisfying their spiritual
hunger outside the walls of family and churches. Therefore, the need for
a wholesome Indian/Pakistani Christian family ministry appears to be
greater than just the development of new churches. It appears that along
with worship experiences, the emphasis of these new congregations should
include Family-based youth ministry, adult educational opportunities,
English as a Second Language classes, parenting classes, counseling services, and English-speaking worship experience within the church for
children and youth that may help them to embrace the best of both worlds.

Where there are no South Asian congregations, the local churches should provide the needed services. Many of our mainstream American congregations provide family ministries to their own members and the youth who come to their churches. By doing this, a large number of the population who do not fit the criteria are overlooked (Dunn & Mohler, (1999). Some churches are not sure how to minister to Indian/Pakistani populations. Dunn and Mohler (1999) state that fear keeps mainline denominations from becoming involved in mentoring relationships with culturally diverse people.

The successful relationship between mainstream society and South Asian Christians can be developed when we create a meaningful interpersonal relationship with families, focus less on diversity, and by walking side by side. Dunn and Mohler (1999) state that theology is a human construct and is therefore always developed with an interpersonal and cultural context. Cultural diversity should be appreciated and celebrated because everyone is a creation of God.

3.    Americans know now that America is the most religiously and culturally diverse nation. To live in harmony, we need to not just rely on churches we, as educators, actually need to take the first step towards helping people who come from backgrounds different than ours. Many of our students, especially in small towns and cities where there is no diversity, come to colleges without any understanding of critical issues as they relate to diversity and diverse people. We, as members of the Christian higher education community, have the opportunity to make a difference. Phan (2004) in his paper, "Cultures, Religions, And Power: Proclaiming Christ In The United States Today," says that "envisioning the new America in the twenty-first century requires an imaginative leap." In order to understand "new America," we need to see new America through the eyes of an immigrant. We, as Christian educators, need to teach our students beyond tolerance and acceptance. Immigrants don't need to be tolerated. They need serious religious and intellectual engagement, which leads the way to interpersonal relationships. They need sincere respect and genuine equal opportunity. Understanding of diverse people and having relationship with them is not the end product of our effects, but it is a process, which needs our constant hard work and an adjustment in our thinking (Phan, 2004).

So what as members of Christian higher education we can do in our colleges and universities? Following are some of the suggestions:

- In order to create a college environment that values differences among students, faculty, and staff, we need to hire faculty that are diverse and/or hire the faculty and staff that have a commitment to a diverse population. We need to promote institutional collaborations that will make a sincere effort to bring diverse faculty in their midst. Sunday mornings, our churches are the most segregated places in the United States; let us not practice this at our Christian colleges and Universities. When you do hire diverse faculty, don't hire them as token but make a sincere effort and do it with genuineness.

- The emphasis on cultural diversity should be evident through our policies, procedures, and practices. The Christian colleges and universities should develop a strategic plan that seeks to address issues of young Christian immigrants. This plan will help young immigrant Christians to have a clear Asian-American identity without losing their rich cultural heritage and fundamentals of Christian beliefs.

- We need to offer courses that focus on diversity. They should be requirements not electives. The colleges and universities should discuss the educational value of diversity-related curricular. The studies show that the students who take diversity education requirement classes exhibited significantly less prejudice and made more favorable judgments (Chang, 2002).

- Student Service Projects should include projects that have the focus on understanding cultural and religious diversity. As much as possible, students should be provided with the opportunities to participate in a variety of experiential learning activities, which provide understanding and appreciation of other cultures, faiths, and struggles.

- We need to recruit students from diverse populations. Not only the population which fits the "Whiz Kids" concept but also students who need to become "Whiz Kids" and don't have resources to do so.

- We need to offer family counseling services to immigrant students and their families who are struggling to fit in mainstream America.

- We need to become a partner with local churches who provide a family-based youth ministry. Our colleges and Uni-

versities do have experts who may extend helping hands to
these churches without charging a fee.

- English departments of our colleges and universities can extend a helping hand to adult education programs that offer
English as a Second Language.
- Many Indian Pakistani students cannot go to colleges and
universities due to their residence status. Many of these students and their parents are struggling to become American
citizens or permanent residents in United States. Some are
pursuing religious asylum due to religious persecution in their
homeland. While waiting for the long process of becoming a
citizen, these students fall through the system's cracks and in
turn either become a part of poor communities or become a
part of a gang community. Therefore, we need to explore
the possibilities of establishing scholarships and financial aid
for the students who are immigrant and not yet citizens who
cannot get federal help.

4.   The idea of America as a Christian country has become a myth
to many. Statistics indicate that there are more American Muslims than
Episcopalians; more Muslims than members of Presbyterian Church
U.S.A.; and as many Muslims as Jews (Phan, 2004). So the relationship
between Christianity and other religions is not only a theological issue
but a practical issue. Therefore, we need to deal with this in a practical
manner. The majority of large universities and colleges (Christian and
non-Christian) have an Indian sub-continental organization. These organizations are a good place for universities and colleges to provide opportunities for inter-religious dialogues among student of diverse faith. These
organizations can be a most important avenue for young people to overcome religious and cultural myths and biases. The interfaith dialogue is a
necessity in the 21st century. The higher education has an obligation and
responsibility to educate all with whom they must come into contact with.
Phan (2004) states that interfaith dialogue must be accompanied by a
comprehensive program of enculturation and by effective solidarity with
the poor people. He also states that interfaith dialogue must not be reduced to intellectual exchange among theologians but must embrace life,
action, theological exchange, and religious experience. Therefore, faculty clubs, staff clubs, and students clubs should be encouraged to engage in activities that promote these dialogues.

5. In order to enhance the white American student and faculty understanding of Asian Christian immigrants, colleges and universities should create an environment that values differences among students of all kinds; that places emphasis on understanding of cultural diversity through their policies and practices; that encourages multicultural activities; and that provides opportunities for faculty, students and staff to fully participate in workshops, seminars, and individual discussions that promote understanding of these differences. The higher education institutes should also provide more opportunities for all students to participate in a variety of experimental learning activities, which provide an understanding and appreciation of other cultures.

# References

Asimi, Alfred Allaud-Dean. (1964). *Christian minority in West Punjab*: The dissertation. NY:The School of Education, New York University.

Brammer, Robert. (2004). *Diversity in Counseling*. Belmont, California: Books/Cole-Thomson Learning Inc.

Chang, Mitchell J. (2002). "The Impact of an Undergraduate Diversity Course Requirement on Students' Racial Views and Attitudes." *The Journal of General Education, 51*, 21-42.

Dharmaraj, Jacob S. (2005). "The Theologies and Missionologies From India." In *Glory Dharmarag Indian and Pakistan* (91-114). New York, NY: The General Board of Global Ministries, The United Methodist Church.

Dharmaraj, Glory (2005). *Indian and Pakistan*. New York: The General Board of Global Ministries, The United Methodist Church Publication.

Dunn, R.R. & Mohler, J.W. (1999). "The Forth Wave: A Theological Perspective On Youth Ministry." *Christian Education Journal 3*, 47-61.

Ellickson, Phyllis L.; Collins, Rebecca L.; Bell, Robert M. (1999). "Adolescent use of illicit drugs other than marijuana: How important is social bonding and for which ethic groups?" *Substance Use & Misuse, 34*(3), 317-346. [*Peer Reviewed Journal*]

Feng, Jianhu (1994). *Asian-American Children: What Teachers Should Know*. Retrieved June 6, 2004 from http://www.ericfacility.net/datbases/ERIC_Digest/ed369577.

Kim, S.C. (1985). "Family therapy for Asian Americans: A strategic-structural framework." *Psychotherapy, 22* (2), 342-348.

Kim, S., Colette, S.D., Williams, C., & Hepler, N. (1995). "Substance abuse prevention involving Asian/pacific Islander American communities." In G.J. Botvin, S. Schinke, & M.A. Orlandi (Eds.) *Drug abuse prevention with multiethnic youth* (295-312). Thousand Oaks, Ca: Sage.

Lee, S.J. (1996). *Unraveling the "model minority" stereotype: Listening to Asian American Youth.* New York: Teachers College Press.

Lee, Angela & Yeh, Christine J. (2002). "Stereotypes of Asian American Students." Retrieved June 14, 2004 from http://www.ericdigests.org/2002-4/asia

Phan, Peter C. (2004 December). "Culture, Religions, and Power: Proclaiming Christ in the United States Today." *Theological Studies, 65* (4) 714, 27

Pang, V.O (1990), "Asian-American Children: A Diverse Population." *Educational Forum, 55,* 49-66.

Ramalshah, Munawar (1998). "Hear the cry—of the Voiceless: Being a Christian in Pakistan." In *Hear The Cry: Standing in Solidarity with the Suffering Church.* Edited by Sharon Sheridan. (39–44) New York, NY: Anglican and Global Relations, ECUSA .

Rathod, E. (2004). *The myth of the "Model Minority."* Retrieved on May 2005 from http://gbgm-umc.org/global_news/full_article.cfm? Articled=2705.

Samuel, John (2004). *A History of Christianity in India.* Retrieved on September 2005 from http://christianity today.com/ch/2005/003/6.html.

Yeh, C.J. (2001). "An exploratory study of school counselors' experiences with and perceptions of Asian-American students." *Professional School Counseling, 4*(5), 349-356.

# Global Christianity: African Christians on American College Campuses

## DR. A. EZEKIEL OLAGOKE

The importance of ethnic religion in the lives of immigrants in the United States cannot be overstated. Significant sociological and historical investigations have been conducted regarding immigrant groups in the United States and the role of religion in their transition to the civic life (Chong 1998; Olagoke 2002; Swierenga 1991; Palinkas 1982; Haar 1998; Ebaugh 2000). Despite this body of literature on the subject, none has examined in depth the role of faith especially among African students on American college campuses, even with the increasing number of African students in the United States over the last twenty years.

During the past three decades, African immigrants in the United States have introduced religious and cultural diversities to the existing mosaic of cultures in the country. Coming from countries such as Nigeria, Ghana, Sierra Leone, Senegal, Kenya, Ghana, South Africa and Zimbabwe, they have dotted cities and college campuses of the United States. Like earlier African immigrants, they are young, ambitious, passionate, and unashamed in their faith. For these immigrants, the impact of Christianity in their transition to the civic, cultural, and intellectual life in the United States is as immeasurable as it is incalculable. African immigrants are part of the global resurgence of the Christian faith, a

**Dr. A. Ezekiel Olagoke**—a native of Nigeria, West Africa—is currently Visiting Assistant Professor of Sociology at Taylor University, Upland Indiana.

phenomenon that is rapidly changing the religious landscape between the countries of the Western world and those of the so-called third world.

Very often, contending theories on globalization (Friedman 1999; Nyamnjoh 2000) see the countries of the third world, especially Africa as passive recipients of social, political, and economic crumbs that fall from the banquet table of the West. The reality for African immigrants in this study, however, speaks differently. The difference between the contending theories of globalization as they relate to globalized African Christianity in this study is reinforced by the opposing views of Anthony Hopkins and Van Binsbergen. While Hopkins sees "globalizing religious projects such as Christianity and Islam; globalizing intellectual projects such as emergence and spread of philosophy and science,"[1] Binsbergen employs the concept of "proto-globalization, defined as the social, including economic, political, cultural and religious effects of dramatic advances in communication technology."[2] For African students on American college campuses, the intersection of "Athens and Jerusalem" in a different cultural setting underscores the importance of an emerging spatial, cultural, and religious dynamics as these students engage the host culture locally and globally. Therefore, they are not passive recipients of religious and cultural histories.

In underscoring the rising force of the Christian faith among Christians from the so-called third world countries, Philip Jenkins stated that, "There is no recognition that the gravest challenge to McWorld" might not come from Jihad, but rather from what we might call the forces of Crusade, from the Christian Third World.[3] African Christians in the United States see the opening words of prophet Ezekiel above as relevant today as these Africans move, live and have their being among the cultured despisers of the faith in the West. To these immigrants, the Christian faith matters, and it matters considerably.

The purpose of this paper is to trace the origin of an African immigrant student's initiated organization, African Christian Student Fellowship (ACSF), its impact on college campuses in the United States, its relationship with the host and dominant culture over the last twenty five years, the spiritual and faith journeys of its members, and its overall impact in the increasing and exponential numbers of African Christian Churches in the United States today. Furthermore, this paper examines the manifold ways in which African immigrant Christians combine faith and ethnic practices in adapting to the civic life in the United States.

Additionally, the paper examines their adeptness in adaptation by the ways which they prepare their immediate and extended families to leave a legacy for the coming generation. Additionally, the paper explores the role of religion in the quest for "tripartite identities" (African, Christian, and American). Finally, the task of transmission of African cultural identities from the first generation of Africans to the second generation is both salient and significant in this study.

Since the early eighties, I have sporadically been a participant observer in many African congregations and Christian student fellowships in the United States. For the purpose of this paper, I was a participant observer at the African Christian Student Fellowship (ACSF) at Oklahoma State University, Stillwater Chapter, Denver Theological Seminary, Wheaton College, and the University of Denver/Iliff School of Theology. I have also participated in their conferences held in many key cities in the US. I am currently in touch with key figures of the ACSF who are now pastors, para-church leaders, or bible scholars in their own right in the United States. Furthermore, I have had contacts with the offspring of these earlier ACSF members, who are now the second generation Africans, holding the fort and the battlement of faith for the coming generations.[4]

In 1967 and 1973, unsuccessful attempts were made by African Christian students in the United States to form a fellowship of Christian students. During the intervarsity convention of 1976, which took place at the University of Illinois in Urbana-Champagne, a group of African students in attendance met and were addressed by the late Bishop Kivizenjere of Uganda.[5] With other African participants, they discussed past efforts and problems of bringing African Christians together, and they longed and looked for a day when such Christian fellowships will be formed.

The Easter Conference of 1977 at University of Wisconsin, Madison, finally marked the inauguration of African Christian Student Fellowship. Participants included Brothers Amaechi, Nwachukwu, and Joshua, all students of Wheaton College, Illinois, at the time. Wheaton College is an evangelical Christian college located in the suburbs of Chicago, Illinois.[6] Subsequently, a committee was set up, headed by Brother Wokoma Wokoma, to write the Fellowship's constitution.[7]

The rationale for the formation of the fellowship was for Africans in a foreign land to be able to gather together to worship God. Some cited bad experiences such as racist and stereotypical encounters about Africa and Africans from some churches in the United States. Rather than abandon the faith that shaped them in their homeland, they felt it was necessary to form a Christian fellowship where their emotional, spiritual, and relational needs will be met, even as they are intellectually engaged in the kingdom of the mind on American college campuses.

The African Christian Student Fellowship is composed of national executive members with regional branches, usually called "chapters." The regions were initially divided into: midwest, southern, southwestern and eastern. The branches/chapters constitute the backbone of the Fellowship. As one member asserted, "Without the chapters, there is no African Christian Student Fellowship" (ACSF). During the formative years, the chapters were located on the college campuses of the following cities and states: Ann Arbor, Michigan; Atlanta, Georgia; Austin, Texas; Baltimore, Maryland; Chicago North, Illinois; Chicago South, Illinois; Columbus, Ohio; Detroit, Michigan; Greensboro, North Carolina; Houston, Texas; Jackson, Mississippi; East Lansing, Michigan; Norman, Oklahoma; Philadelphia, Pennsylvania; San Antonio, Texas; and Tulsa, Oklahoma.

The Stillwater, Oklahoma chapter was one of the most potent chapters in the eighties. It is interesting to note that most of the original members and those who joined from the early eighties still reside in the Texas/Oklahoma regions with significant Christian ministries and vocations. Some left for Africa after graduation and are back in the United States as pastors and assistant pastors in many African-initiated ministries in the United States.

Since its inception, the Fellowship has met yearly in many regions of the United States. For example, the national conference was held in the following cities yearly: Tulsa, 1978; Dallas, 1979; Chicago, 1980, Detroit, 1981; Stillwater, OK,[8] 1982; New Jersey, 1983; Atlanta, 1984; Houston, 1985; Madison, WI, 1986. The ten-year anniversary of the Fellowship was held in New Jersey in 1987. In 1988, the national conference was again held in Tulsa, Oklahoma. Some of the members of the fellowship were students at Oral Roberts University and the University of Tulsa. Since then, the national conference has taken place in many venues in the United States. Tax exempt status for the Fellowship was not granted until 1988.[9]

There seems to be a Babel of conceptual confusion, even among scholars in the field when discussing or classifying Christians belonging to minority groups. African Christians are no exception in this regard. For example, it is not uncommon for people to confuse fundamentalism with Pentecostalism, conservative Christians with right wingers, "holy rollers" with cults etc. (Gifford 1988; Van Dijk 1997). I will now discuss the three strands of Christianity above as these relate to the African Christian Student Fellowship.

First, evangelicalism is now a world wide phenomenon, which some maintained dates back to the Reformation, with expansive domain in Great Britain and the United States, especially through the religious conversion and experiences of John Wesley and George Whitefield.[10] Despite the secularism in Western countries of Europe and the United States, evangelicalism has remained one of the dynamic forms of the Christian faith. The emphasis that evangelicals placed on the Bible is unapologetic, unwavering, and unabashedly missionary. According to Gerrie ter Haar, there are four key elements that define and denote what evangelicalism is in terms of belief system:

> Four key elements are, in the view of evangelicals themselves, crucial to their identity as Christians. These are, in their own words, Biblicism, crucicentrism, conversionism, and activism. This means that evangelicals consider the Bible their supreme authority and the dependable record of God's revelation; that the cross of Christ and the idea of substitutionary atonement which goes with it from the heart of the gospel which, in their view, requires a personal response on the part of the believers, a change of heart which is usually called conversion; and the fruits of that change should be seen in the individual believer's life and consequently shared with others through active evangelism.[11]

For African Christians in the student fellowship, the personal belief and experience of the Bible and the person of Christ seem to be unshakeable as the determination and the desire to communicate that faith to those who have not experienced it. This conviction is reminiscent of a chorus sang in one of the chapters as well as at many of the national conferences:

> There is power in the word of God
> There is power in the name of Jesus
> There is power in telling the story of Jesus
> The power that is greater than the devil
> The power that is greater than nations
> The power that is greater than circumstance
> The power that is greater than Satan
> There is power in the word of God.[12]

From the foregoing, personal and passionate faith in the Christian God is not merely aping and mouthing of the creed of evangelicalism in foreign countries, but a deep conviction that the Christ of the Bible irrupted into human affairs with unmistakable signs and wonders. African variation and inculturation of such conviction vary from one African context, culture, or country. The African adeptness in adaptation, using religious symbols and signs, especially the Christian faith, is one of the central dynamics of faith and spirituality in human affairs.

The role of the Christian faith becomes an adaptive mechanism even as these students move around in the halls of higher learning and the seemingly impregnable achievements of science and technology they observed in the West. As one member proudly observed, "we are not yet bitten by the bugs of secularism or enlightenment that has afflicted the Western countries."

Pentecostalism as a strand of Christian evangelicalism has had tremendous following in many parts of the world, including Africa. This is not to say that there is no difference between evangelicalism and Pentecostalism whether in theology or the form of church organization. A crucial theological difference is the place which Pentecostalism accords the Holy Spirit, or the baptism of the Holy Spirit in the lives of the believers, with a fundamental emphasis of that baptism resulting in "*glossolalia*" or speaking in tongues. The Charismatics, who are the most recent offshoot of the Pentecostal movement, are also committed to the power and gifts of the Holy Spirit.

On one hand, while Pentecostals belong to the more established churches like the Assembly of God or the Foursquare Gospel, Charismatics do operate outside denominational boundaries, in schools, college campuses, para-church groups, and Christian youth movements. Many members of the African Christian Fellowship belong to these strands of evangelical, Pentecostal, and Charismatic groups. According to statements, Fellowship documents, and many years of conference attendance with these ACSF members, various stands of worship are observed and practiced, with the accompanying understanding of not offending the spiritual sensibilities of those with different cultural, spiritual or denominational background. The following statement from the Fellowship archive and conversation summarizes the worship style or doctrinal stance of the fellowship chapters:

Each conference, influenced by the leadership was unique in its setting. Depending on the denominational persuasion, the conference was loud, quiet, or anywhere in between. When there was excessive predominance of one, it offended conferees who were of another persuasion. [13]

For these African believers, the reality of the spiritual and their effect on the natural world they observe and see is a reality that they strongly believe in despite their pilgrimage from a culture where such realities are either ignored or dismissed.

Many of the original founders of the African Christian Student Fellowship (ACSF) have either gone back home to Africa, remained here in the States, or as a result of the political, religious, and economic turmoil in the continent, they have emigrated back to the United States. Since they are no longer students, the original name of the fellowship becomes a misnomer. Therefore, to accommodate those who are no longer students, the name African Christian Fellowship (ACF) was later adopted. This provides a larger umbrella for students, non-students, visitors, guest speakers, evangelists, professionals, and first and second-generation African immigrants to be members.

Some of these earlier members of the African Christian Student Fellowship have now become pastors, preachers, evangelists, or Bible Study leaders with congregations in many cities of the United States. Some have attended seminaries and bible colleges in order to sharpen their spiritual skills to effectively minister, not just to Africans but to other ethnic groups in their communities. Their mission of being a light among the dominant culture has not changed.

The strategic plan of the African Christian Fellowship (USA), presented by the National Board of Directors in 1998, provided a general overview of the fellowship's mission, objectives, and goals as it engages the larger community. There are four aspects of this mission, with implementation not diverging much from region to region, and chapter to chapter. They are the following: first, building the family and the African Christian Fellowship community; second, reconnecting with the continent; third, passing on the legacy; and fourth, building bridges. [14] I will now expound further on each mission and objectives as each relates to the purpose of this paper.

Three key questions will first be raised in examining the relationship between religion and ethnic identity. First, to what extent is religion seen from the standpoint of identity formation related to ethnic identity? Second, how does religion enhance ethnic identity? Conversely, are religion and ethnicity one side of the same coin? According to Williams (1988:12-13), the interaction or intersection of religion and ethnicity can be either an identical interaction, or seen as a precedent to ethnic identity or subordinate to it.[15] For example, while works have pointed to the indistinguishable link between Polish immigrants and Catholicism[16] (Galush 1966), or Dutch and Calvinism[17] (Lucas 1955), for African immigrants, the plurality of their religious milieu makes it more difficult to pin them to a particular denominational affiliation.

Max Weber (1963), a noted classical sociological theorist of religion, discussed the ethical and legitimating roles of religion, as well as its functions as an instrument of protest.[18] Weber, however, discussed in general terms the functional role of religion. For African immigrants, the Christian faith served not only as an ethical or legitimating factor, but it also cements immigrants changing identities as well as a bulwark against the onslaught of marginalization, alienation, and despair associated with leaving the safety net of a traditional, communal society to live in a more individualistic culture.

Likewise, Fenggang Yang (1999) discusses the changing pattern of identities among Chinese Christians in the United States. The cultural Chinese identity is particularly strong among older or first generation Chinese. Other identities reinforcing this sense of self are the Christian and American identities. Yang asserts that in the structure of diverse ethnic groups in the United States, immigrant assimilation can become a complicated process:

> Structurally, assimilation has become "segmented." From the standpoint of immigrants, assimilation is selective. The choices newcomers make will greatly influence their degree of success in the host society. To maximize the chance of socio-economic success, immigrants need to select the subsystem into which they want to assimilate in the host society, control the pace of assimilation and maintain a cohesive ethnic community.[19]

While there are clear differences in the Chinese and African cultures, the immigrant experience of alienation from homeland and the adjustment to new linguistic and cultural conventions are common elements among most immigrants. There is another commonality with African immigrants: the fact of the Christian faith. Like the Chinese Christians whose brand of Christianity is basically the evangelical type in the United States, most of the Africans interviewed for this study oscillate from evangelical forms of Christianity to its Pentecostal variance.

Why do Africans in the United States maintain a spiritual worldview that sometimes defies sociological and psychological explanations of conversion? Why is Christianity so crucial for immigrants, especially in their transition and adjustment in the United States? Furthermore, how is the Christian identity essential in an alien culture for self and collective preservation?

From many years of participant observation in studying African Christian Students in the United States, neither modernity's anti-religious bias nor the traditional sociological accounts of conversion suffices to explain why the Christian faith has become so significant for this group of African immigrants. Dealing with the structure of religion in the African landscape, Bolaji Idowu, the Nigerian theologian and Methodist minister, asserts:

> Taking Africa as a whole, there are in reality five component elements that go into the making of African traditional religion. These are belief in God, belief in the divinities, belief in spirits, belief in the ancestors, and the practice of magic and medicine each with its own consequent attendant cult.[20]

The Enlightenment project with its powerful critique of religion has not had the effect in Africa that it has had in the Western world. As Mbiti argues, the notion of being an atheist or agnostic is foreign to Africa.[21] The importance of religion in the African landscape reverberates among these immigrants in a new transatlantic setting. This is more so bearing in mind that most members and leaders of the African Christian Student Fellowship are graduate students in colleges and universities in the United States, coming from diverse religious milieu, and yet with profound conviction in the Christ of history and His uniqueness in personal and collective lives. Coming from predominantly former European colonies of Britain, France, Germany, Portugal, these immigrants are both products and children of Enlightenment, by education and exposure.[22] The uniqueness and diversity of African religious expression is further amplified by Blakely, who writes:

Even if there is not only one African religious expression, there is an
African "genius for religion"—a shared creativity of Africans in ex-
pressing their individual and collective experiences through religion, a
proclivity to find new expressions for old and new feelings, new answers for old as well as new questions.[23]

It is in this context of new experiences that underscores the central
role of Christian religion for these immigrants as they make the transition into the civic life of the United States. My study of African Christian
Student Fellowship, as well as other church ministries established by
Africans in the United States, revealed that the person of the historical
Jesus, as well as the history of the Jewish people, find a great resonance
among Africans. Respondents identified the Jesus story, as well as other
Biblical stories, resonate with characters and experiences in their own
historical journey, both individually and collectively. For members of
the African Christian Fellowship, Christian religion provides spiritual
nourishment that engenders hope in a different cultural context. Additionally, it also provides a way of dealing directly or indirectly with
some of the political conflicts in their respective countries.

Among African converts to Christianity, Pentecostal forms of Christianity offer more hope and more meeting of aspirations, and they are
more in tune with the African spiritual landscape. Some authors have
questioned the revolutionary potential of this kind of Christianity. For
example, Paul Gifford, writing on Pentecostalism in Nigeria recognizes
the moral power and virtues espoused by the Pentecostal group, but he
emphasizes its limitations:

Whatever the power of the moral vision of civic virtue presented by
Pentecostals, the uses to which it is put in the high politics of the state
rob it of its radical potential, a process of narrowing or flattening of
identity—the closing of plural and lively options.[24]

For the most part, Gifford's assertion emanates from a Western tradition, which is sometimes uncharitable or unsympathetic to the Pentecostal movement because of what they perceive as its lowly origin, un-
critical acceptance of social structures, and disdain for intellectualism.
The examples given by Gifford about Pentecostals in Nigeria are a cari-
cature of ostensible absence of political sophistication associated within
Pentecostals. However, Gifford's critique overlooks the inroads made
by Christians who have fought against the Islamization of the country by

the Muslim north. Some of the most powerful critiques of *Sharia* in Nigeria have come from people with both Pentecostal/evangelical leanings.[25] One of the foremost scholars of Pentecostalism, Walter, J. Hollenweger, provides a counterpoint to Gifford's assertion:

> Pentecostalism is revolutionary because it offers alternatives to literary theology and thus defrosts the frozen thinking within literary forms of worship and committee-debate and gives the same chances to all— including the oral people. It allows for a process of democratization of language by dismantling the privileges of abstract, rational, propositional systems.[26]

Since majority of Africans emigrating to the United States are from a traditional/oral culture, they are likely to identify with the grass root, evangelical principles of Pentecostalism. Many members of the African Christian Student Fellowship (ACSF) came from the historic church background before conversion to the Pentecostal/Charismatic form of the Christian faith. According to them, while they were in the historic/orthodox churches, the Bible remained a closed book until they "met the Lord" or become "born again" in the spirit-filled, Pentecostal churches. Contrary to Gifford's view, this fact does not nullify the possibility that these immigrants have become politically engaged especially during some of the turbulent years in the late 1990's in some African countries.

Furthermore, members of African Christian Student Fellowship also belong to churches that are involved in many ministry groups, including the Women's group, cell groups, prayer groups, and children's groups. These small groups appear to be preparation for future community involvement that may not be necessarily "spiritual."

Songs of praise and adoration at ACSF are interspersed with songs reinforcing the unique notion of Christian identity. As these songs are sung, complementary bodily and hand gestures denote the omnipotence of the personhood of God, and the victory of the believer over sin, Satan, sickness, and every circumstance of life. Sometimes, the congregation is exhorted to dance with a joyous movement to the front of the pulpit, either in thanksgiving or an expression of the Pentecostal belief that they are not the "chosen frozen"—a term reserved for members in historic/orthodox churches where any show of emotion is frowned upon. Pentecostals are not ashamed to expressed themselves in songs, Bible reading and quotation, and demonstrations of affection. A typical song transliterated from Yoruba (one of the African languages) to English goes as such:

*Agbara Esu da, nibiti Jesu gbe njoba*
*Agbara Esu da, kosi o oti wo patapata.*
Where is the power of Satan where Jesus is reigning
Where is the power of Satan, there is none at all whatsoever.
It has been overthrown and fallen flat completely.

The confidence extolled as the song is sung reassures believers, as children of God, that the problem they may be going through is really a stepping stone to greater opportunities in the overarching design of God. Whether the "stepping stone" is difficulty with finances, immigration papers, job, or family, the songs reassure Christians that everything will be all right.

Three-quarters of Africans coming to African Christian Student Fellowship wear their traditional African dresses. Men wear **Dashiki, Agbada, Dandogo, and Buba** while women—**Gele, Iborun, and Iro ati Buba** with designs that are sometimes hand sewn. Most of these clothes are made from cotton materials or other light materials so that even a two-piece or three-piece attire does not adequately provide enough warmth, especially during the cold weather. Nevertheless, members gladly wear them as part of memory of homeland where they come from and to pass on traditional dress codes to the coming generations.

It is not unusual for children to be dressed in attire similar to their parents. Asked why this continuity is important, most members asserted, "this is part of our culture and we must not allow it to die down in a foreign land." Some said that wearing homemade clothes gives them a sense of pride, a sense that they belong, and a sense of continuity of African identity in a place where values from the continent are often relegated to the background.

On one occasion, an invited speaker lamented on the marginalization of Africa and Africans. He drew inspiration from a story in the Bible where the disciples of Jesus questioned each other about the geographic area in Israel, where the Messiah would come from. One of the disciples, Nathaniel, on hearing that the Savior of the world is from the city of Nazareth asked, "Can anything good come out of Nazareth?" The speaker lamented that the same kind of question is often asked by the media and people about Africa. The speaker advised that through their lives of commitment, character and civic responsibilities, members should educate people ignorant of Africa to the values and principles that traditional Africa inculcates. The Africa of CNN, he asserts, is vastly different from the Africa that the speaker knows and comes from. The congregational response to his statement was affirmative.

Whether it is birthday celebrations, wedding anniversaries, cell groups, cultural visits and home visits, African foods are served liberally by the host. Ancient Biblical and traditional African practices are often invoked to underline the significance of food in human interaction. While encouraging members to visit one another and be open to others from a different cultural tradition, speakers in the ACSF often allude to places where Jesus met people as usually saturated with food. Biblical examples include the wedding at Canan, the visit to Peter's house, the visit to Mary and Martha, and the last supper; and, when Jesus resurrected, His gathering with the disciples was around a breakfast meal.

In the African tradition, food also takes on a very important role in gatherings—from the womb to the tomb. During birthday celebrations, marriages, business successes, house warmings, purchase of a new car, invitations to friends to share in one's promotion, and even in death, parties and food consumption can last for days. In some African cultures, it would be offensive to visit somebody's house and refuse to eat what was hospitably offered.

Tedros Kiros examines the traditional African approach to food in the community as an inalienable right as opposed to the modern view which treats food as a commodity. Most members of the African Christian Student Fellowship hold a traditional African worldview, a perspective that emerges from having lived on the farm and seldom having to buy food since most food is grown for consumption. Kiros' description of the two worldviews suggests that certain aspects of traditional worldviews also have Christian underpinnings:

> There was a period in the history of Africa prior to its penetration by colonialism and by the global world economy during which African food producers circulated and consumed food among themselves. The tendency to look at food as a commodity, accessible only to those who have the means to buy food, thereby securing an everyday existence, and to look at those who fail to have the means as predestined victims of poverty famines, starvation, and malnutrition has become almost second nature in the modern age.[27]

Two points need to be made here. First, during the interviews, some of African immigrants expressed amazement at the abundant food supply in the United States, where less than two percent of the population are farmers, and yet there is enough food for a population of over 240 million.

The commercialization of food in the modern economies often makes these immigrants long for the "good old days" in African villages where oranges, mangos, bananas and apples are never placed in the market for purchase. It is in this light that food becomes an essential part of fellowship for these immigrants. They reminisce about the traditional landscape, untouched by modernity and the commercialization of food, where in house gatherings and some church events so much food is provided that the unmarried are encouraged to take food home.

When members contrast the abundance of food in the United States to famines in Ethiopia, Somalia, and other African countries, they often invoke moral lessons of the traditional African worldview through stories. Most members express the view that even underdeveloped Africa can contribute to Western values, especially in areas that are not measured in terms economic or material quantification. Kiros' statement in this regard is instructive:

> In the traditional African life-world technocratic backwardness and the resistance to modernization is balanced by moral richness and charity. Modernity needs to revitalize the moral richness of the prereflective stages of the life-world. Whereas the African peasant's resistance to science as a whole may be criticized, his moral sentiments are admirable, so admirable that they can serve as the foundation of African philosophy.[28]

During gatherings when food is served, Africans pray for those who cannot afford to eat. In addition, concrete measures are undertaken to insure that jobless members are provided for, measures that are reminiscent of the traditional African milieu. Secondly, it is also a time when the African concept of collective **Harambe** is implemented. The Swahili word "**Harambe**" has a Yoruba equivalent "**Ajo**." "Harambe" encourages six or eight person groups to raise five hundred to a thousand dollars a month. One person in the group is given the money to start a business venture or to send home to start building a house or fulfill other family responsibilities. Each participant takes a turn in contributing and collecting at the end of the month until all participants have collected a sum of money. Members who have participated in "Harambe" say that this form of enterprise has enabled them to accomplish goals that would have been impossible otherwise. Such is typical traditional African economics. It also encourages thrift and saving in easing the transition process to a new culture.

Women play a crucial role in this form of cultural continuity at the African Christian Student Fellowship. Peter Goldsmith underscored the central significance of food and the role of women in sustaining ethnoreligious identity and community.[29] Eating together, he argues, creates a sense of community, and the process of food preparation itself fosters a sense of identity in a religious context. Food preparation becomes a "ministry" in the service of others and is often seen as a demonstration of one's God-given talent. Most of these foods are ethnic foods, and because the women shop together for the various ingredients, they regard this as a time of fellowship and problem solving.

One of the women interviewed, who is from the Caribbean and married to an African, complained that so much money is spent by the group in preparing predominantly African food. She asked the president of the group, "Why is it that you do not take us non-Africans by birth into consideration as these foods are prepared and served?" "Why do you not include salad, pizza, sandwiches into your menu?" "Why is it always going to be African food all the time?" In response to the woman's request, the president of the group, who is in charge of allocating money for food, reluctantly designated twenty dollars for American snacks and cookies while the bulk of the money was earmarked for ethnic foods.

This incident met with vigorous protest by other women in the group, and the president had to reconsider his decision. The women stressed the important role they play at home, invoking the often quoted saying that "a woman's work is never completed." Underscoring the importance of women in food preparation, ethnic reproduction, and identity formation, Helen Ebaugh writes:

> Along with participating in the ethno-religious education of children, women's most ubiquitous role within their congregations is that of ethnic food provider. Whether for formal, congregation-wide social events, less formal religious meetings, or family centered but religiously oriented practices, ethnic food consumption marks the most gatherings of fellow ethnic congregational members. Along with the use of native tongue, the collective consumption of traditional foods constitute what are undoubtedly the most significant ways by which

members of ethnic groups define cultural boundaries and reproduce ethnic identities.[30]

Music is another aspect in the reproduction of ethnic identities or cultural continuity. Quite recently, the traditional talking drum, which is one of the ensemble of drums has been recently introduced by some of the newly formed African initiated churches, pastored by past and current members of the Fellowship.

African immigrants, whether those among the African Christian Fellowship or African-initiated churches in the United States see a spiritual vacuum and decadence among the nations of the West. Despite their experience with racism, stereotypical affronts, and other negative experiences, African immigrant churches and ministries do not espouse a particularly Afrocentric worldview. In fact, they are often amazed at the cultural captivity that has resulted in segregation of both black and white churches in the West.

Most African churches and ministries attended for the purpose of this study affirmed their mission and objective to be international, intercultural, and interracial.[31] The avoidance of Afrocentric captivity is noted by the Ghanaian preacher and pastor whose ministries span three continents: Africa, Europe and the United States. He writes:

It is a little wonder that in Ghana, we have a saying which literally translated means; "When you see the white man you have seen your God." That is total blasphemy and an abomination! It is supplanting the image of God with the image of man. In order to change that concept, black people have advocated that Jesus Christ should be portrayed as a black man. That is swinging from one extreme to another. Their frustration is real but the answer is wrong.[32]

The voluntary and massive emigration of Africans whether as students, professionals, or visitors to the countries of the West has taken place in the current era called globalization, a term which according to some scholars "did not exist as a processual term in academic literature prior to 1987."[33] There is no doubt whatsoever that rapid changes in information, technology have shrunk the world into a global village. However, whatever meaning one advances to the concept of globalization, it must be noted that historically, Africans have been involved in global movements, whether it was through forced enslavement, colonial education, modernization, or other forms of trans-Atlantic movement of ideas. What is unique in the current era of emigration is the cultural, political, and religious implications of such movements. These implications are still unraveling especially in its religious forms.

What is evident from the foregoing study, however, is that in the words of Philip Jenkins, it is a "New Christianity, a Southern Christianity, the Third Church, and it is not just a transplanted version of the familiar religion of the older Christian states: the New Christendom is no mirror image of the Old. It is a truly new and developing entity. Just how different from its predecessor remains to be seen."[34] In the meantime, the African Christian Fellowship, as well as other African-initiated churches and ministries, continues to form part of the religious and cultural mosaic in the United States.

# Notes

1. Hopkins, Anthony (ed), 2002. *Globalization and World History*, London: Pimlico.

2. Van Binsbergen, 1999. "Mary's Room: A Case Study on Becoming a Consumer in Francistown, Botswana." in R. Fardon, W.M.J. van Binsbergen & R. van Dijk (eds), *Modernity in a Shoestring: Dimensions of Globalization, Consumption and Development in Africa and Beyond*, Leiden: EIDOS.

————,2003. *Intercultural Encounters: African and Anthropological Towards a Philosophy of Interculturality*, Berlin/Muenster: LIT.

————,2004. *Situating Globality: African Agency in the Appropriation of Global Culture*, Boston: Brill.

3. Philip Jenkins. (2002). *The Next Christendom: The Coming of Global Christianity*, Oxford: Oxford University Press, page 6. For the ongoing religious pluralism especially among recent immigrants, see Helen Rose Ebaugh & Janet Saltzman Chafetz. (2000). *Religion and the New Immigrants: Continuities and Adaptations in Immigrant Congregations*. New York: Altamira Press. See also Lamin Sanneh. (2003). *Whose Religion is Christianity? The Gospel Beyond the West*. Grand Rapids: William B. Eerdmans Publishing Company.

4. In October 2005, one of the key members of the Oklahoma chapter, Festus and Ruth Okiomah celebrated their 25th wedding anniversary in one of the African initiated churches in Grand Prairie. In attendance were many members past and present and two of their four children served as maids of honor. I later had an extended visit with the couple on December 3, 2005 to reminisce on their works. Ruth Okiomah is currently the assistant pastor of Redeemed Christian Church of God in Grand Prairie, TX.

5. Extracted from African Christian Student Fellowship (ACSF) papers, archival documents, and interview with Sam Umunna, the president of the Chicago chapter. He is one of the earliest members of the fellowship based in Chicago, Illinois.

6. As a graduate student at Wheaton College from 1988-1989, I had the privilege of meeting Sam Umunna, the then president of ACSF, and some of the members of the African Christian Fellowship in the Chicago area.

7. Conversation with David Ogbuaku, Sam Umunna, and others who are familiar with the formation, membership, and programs of the African Christian Student Fellowship.

8. In January 1981, I arrived in the United States from Nigeria where I grew up. Like all other Africans, I was warmly welcome and introduced for the first time into African Christian Student Fellowship at Oklahoma State University, Stillwater, OK. It was here that I had my first exposure and experience to the structure, constitution, composition, aims and objectives of the Fellowship. I was a member of the Stillwater Chapter of the African Christian Student Fellowship until I left Stillwater in December 1985 to attend Dallas Theological Seminary the following year.

9. See papers, conference schedules, and agendas, newsletters of regional and national conferences, and interview with past and present members of the Fellowship.

10. Gerrie ter Haar (1999). *Halfway to Paradise: African Christians in Europe*, Cardiff Academic Press, page 12. See also Diane B. Stinton. (2004). *Jesus of Africa: Voices of Contemporary African Christology*. (New York: Orbis Books).

11. ibid, page 13.

12. Regular Congregational call and response chorus

13. See unpublished paper of the history of African Christian Student Fellowship, by Sam Umunna, page 11. These papers and other documents from the many chapters of the Fellowship were collected from the Umunna in 1998, with extensive conversation with him and David Ogbuaku. Both are actively involved in Fellowship activities as well as African Christian ministries in the United States; David Ogbuaku, an assistant pastor, who also work with Ford Motor as a mechanical engineer, currently lives in Inkster, MI. Sam Umunna is actively involved in Chicago, Illinois.

14. ACSF Mission statement is expressed in the unpublished history of the fellowship and it is also found on their website, acf.org.

15. Williams, R.B. 1988. *Religion and Immigrants from India and Pakistan*. Cambridge: Cambridge University Press.

16. Galush, W.J. 1977. "Faith and Fatherland: Dimensions of Polish-American Ethnoreligion, 1875-1975." In *Immigration and Religion in Urban America*, edited by R. Miller and T.D. Marzik, 84-102. Philadelphia, PA: Temple University Press.

17. Lucas, H.S. 1955. *Netherlands in America: Dutch Immigration to the United States and Canada, 1789-1950*. Ann Arbor: University of Michigan Press.

18. Weber Max, (1963). *The Sociology of Religion*, Boston, MA: Beacon Press.

19. Fenggang Yang. (1999). *Chinese Christians in America: Conversion, Assimilation and Adhesive Identities*, University Park: The Pennsylvania State University Press, pages 196-197.

20. E. Bolaji Idowu. (1973). *African Traditional Religion: A Definition*, Ibadan: Fountain Publications, page 133. See also Stephen Ellis & Gerrie Ter Haar. (2004). *Worlds of Power: Religious Thought and Political Practice in Africa*. New York: Oxford University Press.

21. John S. Mbiti. (1970). *African Religions and Philosophy*, New York: Doubleday.

22. It is not that these immigrants do not critique religion as a whole, but they by and large have an aversion to wholesale abandonment of God and spirituality. For the political and religious critics among these immigrants, their position on critique of religion and Enlightenment is reminiscent of Eduardo Mendieta: "The Enlightenment declared the triumph of reason by vanquishing theology and segregating religion into domesticated subjectivity. Today the Enlightenment lives on by recruiting the services of theology to rescue reason through religion by unmasking the idolatry and fetishism of the market and technology, and by returning to the subject of subjective freedom. . . . Today religion lives on because its promise and complaint, its yearning and sigh, have remained unfulfilled and unheard." See Eduardo Mendieta. (2005). *The Frankfurt School on Religion: Key Writings by the Major Thinkers*, New York: Routledge, page 8.

23. Thomas D. Blakely et al (eds.), *Religion in Africa: Experience and Expression*, London: Heinemann Press, 1992, page 18.

24. Paul Gifford, eds., *The Christian Churches and the democratization of Africa*, New York: E.J. Brill, 1995, page 258.

25. David Laitin. (1987). *Hegemony and Culture: Politics and Religious Change among Yoruba*, Chicago: The University of Chicago Press. Apart from the detailed theoretical and sociological analysis of the role of Christians from the middle belt and the southern part of Nigeria in opposing Sharia during the Constitutional Drafting Committee, I also witnessed the debates at the Constituent Assembly, working as an official reporter for the National Assembly from 1978 through 1981.

26. Quoted in Santosh Saha and Thomas Car (eds.), *Religious Fundamentalism in Developing Countries*, London: Greenwood Press, 2001, page 161. See especially the chapter by Harriet Harris, "Black Pentecostals in London."

27.  Tedros Kiros, "Moral Philosophy and Development: The Human Condition in Africa," *Ohio University Monographs in International Studies, Africa Series*, No. 61, page xv.

28.  ibid, page 175.

29.  Peter, Goldsmith, *When I Rise Cryin' Holy: African-American Denominationalism on the Georgia Coast*, New York: AMS Press, 1989.

30.  Helen Rose Ebaugh and Janet Salzman Chafetz (eds.), *Religion and the New Immigrants: Continuities and Adaptations in Immigrant Congregations*, (New York: Alta Mira Press, 2001), page 399.

31.  For a more detailed study of African initiated churches in the United States, see Abolade E. Olagoke. (2002). Unpublished Dissertation, University of Denver/Iliff School of Theology. *Pan Africanism and the New Diaspora: African Christians in the United States*. A whole chapter of the dissertation was devoted to Africans and African Americans

32.  Mensa Otabil. (1993). *Beyond the Rivers of Ethiopia*. (Lanham: Pneuma Life Publishing). For a critique of both Afrocentric and Eurocentric worldview, see Edwin M. Yamauchi. (2004). *Africa and the Bible*. (Grand Rapids: Baker Academic Publishing). The transatlantic movement of ideas especially in the area of religion is not a new phenomenon; it dates back centuries. For a detailed study of Evangelical Pan Africanism, see, Moses N. Moore. (1996). *Orishatukeh Faduma: Liberal Theology and Evangelical Pan-Africanism 1857-1946*. (Lanham: The American Theological Library Association and The Scarecrow Press, Inc.

33.  Waters (1995:2). Quoted in Wim van Binsbergen & Rijk van Dijk, (eds). (2004). *Situating Globality: African Agency in the Appropriation of Global Culture*. (Boston: Brill), page 5. The authors went further to elaborate on the definition of globalization: "Globalization as a concept, a phenomenon, and an ideology." (Globalization constitutes the dominant international system that replaced the Cold War system after the fall of the Berlin Wall (Friedman 1999:7).

34.  Jenkins, page 214.

# Sustainable Development:
# The Great Lie of the 21$^{st}$ Century

## Ms. Joan M. Veon

Sustainable development is a little known, and poorly understood global policy. As such, most Americans are ignorant of its existence. It is not being explained by the news media or from the pulpits. This multifaceted and complex philosophy is an "ism," if you will. Under the guise of "environmentalism," i.e., "protecting the environment from destruction by Man" virtually every aspect of human existence and all of God's earthly creation is targeted for redesign and control. The earth is to be re-created in the image of a handful of powerful, godless men that include the kings, the princes, the presidents and prime ministers and as well as businessmen of the world.

Sustainable development—by its very nature also demands a restructuring of Man's relationship to the Earth and to God. Under sustainable development, human beings cannot be trusted since they are now considered to be the destroyers of Mother Earth. God's millennia-old plan is altered. Man is to be replaced—as the guardian of the earth and of life on earth—by global partnerships of environmentalists, business, and government. And, as with Communism and Fascism, the Creator of the Universe, the God of the Bible, cannot be tolerated. Instead, a new god, the Mother Earth goddess (Gaia), has been scripted to play a vital role in sustainable development. In short, sustainable development is a threat to all civilizations.

**Joan Veon**—who resides in Maryland—is Founder and President of Veon Financial Services, International reporter, and author of several books.

The world stands literally on the brink of that same moment as when Eve was confronted with the lies, deceit, and deception of Satan. The pagan philosophy of Agenda 21 is poised to completely destroy the God-given order of earth as given in Genesis 1, 2 and 3. In order to understand this complex and heinous agenda, it is first necessary to explain the United Nations, the evolution of environmentalism, major players who have fostered and advanced it, and role of powerful foundations in financing it before explaining the philosophy itself. Without the United Nations, Agenda 21 and sustainable development—the philosophy, which claims, "the world has to reduce its population" would not have the central power that it has.

We cannot consider the topic of sustainable development and all that it encompasses without a brief introduction to what the United Nations-UN is. Although it was begun with the idea that it would be a place where the various countries of the world could talk over their differences, over the past sixty years, it has evolved into something far more.

In order to see how vast the UN has become, please go to their website: www.un.org. The UN has a head of state who is appointed in secret by the Security Council as opposed to being elected; a governing body; the General Assembly in which appointed representatives from the 191 countries of the world meet and pass laws which become part of international law; sources of income from member-countries; its own currency called the Special Drawing Right; its own treasury and financial system through the World Bank and International Monetary Fund; its own court system through the World Court and International Criminal Court; its own policing (agreed to September 2005) and military forces(agreed to September 2000 and expanded by the G8 in July 2005); its own flag; and its own oath of allegiance. Furthermore, it has its own constitution, the U.N. Charter. Recently at the 60ᵗʰ General Assembly held in New York City, the presidents, prime ministers, princes and kings of this world went to the UN where they voted to allow the UN to raise monies through the capital markets and to allow member-states to determine if they want to charge $10-$20 on airline tickets to help them meet the UN Millennium Development Goals-MDGs agreed to in 2000.

Beginning in the 1970s, the United Nations held a series of global meg-conferences on the environment (1972), population (1974), women's issues (1975), city planning and zoning (1976) and food (1976). These same meetings were repeated in the 1990's and updates to them are planned for the early 21ˢᵗ Century. This paper will deal with the environmental agenda, which began in 1972 at the UN Conference on the Environment in Stockholm, Sweden. This meeting provided the foundation for the Agenda 21, which was unveiled at the follow-up meeting in Rio de Janeiro at the UN Conference on Environment and Development, dubbed the "Rio Earth Summit." In 1992, Agenda 21 and sustainable development were made public. At the ten-year follow-up to Rio in 2002, sustainable development was further defined and expanded.

Sustainable development is like a prism that changes color when it is turned different ways. The sustainable development prism includes social, political, economic, legal, and environmental facets. It was the 1992 Rio Earth Summit that set the tone and provided the support for the philosophical shift to Gaia—the earth over man. Their phrase, "sustainable development," was first used at the Earth Summit. Before that time, it does not appear that it was used in any of the 1970s or 1980s United Nations documents or reference books.

Agenda 21 sets up the global infrastructure needed to manage, count, and control all of the world's assets. Included are the forests, fresh water, agricultural lands, deserts, pastures, rangelands, farmers' fields, oceans and inland waterways, marine environment, marine life, cities, housing, sewers and solid wastes, methods of production, air, pollution, biotechnology—every aspect of living—farming, production and manufacturing, research and medicine, etc., along with you and me. As a result of advanced technology through computers and satellites—the Geographic Information System (GIS)—the management, count, and control is being done.

The Brundtland Commission has been given credit for developing the definition of sustainable development. This philosophy changes the current world order which has existed from the time of the Garden of Eden, to an old world order (Satan's world order has been around since he rebelled) now called "the New World Order" by the first President George Bush when he addressed the United Nations General Assembly in September, 1991. The commission's definition of sustainable development is:

> Development that meets the needs of the present without compromising the ability of future generations to meet their own needs . . . two concepts: (1) Needs as it pertains to the world's poor to which overriding priority would be given, (2) the idea of limitation imposed by . . . technology . . . on the environments ability to meet present and future needs. . . . At the minimum, sustainable development must not endan-

ger the natural systems that support life in Earth: atmosphere, water, solids, living beings.

At the heart of the sustainable development definition is the issue of overpopulation. Environmentalists believe that the carrying capacity of the earth is about 2 billion people. Currently the earth has 6.4 billion people. The following is a paraphrased version of sustainable development:

> The world has too many people, and if we do not reduce the number of people on planet Earth they will use up all of the Earth's resources so that future generations will be left without any resources. The United Nations is the best global body to monitor, manage, and reserve the resources of the planet (Veon, p.51).

It should be noted that there is no problem with overpopulation. There are many scientists who have proven that overpopulation is a myth. Dr. Jacqueline Kasen from Humboldt University is one of them. She proved statistically that if you were to give all of the people of the world 1200 sq. feet of space, they would fit into the state of Texas. Please refer to her very fine book *The war Against Population*. At every turn, the population of the world is being reduced through abortion, condom distribution, family planning, homosexuality, euthanasia, wars, genocide, famine, plagues, and natural disasters.

Where does the philosophy of sustainable development come from? It is not in the Bible and is not in the U.S. Constitution. In doing some research, Joan Veon found a description in the 1977 Constitution of the Union of Soviet Socialist Republics. Chapter 2, Article 18 describes sustainable development:

> In the interests of the present and future generation, the necessary steps are taken in the USSR to protect and make scientific, rational use of the land and its mineral and water resources, and the plant and animal kingdoms to reserve the purity of air and water, ensure reproduction of natural wealth, and improve the human environment.

Given the fact that the earth has more value than man, what man does, how he lives, the amount he consumes is under the microscope. For all the earth's resources belong to the earth and are not for man's enjoyment. The family dependency ratio and the new accounting system for the earth are all part of the philosophical changes that are part of Agenda 21 and sustainable development.

In the 1995 Fourth Women's Conference Programme of Action, an interesting phrase was used throughout, "family dependency ratio." In an interview with Maurice Strong at a conference that sponsored Mikhail Gorbachev that same year, Joan Veon was able to ask if family dependency ratio was a way to measured the production and consumption of every family on planet earth. He confirmed that it was.

Basically family dependency ratio will look at every household to see if they are using more resources than what they are producing. How will and does this work? The World Bank is looking to assign a value to the jobs the adults in the household have and then assigning a value for everything they do to improve themselves: additional education, community activities, business, volunteerism, etc. They will add up all of the production a household has and then subtract from it what it consumes: electricity, water, mortgage, size of home, food, clothing, etc. If a household uses more than it produces, at some point in our future they may have to provide community volunteerism in order to "make up" the difference or reduce consumption and/or pay heavy fines.

Currently British Prime Minister Tony Blair has introduced a bill into Parliament which would give every person a "carbon allowance" which is a form of energy rationing. If they use too much energy, they would have to pay a tax (*New Zealand Herald*, 7/3/05, p. 1). This is only the beginning of where we are going. You see, when Mother Earth has greater spiritual value than man, everything we do will be subject to the health of the planet. Who will determine the health of the planet? The answer lies in those who formulate and plan how this agenda will dominate the philosophy of life on earth.

In 1993, the World Bank established a division for Sustainable Development. As a result of the philosophy of sustainable development, the Bank has divided the assets of the world as:

1. *Natural Capital*—the mineral of the earth, water, forest, anything natural.
2. *Manufactured Capital*—anything built, such as roads, buildings homes, etc.
3. *Human Capital*—every living person on the earth, including their age, health, experience, education, and ability to work.
4. *Social Capital*—how people think, that is, politically current thinking.

At the 2002 World Summit for Sustainable Development, the ten-year follow-up to the Rio Earth Summit, and at the September, 2005, 60th U.N. General Assembly, sustainable development and public-private partnership were the key themes. Given the fact that everything in the world is being given a value so that a balance sheet of the earth's assets can be put together, The Royal Society for the Protection of the Birds has been working to put a global value on nature—all of the birds, bees, animals, plants, fish, and so forth. In a 2002 interview, Dr. Paul Jeffers from The Royal Society told Joan Veon that they now value the biological diversity of the world at $20T to $38T while other experts who are valuing the earth say that it might be as high at $51T. This figure equates all the monies in the stock, bond markets, and banking and insurance industries. That just may be the reason for the control of the resources—they are an asset. God never put a monetary value any on His creation. When you put a dollar value on life, it becomes expendable.

At the 2002 meeting, a new umbrella organization representing the transnational corporations of the world was set up. The Business Action for Sustainable Development included the International Chamber of Commerce-ICC and the World Business Council for Sustainable development-WBCSD. Bjorn Stigson from the WBCSD announced "We describe ourselves as a catalyst for change." Over 250 public-private partnerships were announced, including the Congo Basin Forest Partnership. This partnership involves a total of 14 governments of which eight are African, with the rest developed countries, 8 key environmental groups like the World Wildlife Fund, IUCN, and Conservation International, along with the American Forest and Paper Association, which has 200 companies as members, representing 1.5 million employees and a French paper association. The partnership involves over 74 million acres of land.

Please refer to the UN Department of Economic and Social Affairs Division for Sustainable Development: http://webapps01.un.org/dsd/partnerships. There you will see many, many public-private partnerships. They include partnerships on Cement Sustainability (1 government, 2 NGO's, and 15 corporations), Cleaner Fuels and Vehicles (8 governments, 5 UN organization, 11 Associations, 8 corporations and 5 NGO's), Appliance Standards Program (9 governments, 9 NGO's, 3 foundations, 2 Institutes and 4 UN organizations), Network of Regional Governments for Sustainable Development (16 governments), Global Conservation Trust (5 governments, 2 corporations, 1 college, 2 foundations and one NGO) and Global Water Partnership (7 governments, 5 UN organizations), to name a few.

Please note that these public-private partnerships are changing the structure of governments. Each of these partnerships has different countries, corporations, foundations, NGOs, and educational entities that have formed partnerships. They are all being legally, politically, and economically interconnected in new legal entities which will supersede the old form of government. How do you separate your assets in a complex public-private partnership if you have a disagreement or want to dissolve?

What is the power of public-private partnerships and sustainable development that have led the way to the major changes in the order of government and the world? At a meeting in July 1997 at the United Nations, independent reporter Linda Liotta reported that "the secretary-general opened the meeting by telling participants that, "You are the agents of change and of a new politics' and that '[g]ood governance and sustainable development are indivisible.'"

At the 60th UN General Assembly in September 2005, the conference Programme of Action, specifically stated,

> We reaffirm that development is a central goal by itself and that sustainable development in its economic, social, and environmental aspects constitutes a key element of the overarching framework of United Nations activities. We reaffirm the universality, indivisibility, interdependence, and interrelatedness of all human rights. We reaffirm our commitment to the global partnership for development.

Sustainable development has come down from the global level through the United Nations mega conferences, corporations, non-governmental organizations, and governments. Every government has embraced sustainable development, including the United States of America. It permeates every level of government, which has adopted sustainable development. It is now taught in our universities and colleges, high schools and junior highs as "Earth Science."

We now hear about "sustainable cities," "sustainable agriculture," "sustainable transportation," and so forth. Everything is now sustainable. In short, "sustainable" also pertains to the "highest and best use." Recently, personal property rights were dealt a severe blow when the Supreme Court ruled in Kelo versus City of New London that the city had the right to use eminent domain to force highest and best use of property that would create jobs and increase tax revenue for the public good.

Nothing is sacred if highest and best use now measures Constitutional rights and the value of man.

In order to overcome the adverse effects of sustainable development and become spiritually sustainable, as well as responsible citizens, we will need truth and wisdom from the Creator.

# References

Dewar, Elaine. (1995). *Cloak of Green*. Toronto: James Lorimer & Company.

International Union for Conservation of Nature and Natural Resources (IUCN). *World Conservation Strategy*. 1980.

Lovelock, James. (1987). *Gaia A New Look at Life on Earth*. New York: Oxford University Press.

Lovelock, James. (1988). *The Ages of Gaia A Biography of Our Living Earth*. New York: W.W. Norton & Company.

Schumacher, E. F. (1973). *Small is Beautiful*. New York: Harper & Row, Publishers.

United Nations Conference on Environment and Development (UNCED). *Agenda 21: Programme of Action for Sustainable Development—Rio Declaration on Environment and Development Statement of Forest Principles—*The final text of agreements negotiated by Government 3-14 June 1992, Rio de Janeiro, Brazil.

Veon, Joan. (1998). *Prince Charles the Sustainable Prince*. Oklahoma City: Hearthstone Publishing.

Veon, Joan. (2000). *The United Nations' Global Straitjacket*. Oklahoma City: Hearthstone Publishing.

World Summit on Sustainable Development. "A Framework for Action on Biodiversity and Ecosystem Management." August, 2002.

# Websites

Agenda 21: www.un.org/esa/susdev/sdissues

Earth Charter—www.earthcharter.org

Global Biodiversity—www.biodiv.org and www.wri.og

International Development Research Centre—www.idrc.ca

Intergovernmental Panel on Climate Change—www.ipcc.ch
UN Department of Economic and Social Affairs, Division for Sustainable Development—webapps01.un.org/dsd/partnerships/public/simpleSearch.do?di . . . www.reformed-theology.com

# Salaam Aleykum Y'All: Being Muslim in the Central Texas "Bible-Belt"

## DR. A. CHRISTIAN VAN GORDER

There are between 6 and 7 million Muslims in America worshipping in over 1200 masjids. More than half of these masjids have been founded within the last 20 years. Islam is the fastest growing religion in the country with twice as many adherents as Judaism. Texas is home to 70 masjids and between 600,000-700,000 Muslims, more than half of who live in Houston and Dallas. Between 80-90% of Texas Muslims are Sunni with the remainder being Shi'a and members of the Nation of Islam.[1]

There are between 15,000-20,000 Muslims in Central Texas.[2] These Muslims share a fascinating story of interfaith and intercultural engagement with Christians in the heart of America's "Bible Belt." This research focuses on the nature and character of Central Texas Islam and, more specifically, on the way that this emerging faith community relates to issues of interaction with and among Christians (and Jews).

Senora Martinez is one of many Central Texans who has left Christianity to convert ("revert") to Islam.[3] Most of these are African-Americans (the first Texas African-American Masjid was formed in Dallas in 1950). Every year between 25,000-30,000 Americans convert to Islam. Texas Islam experiences about 1,000 conversions a year. The story of African-American Islam is unique and multifaceted. African-American

**Dr. A. Christian van Gorder** is Associate Professor of Religious Studies in the World Religions Department of Religion at Baylor University in Waco, Texas.

Muslims face challenges and racialized stereotypes from both Muslims and others in America. Many African-American males have become Muslims through prison outreaches, but there are an equal number of people who make this decision from other circumstances. European-American converts, like Latifah Taoramina, have also complained of experiencing prejudice among their Muslim brothers and sisters because of their ethnic background.

Islam is dramatically growing among Latin Americans. Muslims in Central Texas have printed event fliers in Spanish and posted them in Spanish-speaking neighborhoods. An open-house for Mexicans in a Dallas masjid attracted 150 visitors. "Central Texan Latin American Muslim" Amanda Martinez converted while a student at the University of Texas in Austin. At her conversion, her grandmother asked her to leave her house and stopped financing her education.[4]

Most Central Texas Muslims are immigrants from South Asia, but there are also a few from the Middle East. Prior to coming to the United States, most of these individuals had little interaction with Christian communities. Pakistani and Indian Muslims began to come to Texas in significant numbers after President Lyndon Johnson signed the Immigration and Nationality Act of 1965. Many South Asians first came as students or businesspeople and, at the time, may not have been very interested in religious issues. Islam was often taken for granted. These Muslims wanted to merge into American society but were forced to confront their identity after the events of September 11, 2001.

One of the most important ways that Muslims affirm and strengthen their community and the faith of their children is through the observance of the various Islamic festivals. It is a time for children to eat special foods and be proud of their cultural identity. It is also a time for Muslims to reach out to their neighbors. The Islamic Society of Waco and the Masjid al-Siddiqi hosted a meal every evening during Ramadan and had students from neighboring Baylor University and invited church groups from the Waco community who sat with them and learned more about their faith. These festivals are also an important time for South Asian merchants and professionals to build business networks and friendships. The Austin Islamic community invited area Jews and Christians to join them in their Eid al Fitr celebration. The local Rabbi said of this experience that his participation reflected his desire to promote religious pluralism and respect among various American faith traditions.[5] Islamic festivals also create challenges for children in school, workers and friends in awkward social settings who may not understand their practices. Festivals are also a time for delicious delicacies that underscore Texas Islamic diversity. Katrina Ruiz adds her native Colombian delicacies to the Iftar table of Austin already filled with Pakistani and Malay appetizers. For Ruiz and others it is a beautiful time for intercultural bonding within the Texas dar-al Islam."[6]

Muslims in Central Texas face a host of unique challenges in the area of interfaith engagement. Many of these relate to the political climate since 9/11 and the general widespread support (excepting Austin) for President Bush's policies in the Middle East. September 11th has actually served to galvanize the faith and community activism of most Muslims in Central Texas. One estimate claims that only between 10-20% of American Muslims were devout or active in their Masjids. One 17-year old Texan described feeling ashamed when he could not answer questions about his faith after 9/11: "I felt ashamed for myself because I did not know how to answer. It was like if any of my friends talked about sports right then I would know but about my own religion, I did not know."[7]

Since these Muslims live in the heart of largely Christian communities, they also have to respond to scores of evangelistic efforts, which seek their conversion. On the other hand, Muslim-Christian interaction has expressed itself in a host of other ways including mutual projects for social justice or intercultural education. Al Siddiqi, a mechanic in Waco, has led his masjid to be actively involved in the Waco Habitat for Humanity and has been a frequent guest speaker about the nature of Islam in countless classrooms at the faith-based Baylor University. In these presentations Mr. Siddiqi often deals with stereotypes about terrorism, sexism and loyalty by stressing his own military career in the United States Army stationed in Korea. One Muslim presenter at Georgetown University began his remarks by stating: "This is my country. I am going to live here and die here and be buried here."[8]

Christians in the Waco community have conducted joint worship services. Joint prayer services have also been held on the capitol steps in Austin near the yearly anniversary of 9/11. Mohsin Lari of the Austin Muslim Community Support Services states, "I think it is very important to hold these kinds of activities more often. We need to talk to each other and understand each other."[9]

Baylor University and the University of Texas have taken varying degrees of effort to help Muslim students in their midst feel welcome. Neither University has reported any recent instances of harassment of

Muslim students. Baylor University has yet to hire Muslims to teach or charter a Muslim student association, but there seems to be a strong desire to address the need to provide a hospitable learning environment for all of its students. The Indian Student Association of Baylor has a number of Muslim students who are considering initiating their own Muslim Student Association. These students are also seeking dedicated space within the University to fulfill their obligations for prayer.

Interreligious tensions in Central Texas can take on the form of violent attack, and there have been a number of hate crimes against Texas Muslims. This has led police in various communities such as Austin and Waco to monitor Masjid parking lots at certain times of the year to reassure Muslim worshippers. San Antonio experienced a serious of hate-related arson attacks against Pakistani business properties. Three fires resulted in a quarter of a million dollars in damages. Vandals have spray-painted derogatory terms on the Lubbock masjid home to about 700 Muslims. A Pakistani convenience store clerk was killed in Mesquite, and a mosque in Denton was firebombed. Bullets were fired into both the Islamic center of Irving and a Middle Eastern restaurant in San Antonio. Other Pakistani gas stations have been firebombed, and authorities have determined these attacks to be hate crimes.[10] Antonio Flores, of El Paso, will serve 14 years for attempting to bomb the mosque in that city.[11] Another bomb exploded outside a mosque in Houston.[12] Severed rams-heads were left at the ICGA (East Austin) after it was burglarized on one occasion.[13] In addition, a number of hate-groups exist in Texas which promote acrid diatribes against Islam and Muslim immigrants in their midst.

While these dramatic cases are appalling, Muslims in Central Texas often experience harassment of a much more pervasive nature. To address this, the Austin Area Interreligious Ministry has established numerous volunteer programs to help Pakistanis and other Muslims to deal with possible harassment. The four main dimensions of harassment for Muslims: 1. Racial profiling at area airports, 2. Surveillance or a perceived sense of suspicion, 3. Hesitancy to hire Muslims, and 4. Actual interaction with authorities. Jim Harrington of the Texas Civil Rights Project said "There is Islamaphobia here in Austin. I don't think there is any doubt about that . . . but [it's] sort of indirect words, sort of indirect pressure, unwelcome suspicion . . . that make people feel very uncomfortable. When you put that together with government policy, people would rather go somewhere else and that is a loss to us."[14]

Muslim women in Central Texas who wear the hijab (veil) often experience harassment. Some women do not like to talk about this problem because according to Nahid Khataw "some women are embarrassed to ask for help."[15] Others take the path of least intercultural resistance. Nahid Khataw stopped wearing the hijab after her child was mocked in an Austin public school: "I was scared. I heard so many cases that people were being harassed because they were wearing hijab. Children were pulling the hijab off and hurting them. I thought it would be better for me and my family not to wear it. They would be portrayed as a terrorist if they're wearing it-Muslims who wear a hijab-they are not bad."[16]

International students and local Muslim businessmen have been the focus on FBI scrutiny. A full-time member of the University of Texas Police Department has been assigned to a task force to identify "potential terrorists." The United States Patriot Act has led to students at UT Austin having their records scrutinized as well as the arrest, and later release of Tahir Ibrihim Aletewi, a 30 year old student at the University of Texas.[17]

Politically, Central Texas Muslims tend to support the Democratic Party. South Asian Texans have registered thousands of democratic voters, and Texas brought the largest number of Muslim delegates to the 2004 Democratic National Convention.[18] In recent years Texas Muslims have become increasingly active and are voting, financing and supporting campaigns with more fervor. Most Central Texas Muslims are critical of Bush. However, this has not always been the case, and their overwhelming support for Bush in Florida may have made the difference in the 2000 Presidential election. Bush had strong support because he was a foe of abortion and considered a conservative person who promoted the family values that Muslims appreciate. An example of this is the active support that Texas Muslims gave to the 2004 attempt to create an anti-gay marriage amendment to the state constitution.[19] The main reason that Central Texas Muslims do not support Bush is usually American policy toward Iraq and Israel. These issues often come up in conversations with their neighbors.

The recent earthquakes in Pakistan, the legacy of Hurricane Katrina and the South Asian Tsunami of December 2004 have all resulted in the Muslims of Central Texas to play a visible and supportive role both to those in need and to model to the local community the compassionate nature and their rootedness in the local community. Masjid al-Siddiqi in Waco hosted countless hurricane evacuees, as did the masjids throughout the region. "It's just part of our religion to help our neighbors in need no matter what their faith is said Dr. Jason Black (33) a self-described Army brat who converted to Islam 12 years ago."[20]

Muslims in Central Texas come from all walks of life. Most of them are nominal and are well ensconced on the road to acculturation and social conformity and want simply to be Texans and Americans. They are soccer moms, physicians, office workers, lawyers, mechanics, teachers and students who know where to eat good barbeque and cheer for the Cowboys.

The goal of this research has been, as far as is possible, to provide a Muslim viewpoint on their experience living among the predominant Christian communities of Central Texas. Relations between Muslims, Jews and Christians in this area continue to improve at a glacial pace. The first task is for both communities to take the initiative to better understand and appreciate each other's experiences of faith and life. The challenge is to nurture and sustain these efforts and to encourage Central Texas Christians, Jews and Muslims to be more proactive in promoting interfaith understanding. Interfaith worship and discussions and shared Muslim-Christian-Jewish social justice initiatives have been some of the ways that Central Texas Muslims, Jews and Christians have begun this process.

# Notes

1. Jiti Hinigorani, "Islam Post 9/11: Unveiling the Face of Islam in Austin," *News 8 Explores*, Austin, November 28, 2004.

2. Central Texas will be defined as the Austin, Killeen, Fort Hood, Temple and Waco area. The number 15,000-20,000 is widely held and is cited in the Austin News 8 report of November 28, 2004.

3. http://www.channel4.com/culture/microsites/T/thinktv/comments/0104_tmit.html

4. Chris Jenkins, "Islam Luring More Latinos," *Washington Post*, January 7, 2001.

5. Antonio Castelan, "Austin Area Interreligious Ministries," December 17, 2001, http://www.aaimaustin.org

6. Marium F. Mohiuddin, "Daily Fasts During Ramadan Focuses Muslims on Beliefs and the Nightly Feasts," *Cox News Service*, October 26, 2005.

7. Shomial Ahmad, "Awakening Islam," *The Fort Worth Weekly*, November 9, 2005.

8. Dick Stanley and Mary Ann Roser, *Austin American Statesman*, September 21, 2001.

9. Janet Jacobs, "A Changed World But Still One Family: Tragedy Can't Spoil the Unity of Faith." *Austin American Statesman*, November 19, 2001.

10. T. A. Badger, "Police Say Arson Fires At Business Likely Hate Crimes Against Muslims," *The Daily Texan*, April 8, 2004.

11. Muslim Public Affairs Council, http://www.mpac.org/community_article_display.aspx?ITEM=785

12. Council of American-Islamic Relations Statement, July 7, 2004, www.notinourname.net

13. Kim Sue Lia Perkes, "Islamic Worshippers Uneasy After Four Severed Rams Heads Left on Grounds," *Austin American Statesman*, May 30, 1998. The ICGA is on 1906 Nueces Street, Austin, TX 78705, phone: 512-476-2563. They also maintain the main Islamic cemetery for members of the local communities

14. Jiti Hingorani, "Islam Post 9/11: Islamaphobia in Austin," *News 8 Explores*, November 30, 2004.

15. Kim Sue Lia Perkes, *Austin American Statesman*, October 7, 2001.

16. Jitin Hingorani, *News 8 Explores*, November 30, 2004.

17. Source: http://www.utwatch.org/security/jttf.html

18. Kaukab J. Smith, "U.S. Muslims Grown More Politically Active," March 31, 2005.

19. Jeff Mosier, "Muslims Torn: Civil Liberties or Social Concerns," *The Dallas Morning News*, November 6, 2005. Nawal Suleiman, a substitute teacher said in 2000 she voted for Bush but that "he turned 180 degrees against Muslims and Arabs. If one Israeli dies it is a tragedy. If one hundred Muslims are killed it is no big deal." Jamal Obied of Grand Prairie said, "We love what the Republican Party stands for."

20. Nathan Diebenow, "Faith in Action: Texas Muslims Seek to Rebuild Trust through Relief Efforts," *The Lone Star Iconoclast*, September 7, 2005. Dr. Black is a member of the Irving Masjid that opened at SH183 to serve the 150,000 Muslims who live in the DFW area. Between 1700 and 2000 Muslims come to this Masjid for Friday prayers.